GW00384529

Contents

The **Windows**®**95** Black Box

The **Windows**®**95** Black Box

Tips & tricks for windows mastery

Rob Young

PRENTICE HALL

LONDON   NEW YORK   TORONTO   SYDNEY   TOKYO
SINGAPORE   MADRID   MEXICO CITY   MUNICH   PARIS

First published 1997 by
Prentice Hall Europe
Campus 400, Maylands Avenue
Hemel Hempstead
Hertfordshire, HP2 7EZ
A division of
Simon & Schuster International Group

Typeset in Frutiger and Melior
by The Works, Dunstable, Beds.

Printed and bound in Great Britain by
T.J. Press (Padstow) Ltd

Library of Congress Cataloging-in-Publication Data

Young, Rob.
    The Windows"95 Black Box / Rob Young.
        p.   cm.
    Includes index.
    ISBN 0-13-616558-3 (pbk. : alk. paper)
        1. Microsoft Windows (Computer file)   2. Operating systems
(Computers)   I. Title.
    QA76.76.063Y698   1996   96-38420
    005.4 469–dc20   CIP

British Library Cataloguing in Publication Data

A catalogue record for this book is available from
the British Library

ISBN 0–13–616558–3 (pbk)

---

1 2 3 4 5   01   00 99 98 97

Trademarks

All product and company names are [TM] or [R] trademarks of their owners.

Microsoft, Windows and **MS-DOS** are registered trademarks of Microsoft Corporation.

4 Files & Folders

5 Applets & Accessories   122

7 Dial-Up & The Internet

8 The Registry & Policies   211

10 Bootup & Shutdown

12 Odds & Ends

Get in touch – we'd like to hear from you!

Your opinion counts

If you have any comments about this book – positive or negative, long or short – please send them in. We want to refine our books according to the needs of our readers, so do tell us if there is something that you would like to see in future editions of this book. Your input could well appear in print! We genuinely appreciate it when people take the time to contact us, so every month we give away a free Prentice Hall computer book for the most helpful and comprehensive comments.

Please feel free to e-mail me personally with your comments:

feedback@prenhall.co.uk

Or you can write to me:

Jason Dunne
Prentice Hall
Campus 400
Maylands Avenue
Hemel Hempstead
Herts.
HP2 7EZ
United Kingdom

Please note that Prentice Hall cannot serve as a technical resource for questions about hardware or software problems.

We would also like to hear your ideas for new books, whether it is just for a book that you want to see in print or one you intend writing yourself. Our guide for new authors can be found in the back of this book.

Thanks for choosing Prentice Hall.

Jason Dunne
Acquisition Editor, Prentice Hall

jdunne@prenhall.co.uk

Introduction

Welcome to *The Windows95 Black Box*!

Keen as you probably are to skip the inane ramblings that always preface Chapter One and just start 'tweaking', please take a few moments to read the following pages, containing a definition of 'your computer' for the purposes of this book, and a few extra tips concerning preparation and caution. Reading, and acting upon, this advice could help you avoid potential catastrophes further down the line.

What this book *isn't* . . .

Windows95 is easy to use. It was specifically *designed* to be easy to use. Okay, it might have taken you a week or two to discover the ins and outs of the Desktop, to understand the concept of shortcuts, and to start making the most of the right mouse-button, but now you're probably opening, saving and creating files without thinking twice, and that's what it's for. However much you grow to regard *Help* as a misnomer, it guides you through the basics and elevates you from 'beginner' to 'user' status sufficiently painlessly to make a 'How Do I Use It?' book unnecessary to most.

What this book *is* . . .

But does *Windows95* really do everything you want it to? Does it let you work as fast as you need to, or as easily? Is it tuned to suit your way of working? At this point, you've probably started to become aware of the inconsistencies, oddities and plain annoyances in the software: copy/move anomalies, customization restrictions, rearranged Desktops, spectacularly poor documentary support – what *Windows95* gives with one hand it seems to take away with the other. Much of the reason for this, ironically, is down to its in-built ease of use: if you can't touch it, you can't break it.

As a *Windows95* user you probably have a kind of mental 'wish-list', a collection of things you'd like to change. With a little judicious experimentation, you might even have set about changing some of them when they finally became intolerable. Even so, there's sure to be a whole host of undocumented or badly documented features which, if you only knew what they were and what they're for, you'd probably have added to the wish-list!

The Black Box puts an end to the *Windows95* wish-list with clear step-by-step tips to help you advance to power-user status by adding, fixing, or customizing the features you need, or indeed just *finding* them! Each tip includes a concise explanation of its value and use to help you decide whether it's relevant to you, together with examples and cross-references where applicable. The layout should be intuitive, but since many of the tips could have been included in any one of several chapters, check the Index if you can't find what you need – if you want to do it, and it can be done, it's almost certainly in here somewhere!

Your Computer

Meet *The Black Box* ...

The Black Box is geared primarily towards users of stand-alone (as opposed to networked) computers. Nevertheless, the tips contained here will help to elevate all *Windows95* users (networking or otherwise) to 'power-user' status.

A presupposition of the book is that you have the final-release version of Microsoft *Windows95* (build 950 or 950a) installed on your computer. Certain tips and features may not apply or may give unexpected results in earlier builds and betas. Tips relating to the optional *Plus!* pack are included alongside Windows tips and are noted as such.

It should also be borne in mind that, due to the many possible system configurations and the unknown variables produced by the interaction of installed software and hardware, no guarantee can be made of the effectiveness of any particular tip on any individual system.

Meet Your Computer ...

Throughout the book, the assumption is made that your hard-disk is **Drive C:**, your CD-ROM drive is **Drive D:**, and your floppy drive is **Drive A:**. It's also assumed that you installed *Windows95* into a folder called **C:\Windows**. These assumptions are made in order to provide a clearer overview of file/folder locations, and will be relevant to the majority of *Windows95* users – if your setup differs from these defaults, substitute your own drive- and folder-names when following the tips.

Meet Your Mouse ...

For similar reasons, references to mouse-buttons follow the arrogant assumption that your primary button is the left button.

Meet Your Registry Key ...

Many of the Registry hacks included in *The Black Box* involve editing data particular to each *user* rather than data affecting the *system* as a whole. The instructions given for these tips assume that your computer is *not* set up for multiple-user profiles and specify the key **HKEY_CURRENT_USER** for editing. If you are using multiple profiles, and you want your changes to apply to each, you'll also need to visit the **HKEY_USERS** key and make the same change in the profile-keys listed beneath it.

Meet Your Window Views ...

When you view the drives, folders and files on your system you can do so by double-clicking My Computer or by running Explorer. While these views differ in that the latter gives a split window with a tree-structure in the left pane, both are actually supplied by a program called Explorer.exe. A number of different names have arisen to differentiate these windows, the most popular being *Open-view* and *Explorer-view* respectively. However, since both Explorer and the act of opening items are going to be mentioned a lot in this book, things could get confusing. As an aid to clarity, both window-types are referred to as *Explorer-windows* since it usually doesn't matter what the window looks like as long as you find what you're looking for! In the few cases where a distinction is important, the self-evident terms *single-pane window* and *dual-pane window* are used.

How To Proceed ...

Before making any changes to any part of your system, it's strongly recommend-ed that you

❑   read the *whole* of the tip (and any notes that accompany it);

❑   make sure you know how to reverse any alterations you carry out (which may range from just clicking a check-box to restoring Registry data);

❑   note the original settings before making any changes to them; and

❑   crucially, make backups of any files to be changed.

Before editing *any* part of your system, follow the step-by-step instructions in 'The First Move' on page xlvii to ensure that, should disaster strike, you're covered.

Explanations

Throughout this book icons are used to give a quick comparison between tip-types, to highlight important points to consider, and steer you towards alternative or related tips and methods.

An advanced tip – these are suited to users who are used to working with *Windows95* or are more familiar with computing generally. Advanced tips may carry a certain risk to system-files or may be more complicated to carry out.

Also an advanced tip, but one that will specifically involve editing the Registry. The Registration Editor is very simple to use and the data easy to edit. However, this ease of use tends to belie the fact that the integrity of this data is fundamental to the smooth-running of the system. Casual or careless experimentation is not recommended!

A footnote to a tip, usually highlighting problems or variations that may be encountered, or points to consider before implementing the tip.

A reference to a related tip or topic elsewhere in the book. It's well worth checking this reference before implementing a tip – there may be an easier method, or a way of achieving a more permanent or suitable result.

Keep an eye on the 'Related Tips' section at the end of most chapters, containing a list of tips and subheadings covering similar topics elsewhere in the book.

Finally, this is not intended to be a technical book – it's a 'getting results' book! To get results, you don't want to wade through oceans of technical gibberish first, and usually you shouldn't have to. Where some background detail is required, it's included amongst the related tips in as digestible a form as possible. The rest has been banished to the Glossary, together with additional definitions and explanations related to Windows-based computing.

The First Move

> Some of the information in this book remains undocumented by Microsoft with good reason; certain core system files are 'hidden' by default for the same good reason: *Windows95*, like any operating system, can just cease to operate if vital data is edited incorrectly.
>
> Someone, somewhere, reading this book, is going to screw up; it's absolutely guaranteed. This isn't the innocent mistake that makes the operating system stop operating – many of us have made that one, and survived. This is the supreme idiocy of having no way to make it start again. So the following is a guide for smart people only . . .

Follow these simple instructions to create and test a system-disk (to restart your computer in the event of a problem occurring with the startup files on your hard-disk), and create backups of the vital system files.

There are four tasks which should take about 15 minutes to complete, and could save you hours, days, or even weeks of grief and aggravation.

1 Create A System Disk

Grab a new, formatted, high-density floppy disk, and your *Windows95* installation disks or CD-ROM. Double-click on **Add/Remove Programs** in the Control Panel and click the tab labelled **Startup Disk**. Click on **Create Disk** and follow the instructions.

Now check that the startup disk works. Choose **Shut Down** from the Start Menu, click on **Restart the computer** and **Yes**, leaving the floppy-disk in the drive. When the computer restarts, the system should boot from this disk leaving you at the MS-DOS command prompt (**A:\\>**). If it does, the disk is working fine.

Remove the startup disk from the drive and restart your computer. Write-protect and label this disk, and put it somewhere safe!

If, for some reason, you don't have the *Windows95* installation disk(s), follow the tip titled 'No Installation Disks?' on page 250 to achieve a similar result.

2 Backup The Registry Files

First, make sure Explorer is showing hidden files: select **Options** from Explorer's 'View' menu and check the radio-button beside **Show all files**.

Next, slip another clean high-density disk into the floppy-drive, and open your Windows folder (usually C:\Windows). Copy the files **System.dat** and **User.dat** to the floppy-disk. Remove the disk from the drive and, again, write-protect it, label it, and put it with your Startup Disk.

Before making any changes to the Registry, read the chapter titled 'The Registry & Policies' on page 211 to make sure you understand the various methods of restoring this data, and make extra backups in the formats covered on pages 219–23.

3 Backup Vital System Files

This operation requires a third floppy-disk, and comes in two parts. First, copy the following files to your floppy-disk:

C:\Autoexec.bat
C:\Config.sys
C:\Msdos.sys

Second, select **Find** from the Start Menu. Make sure your boot-drive and any logical drives are selected in the **Look In** box (for example **C:\;E:**), type ***.ini** in the **Named** box, and click **Find Now**. When the search is complete, scroll to the end of the list of files, hold *Shift* and click on the last filename in the list (or just hit *Ctrl + A*) – every filename should now be selected. Now right-click on any filename and choose **Send To** and **Floppy Disk** from the context-menu to copy all these **.ini** files to the floppy disk.

Write-protect and label this disk too, and start practising your smug look: you'll be able to use it to great effect when friends and colleagues tell you they can't start their computer!

4 And Finally . . .

Be prepared! Any problems you encounter are likely to be minor and easily resolved, but nothing's easy if you don't know how to do it! Here are three principles it pays to check out while you have a fully working system and a normal heart-rate:

❑ **Know Your Keyboard Shortcuts**
Just occasionally, an operation as seemingly innocuous as installing a new printer can make your mouse kick its little legs in the air and die. If your mouse should breathe its last and stop responding, make sure you know how to move through menus, dialogs and tabbed pages using the keyboard – chiefly you'll want to complete or cancel the current task, save any open work, and restart the computer to rejuvenate your rodent. A few minutes' experimentation with the Control Panel and Explorer will teach you most of the required moves.

❑ **Know Your Boot Options**
Being able to boot to the command-prompt and to start *Windows95* in Safe Mode are vital in times of trouble, so make sure you know how to display the *Windows95* Startup Menu and select options from it.

❑ **Know Your MS-DOS Commands**
If for any reason you can't boot to *Windows95*, you'll need to do all your troubleshooting at the DOS-prompt. Make sure you know how to move between drives and folders, use Help and Edit, and handle basic file commands such as **ren**, **copy** and **attrib**. For experimentation purposes, create a couple of text files on two different drives, open a DOS-prompt window, and spend a few minutes copying, editing, replacing and renaming them and changing their attributes. (If you don't have a previous version of MS-DOS on your computer, you can find the two DOS Help files on the *Windows95* installation CD-ROM – they refer to an earlier version of DOS, but they're well worth having. See 'Missing?' on page 289 for more details.)

By following the procedures outlined above and on the previous pages, you'll find it easy to 'power-up' your *Windows95* environment while keeping the risk to a minimum, making your Windows sessions both more productive and more enjoyable. Happy 'tweaking'!

1

Start Menu & Taskbar

The Start Menu

Put It On The Menu

Items on the Start Menu itself are far quicker to get at than items tucked away in its **Programs** subfolder, so this is the ideal location for the files and applications you use most often.

The quickest method of adding new items to your Start Menu is to open an Explorer window, locate the item you want, and drag & drop the file onto the Start button – this will automatically create a shortcut rather than copying or moving the file itself.

Fast Folder Views

But why stop at documents and applications? If you find yourself hunting through Explorer for the same folder over and over again, drag that folder onto the Start button in the same way: one click, and the folder's contents is displayed in a new window.

Truncated Start Menu?

If you've spent a session adding new items to the Start Menu in this way, you could find that when you click Start some of the items at the top have gone missing – the Start Menu is a finite size and can't 'squeeze' the items together to make room for them all. If this happens, go to **Start / Settings / Taskbar** and choose **Show small icons in Start menu**.

If you still can't see all the items you added you'll need to reduce the quantity you're trying to display. The easiest way to do this is to group them within subfolders; right-click on the Start button and choose **Open**. Create a new folder by right-clicking in the window and choosing **New** and **Folder**. Give the new folder a name, and drag items onto it to move them.

The size of your Start Menu (and therefore the number of items it can display) is directly related to your screen-resolution: the higher the resolution, the more items you can add. You could also reduce the font-size for the 'Menu' item in Control Panel's **Display / Appearances** to cram in more items, but you might not like the effect this has on Windows' other menus.

Take a look at 'The Missing Column' on page 20 and 'Extra Organization' on page 21 for more about Start Menu subfolders.

One option available, if you really must have more room on your Start Menu, is to remove the Run, Find and Settings entries. See 'Remove The Run Command' and 'Remove Run From The Registry' on page 12.

Folders Or Subfolders?

Placing shortcuts to your most-used folders on the Start Menu is practical, and a doddle to do but there's another choice to be made. Do you want the contents of these folders to be displayed in a window (the result of following the previous tip) or would you prefer the contents on a cascading subfolder (for a one-click launch)?

To create a cascading subfolder on the Start Menu, right-click on Start and choose **Open**, then click inside the window and select **New** and **Folder** from the context-menu. Give this folder the same name as the Explorer folder containing the items you want to display. Next, open an Explorer window to display the items you want to add, press *Ctrl + A* to select them all, and use the right mouse-button to drag them into your subfolder selecting **Create Shortcut(s) Here** from the context-menu.

Adding Single Items

If you don't like the drag & drop method of adding shortcuts to Start Menu subfolders, there's an alternative: right-click inside the subfolder, choose **New** and **Shortcut**, and just follow the instructions from the Shortcut Wizard. Rather than type in the whole path to a file you can use the **Browse** button to locate it, but shortcuts to folders have to be entered by hand.

Resurrect Your Program Manager Groups

If you installed *Windows95* over *Windows 3.x*, your old Program Manager groups should have been recreated as subfolders in **Start Menu / Programs**. If they weren't (or you've accidentally deleted one) replacing them is easy: the **.grp** files still live in your Windows folder – just locate the group-file you need and double-click it.

Bypass The Start Button

Corners of the screen are not the most user-friendly of places to have to access with a mouse and, try as you might, that's where the Start button always ends up. To avoid unnecessarily exercising your rodent, use the *Ctrl + Esc* key-combination to open the Start Menu.

What's In A Name?

Sometimes very little! When you drop an **.exe** (executable) file onto the Start button, for example, your Start Menu might display an 8-character name that bears not much resemblance to the application's name.

To change the 'titles' of these shortcuts, right-click on the Start button and choose **Open** or **Explore**. Highlight the offending icon, press *F2*, and type in a new name of up to 255 characters, including spaces.

Quick-Launch Tip

Create shortcuts to your most-used applications on the Start Menu (rather than in its **Programs** subfolder) and number them as shown in Screen 1.1. To launch an application quickly, just press *Ctrl + Esc* followed by the application's number.

Screen 1.1 – **Numbered application shortcuts on the Start Menu**

Quick-Launch Alternative

Provided each Start Menu shortcut's name begins with a different letter, press *Ctrl + Esc* followed by that initial letter to launch the program. For example, the standard Start Menu commands can be accessed by *Ctrl + Esc* followed by R for **Run**, H for **Help**, S then T for **Settings / Taskbar**, and so on.

If you have several items on the menu with the same initial, such as 'Documents', 'Desktop' and 'Dial-Up', repeatedly pressing D will toggle between them. Press *Enter* to launch the one you want.

Registry
Tip

Turbo-Charged Start Menu

After clicking the Start button, holding your mouse-pointer over any nested entry will bring up its cascading menu. However, the delay between pointing at the entry and the menu actually appearing can seem pretty sluggish. You can speed it up (or slow it down even more if you want to!) via the Registry.

I   Open the Registry Editor (type **regedit** on the **Run** command-line).

2   Expand **HKEY_CURRENT_USER** by double-clicking it.

3   Expand the key named **ControlPanel** and click on the **Desktop** key.

4   Look in the right pane for a string-value named **MenuShowDelay**. If it isn't there, right-click on the **Desktop** key and select **New** and **String Value**. Name this new string **MenuShowDelay**.

5   Double-click on **MenuShowDelay** and a dialog-box will appear. Replace the value in the box with any figure from **0** (for instantaneous) to **100000** (for some time next week) – this is the delay-time in milliseconds. A setting of around 30 is a good starting point: very low values might be as infuriating as high ones! Click on **OK**.

6   Close the Registry Editor. For this setting to take effect, you'll have to restart *Windows95* (press *Alt + F4, R*, then *Shift + Return*).

Getting Keyed-Up

For the keyboard-fans out there, use *Ctrl + Esc* followed by D or P to access the **Documents** or **Programs** menus respectively. You can then use the four arrow keys to navigate the menus and *Enter* to launch a selected program or document. If you change your mind, repeatedly pressing *Esc* will close each successive menu column followed by the Start Menu itself.

Cascading System Folders

Tired of having to delve into **My Computer** or **Start / Settings** to get at Control Panel or Dial-Up Networking? Here's a method of making these (and others) more accessible by creating cascading Start Menu subfolders for them:

Right-click on the Start button and click **Open**. Create a new folder named:

> **Control Panel.{21EC2020-3AEA-1069-A2DD-08002B30309D}**

Note the inclusion of the full-stop after 'Control Panel' and the curly braces. (The hex-codes associate this folder with an entry in the **Registry**.) This adds a copy of the **Control Panel** folder to your Start Menu, although you can just as easily create it in another folder such as Start / Programs / Accessories if you prefer.

Other 'virtual' folders can be created in a similar way by using these self-explanatory folder names:

> **Printers.{2227A280-3AEA-1069-A2DE-08002B30309D}**

> **Dial-Up Networking.{992CFFA0-F557-101A-88EC-00DD010CCC48}**

> **Recycle Bin.{645FF040-5081-101B-9F08-00AA002F954E}**

 (i) If you've renamed your Recycle Bin (following the tip 'Trash The Bin' on page 50), type its new name instead when creating a cascading folder for it.

(ii) A cascading Bin folder isn't the most useful thing you can spend your time creating: clicking an item within it simply displays the item's Properties page!

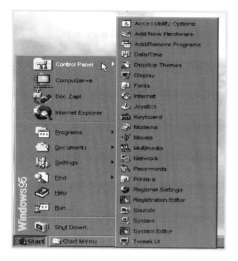

Screen 1.2 – **Cascading Control Panel on the Start Menu**

With almost no effort, you can create your own customized Control Panel instead, and make it the way it should have been from the beginning. Take a look at 'Fake Control Panel' on page 54.

Remove The System Folders

As a form of security on shared systems, **Policy Editor** allows certain elements of the shell to be disabled. Follow this tip to hide the system folders (such as Control Panel and Printers) located in **Start / Settings**.

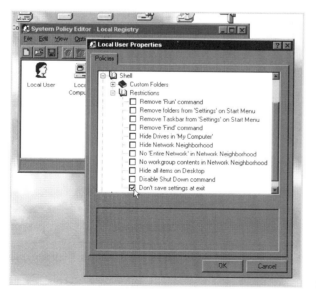

Screen 1.3 – **Policy Editor**

I   Start **Policy Editor** (see page 227 for details on installing this program from the *Windows95* CD-ROM if you haven't already done so).

2   Select **File / Open Registry**.

3   Double-click the **Local User** icon.

4   Expand **Shell** then **Restrictions** and click the checkbox next to **Remove folders from 'Settings' on Start Menu**.

5   Click **OK**, click the **Close** button and hit *Return* to save the settings.

6   Restart Windows for the change to take effect.

To restore these folders to the Start Menu, follow the same routine but this time *clear* the checkbox in step 4.

Once removed from the Start Menu, these folders also vanish from within the **My Computer** and **Explorer** views of the system, and any shortcuts you'd previously created (for example, to individual Control Panel applets) are non-functioning.

If you don't have Policy Editor you can still remove the system folders by using the Registry. Follow the tip 'Remove Run From The Registry' on page 12, but call the new DWORD value **NoSetFolders**.

Getting Help

You can get **Help** from the Start Menu by clicking it, or by pressing *Ctrl + Esc* followed by H. But a far quicker method is just to press *F1*. This is a great habit to get into since most Windows applications provide context-sensitive help at the press of this key. For more on **Help**, see page 147.

If the focus is on the Taskbar (after minimizing a window for example), pressing *F1* will have no effect. In this case, you have to click once on the Desktop first to shift the focus.

The Documents Menu

What Is It?

The **Documents** menu on the Start Menu holds shortcuts to the fifteen files you've opened or created most recently – to re-open one, just click it. Files opened or created in 16-bit Windows applications won't appear here though, unless you double-clicked the file in an Explorer-window to start the program.

These shortcuts are created automatically by *Windows95* in a hidden subfolder of your Windows folder called 'Recent' (unless your computer is set up for multiple users as in 'Desktop Duality' on page 36 – the active 'Recent' folder is then a subfolder of your user-folder in C:\Windows\Profiles).

Tip

Zap The Docs

The Documents menu can sometimes be more of a hindrance than a help, and could be a security risk on a shared computer. For example, some of the files you work with may be 'Hidden', but the shortcuts created in the Recent folder aren't – they'll still show up on the Documents menu.

Apart from the obvious method of clearing the menu (**Start / Settings / Taskbar / Start Menu Programs / Clear**), you could navigate to the hidden C:\Windows\ Recent folder and delete its contents. But both of these are long-winded, click-hungry methods. A quicker method is to use a batch-file:

1   Open **Notepad**.

2   Type the line: **echo y| del c:\windows\recent*.***

3   Choose a name such as **Doc Zap.bat** and save the file into any convenient folder.

4   Create a shortcut to **Doc Zap.bat** on your Desktop called **Doc Zap**.

5   Right-click the shortcut and select **Properties / Program / Run / Minimized**.

6   Check the box marked **Close on exit**.

7   Choose a snappy new icon by clicking the **Change Icon** button.

8   Click **OK** to finalize.

Double-clicking the Doc Zap icon will automatically clear your **Documents** list.

Tip

Clear The Lot

If you want to economize on the clicks still further, use the batch-file to empty your Recycle Bin at the same time. Just add a second line to the batch file that reads: **echo y| del c:\recycled*.*** (Add extra identical lines for any other hard drives or logical drives on your system if you configured their Recycle Bin settings differently, just replacing the **c:** with the drive's identification letter.)

Pick & Choose

If you find the Documents menu useful, but you'd prefer that certain documents weren't there, you can remove individual items. The easiest way to do this is to create a shortcut to C:\Windows\Recent on your Desktop or Start Menu. You can then open the folder easily and delete the shortcuts you don't want.

The Run Command

Running Fast

The **Run** command can be a great time-saver when the alternative is to trawl through Explorer to find a particular file. Click on the Start button and **Run** (or press *Ctrl + Esc* followed by *R*) and type in a filename such as "**C:\Program Files\Accessories\MSPaint**" and hit *Return*. If the file's path is specified in a SET PATH = line in your Autoexec.bat you need only type the file's name (for example, try typing **faq.txt**).

Remember this is a DOS command-line, so files, folders and paths involving *Windows95* long filenames must be enclosed in 'quotes', as in the first example above. For the same reason, the commands are not case sensitive.

To find out more about the path statement, go to page 265.

Open Folders Fast

Use the **Run** command to open any folder quickly. Following the points above, type in a folder name (such as "**C:\Program Files**"); a single-pane view of that folder's contents will open.

Open Hidden Items

Certain files and folders within C:\ and C:\Windows are hidden to prevent accidental deletion. You may also have assigned the Hidden attribute to files and folders of your own for security reasons. To view these files (or the contents of the folders), type the full path and name on the **Run** line.

 Turn to page 91 for more details on showing and hiding items.

Running Favourites

The **Run** applet stores your most-recent commands, the latest successfully executed command being shown as the default. Open the drop-down box to select one of these without having to retype it.

Roll 'Em!

To scroll through the list of previously used commands in the **Run** dialog, just use your Up & Down arrow keys, or press *F4* to drop the list – it's easier than trying to click that little 'expand' button!

Shorten The Run List

The drop-down list of recent commands in **Run** can be immensely useful as a kind of 'in-between' storage space: some items aren't accessed often enough to require their own shortcut, but when you do need them it saves you trying to remember their filename or path.

Unfortunately there's no built-in method of limiting which commands are saved, so you might end up with the path to a folder on a long-since formatted floppy-disk, a disappointing website and all kinds of paraphernalia. Follow these steps to remove those unwanted items (and to shorten the list):

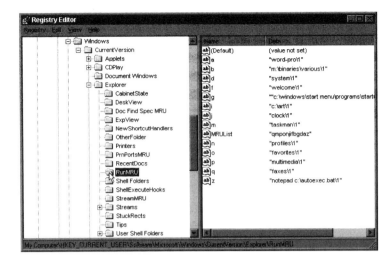

Screen 1.4 – **The Run list in Registry Editor**

1   Open the Registry Editor.

2   Expand **HKEY_CURRENT_USER.**

3   Find and expand **Software \ Microsoft \ Windows \ CurrentVersion \ Explorer.**

4   Click on the key named **RunMRU**, shown in Screen 1.4.

5   In the right pane you'll see a list of the entries in your **Run** drop-down. Just click on an entry you want to remove and press *Delete*. Click **OK** when prompted. Do the same for other entries you want to lose.

If you want a completely empty Run 'list', delete everything in the right pane except the **(Default)** entry.

Registry Tip

Customize The Run List

To customize the **Run** drop-down list, first follow the steps outlined above to find the right point in the Registry and delete any **Run** references you no longer want.

The Run box displays the commands in the order specified in the **MRUList** string. If you want your commands displayed in a particular order, double-click on **MRUList** and type your preferred order (for example, **bgedaz**).

The next time you type a new command on the **Run** line, it will be assigned the first available letter (**c** in the above example) and this letter would be inserted at the beginning of the **MRUList** to make it the default command.

Run A Website

If you use **Internet Explorer** (from the *Plus!* pack), you can use the **Run** command-line to jump straight to a WWW site. Type (or paste) in the URL, hit **OK** and **Internet Explorer** will do the rest.

The Path Trick

Drag and drop a document or application onto the **Run** dialog, and the full path of the file, including the extension, will be displayed.

Tip

Remove The Run Command

Do you have some deep-rooted grievance against the **Run** command? Okay, let's get rid of it:

1   Start **Policy Editor** (if you haven't installed this program, see page 227 for details).

2   Select **File / Open Registry**.

3   Double-click the **Local User** icon.

4   Expand **Shell** then **Restrictions** and click **Remove 'Run' command**.

5   Click **OK**, click the **Close** button and hit *Return* to save the settings.

6   Restart Windows, and take a look at the Start Menu: it's Run-less!

  To restore the **Run** command to the Start Menu, follow the same routine but this time clear the checkbox.

Registry
Tip

Remove Run From The Registry

If you installed *Windows95* from floppies and don't have Policy Editor, you can still remove the **Run** command by editing the Registry.

1   Open the Registry Editor.

2   Expand the keys **HKEY_CURRENT_USER \ Software \ Microsoft \ Windows \ CurrentVersion \ Policies.**

3   Right-click on the **Explorer** key, and choose **New** and **DWORD** value.

4   Name this new value **NoRun**.

5   Double-click on **NoRun** and type **1**. Press *Enter*.

6   Close the Registry. Click once on the Desktop, press *F5* to refresh and click on the Start button. If the **Run** command is still there you'll need to restart Windows for the change to take effect.

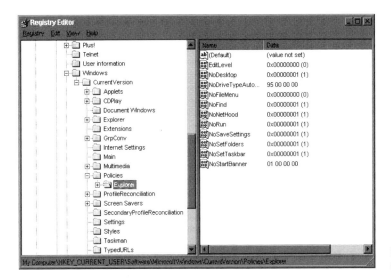

Screen 1.5–**A change of Policy in Regedit**

You can use the **Policies** key in the Registry to carry out other 'removals' mentioned elsewhere in this book. Just substitute the DWORD Value name in steps 4 and 5 with one of these:

❑   **NoFind** – removes the Find command from the Start Menu

❑   **NoDesktop** – removes all icons from the Desktop

❑   **NoSetFolders** – removes the system-folders from Start / Settings

❑   **NoSetTaskbar** – removes the Taskbar edit-page from Start / Settings

❑   **NoSaveSettings** – prevents Windows saving your settings on shutdown

❑   **NoStartBanner** – gets rid of the 'Click here to begin' startup message

(i) Some of these values are included in the **Policies** key by default – if the one you want is there already don't add it again, just edit it.

(ii) Though the results are similar, using **Policy Editor** to toggle these settings on and off is a great deal more convenient than editing the Registry. If you do intend to use the Registry, take this idiosyncrasy into account: With each of the seven values covered in this tip, you can switch its value-data to either **1** (for 'yes, remove it') or **0** ('put it back'). However, with the exception of the last two in the list, when you set the value-data to **0**, and close or refresh the Registry, Windows figures that if you want the default setting you don't need the item listed any more – next time you look it's gone! So you might as well just delete it yourself – it's quicker, and if you want to switch back to **1** in the future, you'd have to re-enter the DWORD Value again anyway.

The Find Command

Finding Hidden Items

Unless **Show all files** is selected (on Explorer's **View / Options** page), **Find** will not locate hidden files or files within hidden folders.

Minimizing Searches In Find

Using **Find**'s drop-down drive list, you have the option to search the entire computer (including CD-ROM and floppy drives) or individual drives. To narrow down the search (and therefore speed it up!) type a starting folder in the **Look in** box. If you're sure the file you want is in this folder rather than one of its subfolders, clear the **Look in subfolders** checkbox before clicking **OK**.

Maximizing Searches In Find

For a fully-maximized search, select **My Computer** from the drop-down drive list in **Find**. However, this wastes time trying to access floppy and CD-ROM drives. To limit your search to hard-drives only, enter the drive-letters separated by a semicolon. For example, to search two drives named C & E, type in **C:;E:**. In the same way, you can list specific folders by entering, for example, **C:\Reports;C:\Current;E:\Oldstuff** (see Screen 1.6).

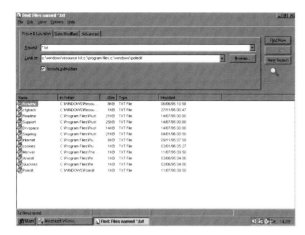

Screen 1.6 – **Searching multiple folders**

Oddly, highlighting two drives or two folders in an Explorer-window and choosing **Find...** from the context-menu doesn't automate this selection process; instead you get two instances of Find, one hiding the other, rooted to your two selected items.

Remember that **C:** is a folder – if **Look in subfolders** is unchecked, the search will be confined to the root folder of drive C rather than hunting through the entire drive. (In **Find**, entering **C:** functions in the same way as entering **C:**.)

Using Wildcards In Find

The wildcard characters (**?** and *****) can be used to replace unknown letters in the **Named** box, or to widen the search.

❑ The asterisk (*) replaces multiple letters: a search for ***.doc** would find any file with the .doc extension. Searching for ***95.txt** would turn up any text file whose name ended with '95'. Searching for ***letter*.doc** would find any **.doc** file with the word 'letter' somewhere in its name.

❑ The question-mark (?) replaces individual characters, so a search for **???ai*.exe** will show any **.exe** files whose fourth and fifth letters are 'ai' (one of which should be Mspaint.exe). A search for **???.exe** would turn up any **.exe** file with a three-character name (such as Ftp.exe or Gdi.exe).

❑ Entering a group of letters without wildcards will find any file or folder names containing those letters in any position. For example, entering **fil** will find the 'Program Files' folder and Winfile.exe.

Multiple Searches

You can use **Find** to search for more than one type of file at a time. Simply type all the required search strings into the **Named** box, each separated by a space. Screen 1.7 shows a multiple search in action, with examples taken from the tip above.

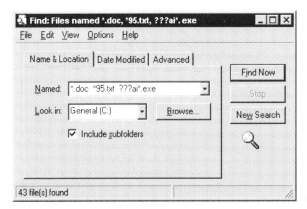

Screen 1.7 – **A multiple search in 'Find'**

Text Search

You can use **Find** to search for files containing a particular word, phrase, numeric sequence etc: click the **Advanced** tab and type in the text to be found. Selecting the known file-type from the drop-down list will speed up the search, as will entering specific details under the **Name & Location** tab.

 If the text-search isn't locating all the examples you think exist, make sure **Case Sensitive** on the **Options** menu is unchecked.

Searching For File Types

To find all the bitmap files on your system you could type ***.bmp** in the 'Named' box, but you can also do it without typing anything at all. Just click the **Advanced** tab, and choose **Bitmap Image** from the 'File Types' drop-down.

This highlights the difference between file *extensions* and file *types*. Some applications grab a bundle of file-extensions for themselves when you install them, so you might find, for example, all your **.gif**, **.jpg**, **.wmf** and **.tif** files associated with Paint Shop Pro. A search for 'Paint Shop Pro Image' files under the **Advanced** tab would turn up any file with one of these extensions; to find just **.gif** files would entail typing ***.gif** into the 'Named' box instead.

Finding Find

Pressing *F3* while on the Desktop or in any Explorer window will bring up the **Find** dialog. If you're working in a particular folder-window, **Find** will default to this folder as the root for the search. (If the focus is on the Desktop rather than the Taskbar or an Explorer-window, the starting point will be C:\Windows\ Desktop which is about the last place you'll ever need to search!)

❑ To launch **Find** quickly from within an application, click once on an empty area of the Taskbar and then press *F3*.

❑ To quickly search the entire system for a file or text-string, right-click on the **My Computer** icon and select **Find...** from the context-menu.

Screen 1.8 – **Using 'Find' from the context-menu**

❑ To search a specific drive, you can use the same method when right-clicking a drive icon in **My Computer** or in any Explorer-window.

❑ To root the search to a particular folder in an Explorer-window, right-click the folder and select **Find...**

Save Search Configurations

If there's a particular multiple search you carry out regularly, or you often search specific multiple folders or drives, it makes sense to save the search and avoid a lot of typing in the future.

Set up all the search parameters as you want them, and then select **File / Save search**. This creates a file on your Desktop with a **.fnd** extension which, when double-clicked, will re-launch **Find** with these parameters already set. (You can rename this file by highlighting it and pressing *F2*.) The 'sort' settings will also be saved with the file, so you can sort these files by Name or Modified date.

If you end up with a little bundle of **.fnd** files that you use regularly, why not create a new subfolder on the Start Menu and move them into it?

Using Find Results

The results of the search, displayed in a (stretchable) window can be treated just the same as files in any Explorer window. In other words, double-clicking a file will launch it with its associated application; right-clicking a file gives you the usual options including Cut, Copy, Rename, Delete, Create Shortcut and Properties.

In this way, **Find** is a useful starting point to creating folders containing certain types of file. Say, for example, you want a folder containing shortcuts to every **.wav** file on your hard-disk. After creating the new folder, run a search for ***.wav** (or click the **Advanced** tab and choose **Wave Sound** from the 'File Types' box).

Scroll to the end of the resulting list, press *Shift* and left-click on the last file (or just hit *Ctrl + A*) – this will highlight every file in the list (see Screen 1.9). Now right-click on one of the highlighted files, move the pointer onto your new folder and drop the files, selecting **Create Shortcut(s) Here** from the context-menu. Hey presto – a folder containing shortcuts to every **.wav** on your system: not bad for thirty seconds' work!

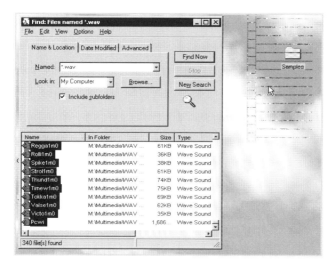

Screen 1.9 – **Dragging shortcuts from 'Find'**

For a different, slightly neater, way to do the same thing, read 'Quick Catalogues' on page 317.

Un-founded?

Yes, you can lose the **Find** command just as easily as **Run**: follow the same routine as in 'Remove The Run Command' on page 12, but when you get to step 4 click the **Remove 'Find' command** checkbox instead.

Two curiosities of this facility: first, while the Find command is no longer accessible from the Start Menu, it *is* still available by pressing *F3* in all the usual situations; second, if you like to right-click on the Start button to edit your Start Menu folders, you'll no longer be able to do so.

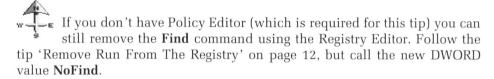

If you don't have Policy Editor (which is required for this tip) you can still remove the **Find** command using the Registry Editor. Follow the tip 'Remove Run From The Registry' on page 12, but call the new DWORD value **NoFind**.

Shorten The Find List

The most recent entries in Find's drop-down list are stored in the Registry, along with the order in which they're displayed. Start **Regedit**, and go to **HKEY_CURRENT_USER \ Software \ Microsoft \ Windows \ CurrentVersion \ Explorer \ Doc Find Spec MRU**.

Delete any entries you want to from the right pane, except the one named (**Default**). If you want to edit the display order, double-click on **MRUList** and retype the letter-references in your preferred order.

This procedure is identical to that for the Run-command's list, which is explained in more detail on page 10.

The Programs Folder

Full Folder?

Is your cascading **Programs** folder on the Start Menu getting too full of items to be able to find anything quickly? Maybe the whole nested collection of subfolders within the **Programs** folder is getting untidy?

When you install new software, some applications place an icon directly into the **Programs** folder itself and its menu can soon expand to a second or even a third column. Other applications have the grace to create their own subfolders within **Programs**, but then fill it with links to Help and ReadMe files that you'll probably never use.

In most cases the single useful item is the shortcut to the application itself, so why not create a folder called **Applications** and move all your app shortcuts here? If you have a lot of apps, create further folders inside **Applications** called **Word Processing, Graphics, Internet** and so on to make items easier to find. Then delete all the empty subfolders and unnecessary ReadMe shortcuts to give yourself a more streamlined 'fast-access' menu.

 When clearing out your **Programs** folder, don't move (and certainly don't delete) your **StartUp** folder, even if it's empty!

The Missing Column

If you use the **Programs** folder as the base for everything you add to the Start Menu, you're adding 'navigation time' and wasting the first 'column'. Move your most-accessed folders from the **Programs** folder to the **Start Menu** itself (see Screen 1.10).

You can then keep the Programs folder as a repository for the lesser-used items to keep them out of the way, and get to everything else a whole lot faster.

If you've set up hotkey combinations for some of the shortcuts you move, you'll probably have to renew them. In fact, they're still there but Windows temporarily loses track of them. Right-click an item with a hotkey combo and choose **Properties** then **Shortcut**. Check the combo is still listed, click **OK** to close and Windows will update its records.

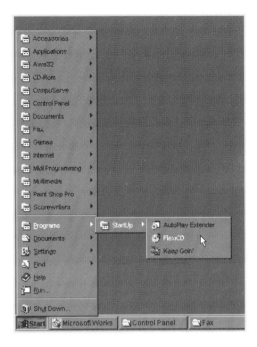

Screen 1.10 – **Making the most of the Start Menu**

Extra Organization

A useful one-stop trick to tidy your Programs folder-nest is to create a subfolder called **Extras**. In this, place all the applications, accessories and utilities that you rarely use but want to be able to find when you *do* need them.

The StartUp Folder

What Is It?

Items placed in the **StartUp** folder are launched automatically as *Windows95* finishes loading. These may be accessories that you keep running in the background (to constantly monitor system resources for example), or applications you would always run at the start of a Windows session (such as an appointments scheduler), saving you the trouble of finding and double-clicking them.

Using StartUp

The **StartUp** folder (C:\Windows\Start Menu\Programs\StartUp) functions in just the same way as any other folder: use the right mouse-button to drag items into it and create shortcuts. Aside from the items mentioned above, here's a few other ideas you might want to use:

❏   If you find that every Windows session involves some digging around inside Explorer, add a copy of your Explorer shortcut here.

❏   If you opt for a multi-user setup to let you have different settings for different types of Windows session (see 'Desktop Duality' on page 36), customize the StartUp folders for each 'user' to automatically run the applications you use for that type of session. (Note: you must select the *Include Start Menu groups* option in **Passwords** for this to have an effect.)

❏   If you want an application to be opened automatically with a specific file (such as **WordPad** with a file named 'Letterhead.doc') use a shortcut to the file instead of the application.

❏   If you have a folder in Explorer containing all the documents you use regularly, drag this into the **StartUp** folder to create a shortcut to it: its contents will be displayed every time you start Windows ready for you to begin work.

❏   For the security-conscious, add a shortcut to one of the **.bat** files covered on pages 8 and 9 to ensure that your Documents list and/or Recycle Bin are always emptied on startup.

Of particular use in the **StartUp** folder is the ability to choose how an application should be run, Maximized, Minimized or Normal. See the 'Running Applications' subheading on page 97.

Overriding StartUp

If you want Windows to ignore the items in your **StartUp** folder (to save resources or perhaps as an aid to troubleshooting), just hold *Ctrl* as Windows loads.

If you want to run your StartUp programs in a particular order, or pick and choose which to run and which to ignore, you can create a DOS batch-program to do the job. Take a look at 'StartUp Control' and 'Custom StartUp' on page 294.

What Happened?

If you arrive in *Windows95* after booting up to find your screen smothered in application-windows, you've probably deleted your **StartUp** folder. With no StartUp folder to use, *Windows95* defaults to using the Programs folder instead!

To solve the problem, open your Windows/Start Menu/Programs folder and create a new folder inside it called **StartUp**, then choose 'Restart' from the **Shutdown** menu to close all these windows in an orderly (and automatic) fashion.

The Taskbar

Taskbar Clicks

Right-click on an empty area of the Taskbar to show a list of options relating to all open windows: **Minimize All Windows** is a handy way to get back to your Desktop in a hurry, and the **Tile** options make for easier drag & drop between windows. The **Properties** selection is a quick route to the **Start / Settings / Taskbar** page.

You can also reach the **Taskbar Properties** page by clicking once on the Taskbar (to 'select' it) and pressing *Alt + Enter*.

Right-clicking an iconized application on the Taskbar gives a list of options for that app such as **Maximize, Minimize, Restore**. Selecting **Close** will shut the window or application after giving you the chance to save any unsaved work.

Taskbar Travels

By default, the Taskbar lives at the bottom of the screen, but you can move it to any edge of the screen by left-clicking and dragging it to where you want it (see Screen 1.11). The Start Menu will adjust its direction accordingly, and any open windows will move to make room for it.

Stretching It

As soon as you have more than four or five windows open, the buttons on the

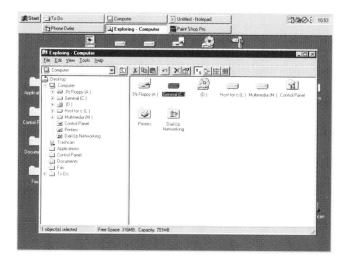

Screen 1.11 – **The Taskbar, moved & stretched**

Taskbar begin to shrink to make room for new ones, making the applications' titles hard to read. To make extra space (as shown in Screen 1.11), move the pointer to the edge of the Taskbar (the pointer will change to a double-headed arrow) and drag to expand it one 'row' at a time.

Avoid Stretching It

As soon as you stretch the Taskbar, of course, your working screen-area becomes smaller – this is the last thing you need when you've got so many objects open !

As long as you can put up with the way those little huddled Taskbar icons look, you can still find out what each one represents: just hold your mouse-pointer over one of the icons for a moment and a pop-up tooltip will reveal all.

Reduce Mouse Mileage

If you prefer to work with the Taskbar hidden (**Start / Settings / Taskbar / Auto Hide**), save yourself the frequent mouse-excursions to the bottom of the screen to bring it back: press *Ctrl + Esc* and up pops the Taskbar with the Start Menu selected.

The Thin Line

When you work with the Taskbar set to **Auto Hide**, it collapses to a thin line at the bottom of the screen and waits for your pointer to land on it. To change the size of the line, right-click on the Desktop, select **Properties**, click the **Appearance** tab, and select **Active Window Border** from the **Item** box. You can then increase or decrease the value in the **Size** box to its right.

I *Know* Where To Click!

If you still have that irritating bouncing message on startup that reads 'Click here to begin', and feel you can now remember where to click unassisted, here's the way to remove it:

1   Start the Registry Editor (type **regedit** on the **Run** command-line).

2   Expand **HKEY_CURRENT_USER** and navigate to \ **Software** \ **Microsoft** \ **Windows** \ **CurrentVersion** \ **Policies** \ **Explorer**.

3   Click on the **Explorer** key and look in the right pane. You should see a string named **NoStartBanner**. If you don't, right-click on the **Explorer** key, choose **New** and **Binary Value**, and name this new value **NoStartBanner**.

4   Double-click on **NoStartBanner** and a dialog-box will pop up with the cursor flashing in the correct position.

5   Press *Delete* once, and then type **01** (i.e., zero, one). Click **OK**. The entry in the right pane should now read **01 00 00 00**.

6   Press *F5* to refresh the Registry settings.

7   Close the Registry Editor. Next time you start Windows, you'll have to decide for yourself which button it is you're supposed to click...

If you have one or more items in your StartUp folder, or programs that log themselves in the Tray on startup (such as **System Agent** in *Plus!*), you won't see this message.

Remove Taskbar Properties Page

The Taskbar properties item can be removed from the **Start / Settings** menu using Policy Editor as covered in 'Remove The Run Command' on page 12. Follow the same instructions, but in step 4 click the checkbox beside **Remove Taskbar from 'Settings' on Start Menu**.

The **Taskbar Properties** page and the **Add/Remove Start Menu Programs** dialog can no longer be accessed by right-clicking the Taskbar or Start button, but items can still be added to the Start Menu from within Explorer (C:\Windows\ Start Menu).

If you don't have Policy Editor you can still remove the **Taskbar Properties** page via the Registry. Follow the tip 'Remove Run From The Registry' on page 12, but call the new DWORD value **NoSetTaskbar**.

The Tray

Clocking Off

If you have your own preferred **Clock** utility, you can remove the clock from the Tray (aka the 'Notification Area') and gain a little extra space on the Taskbar. Open **Start / Settings / Taskbar** (or right-click on the Taskbar and select **Properties**) and clear the checkbox for **Show Clock**.

Date Doubt?

Hold your mouse pointer over the clock in the Tray to see today's date. Double-clicking the clock will produce a full calendar to let you change your system-time and date. Make sure you click **Apply** to actually make the change – if you just click **OK** the applet will quit without altering your settings.

Customized Date

It isn't immediately obvious, but the date you see when you hover the pointer over the Tray's clock can be customized – go to **Regional Settings** in the Control Panel and click on the **Date** tab. In the area marked 'Long date style' you can type in your chosen format. You can right-click on the words 'Long date style' for instructions. A few examples are shown in Fig. 1.1

Fig. 1.1

Entry	Result
dddd, d MMMM yyyy	Friday, 8 September 1995
MMMM dd, yy '('dddd')'	September 08, 95 (Friday)
dd-MM-yy	08-09-95

You can add text to the date by enclosing it in single-quotes ('), but certain characters can't be used, such as **&** and **?**. And don't get too carried away – the format you choose will appear on Properties pages too!

Screen I.12 – **Want to add spice to your dates?**

Spaced Out

Do you find it irritating that the tooltip-date appears on the far right of the screen when you hold the pointer over the clock? Suffer no more . . .

When you've set up the date format you want, as in the previous tip, just add spaces to the end of the line. Add about 25 to move the text roughly an inch to the left.

 This will tend to mess up the date and time displayed on Properties pages, but they'll still be shown correctly in Explorer's details view.

 You can also increase the text-size of the tooltip date (see 'Tooltips' on page 173).

Time Zone Fun

Double-click the clock in the Tray, and select the **Time Zone** tab. Click anywhere on the map to see the time-zone of any part of the world (useful for planning international phone-calls) and to learn a little geography in the process. (Make sure you don't click **Apply** before you close the applet if you don't want your system-time changed !)

Screen 1.13 – **Time-travel**

 Is your Time Zone too vague? See 'My Very Own Time Zone' on page 318 to add a little more detail.

Use The Loudspeaker

Left-click the loudspeaker icon in the Tray to control the volume of your soundcard. Double-clicking the icon brings up a complete mixing desk of individual volume and balance controls, together with an **Advanced** option for altering tone (see Screen 1.14).

Lose The Loudspeaker

Had enough of the loudspeaker icon in the Tray? If you prefer to use the volume controls on your speakers or amplifier instead, go to **Control Panel / Multimedia / Audio** and click on **Show volume control on the taskbar** to clear the checkbox.

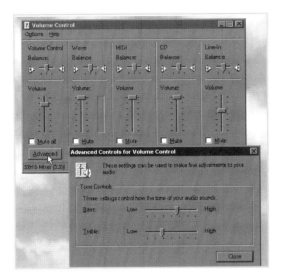

Screen 1.14 – **The mixer and tone controls from the Taskbar volume-icon**

Mixer On Tap

If you don't want the loudspeaker icon in the Tray but you'd still like to get to its mixer-control page once in a while, create a shortcut to **Sndvol32.exe** (from the Windows folder) somewhere convenient such as your Fake Control Panel (see page 54). Running this app bypasses the simple volume-slider and opens the mixing-desk directly.

Use The Modem

If you use **Dial-Up Networking**, you'll see a modem icon arrive in the Tray when a connection is made to indicate data-transfer. But the modem does more than just indicate data in/out. Hover your mouse-pointer over the icon for a count of the total data transmitted and received during the current session.

Ins & Outs Of The Modem

For a more graphic depiction of modem-action, double-click on the Tray-icon: a movable diagram will keep you notified about your connection-time and total data transmitted and received (see Screen 1.15).

Screen 1.15 – **Double-click the modem Tray icon for data details**

Lose The Modem

If you have an external modem and one set of lights is enough for you, here's how to remove this little chap:

1   Go to **Control Panel / Internet**.

2   Select the connection you want to change.

3   Click on **Properties...** then on **Configure**.

4   Select the **Options** tab and clear the **Display modem status** checkbox.

5   Click **OK** twice to close each page.

6   Repeat steps 2–5 for each connection you want to change, or click **OK** again to finish.

This routine applies only to Dial-Up Networking connections: if you want to do the same with Hyper-Terminal connections, right-click the connection and go to **Properties / Phone Number / Configure / Options** and clear the same checkbox. (Once again, you need to do this with each individual connection.)

Print Control

Whenever you choose the print command in an application, you'll see the printer icon appear in the Tray. This little icon is more than just decorative: hold your mouse-pointer over it and you'll get a tooltip telling you how many documents are waiting to be printed (handy if you use a shared printer).

Screen 1.16 – **The Tray displays its wares**

Double-clicking on the icon brings up the printer window from which you can pause, resume, or cancel printing, and change the print-priority of the remaining documents without having to leave or minimize your application window.

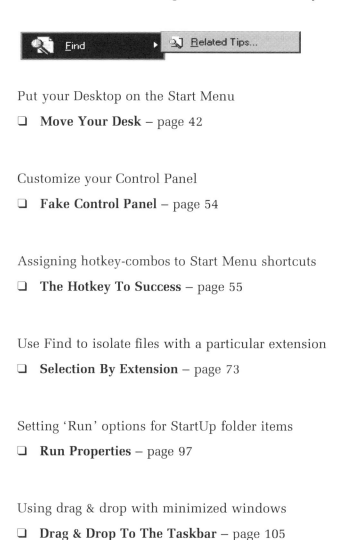

Put your Desktop on the Start Menu

❑ **Move Your Desk** – page 42

Customize your Control Panel

❑ **Fake Control Panel** – page 54

Assigning hotkey-combos to Start Menu shortcuts

❑ **The Hotkey To Success** – page 55

Use Find to isolate files with a particular extension

❑ **Selection By Extension** – page 73

Setting 'Run' options for StartUp folder items

❑ **Run Properties** – page 97

Using drag & drop with minimized windows

❑ **Drag & Drop To The Taskbar** – page 105

Reorganize your HyperTerminal connections

❑ **Whose Crazy Idea...?** – page 129

Put your Internet Explorer 'Favorites' on the Start Menu

❑   **Cascading Favorites Folder** – page 196

❑   **Move Your Favorites** – page 196

Additions to the customized Control Panel

❑   **Keep 'Em Together** – page 251

Find the largest file on your system

❑   **The Big One** – page 313

Working with shortcuts

❑   **'SHORTCUTS'** – page 52

Using Help files

❑   **'HELP TIPS'** – page 147

The Shutdown command

❑   **'SHUTTING DOWN'** – page 270

2

Desktop & Shortcuts

The Desktop

Fast Access To The Desktop

Getting back to the Desktop when you've got a bunch of applications and windows open can be a struggle – right-clicking on the Taskbar and selecting **Minimize All Windows** does the job, but may not do it quickly enough. The speedy solution is to put your Desktop on the Start Menu:

1   Right-click the Start button and click **Open**.

2   Right-click on an empty space and select **New** and **Shortcut**.

3   In the command-line box type:

        C:\Windows\Explorer.exe /n, C:\Windows\Desktop

     (making sure there's a comma and a space after the '/n' switch). Click **Finish** or hit *Return*.

4   Select a name for the shortcut (such as Desktop) and click **Finish**.

5   To select a different icon for the new shortcut, right-click the Desktop shortcut and select **Properties**. Click the **Shortcut** tab, followed by **Change Icon** and choose a new one.

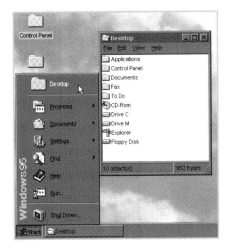

Screen 2.1 – **Quick access to the 'Desktop'**

When you want to see the contents of your Desktop in a hurry, just click on Start and your new Desktop icon (see Screen 2.1). Keeping its window minimized on the Taskbar will give even quicker access.

 One of the items missing from this folder is **My Computer**. This is another good reason to create a 'Fake Control Panel' (see page 54). You can then add shortcuts to some of the missing elements such as drives, printers and Dial-Up Networking connections to keep everything available from the Start Menu.

 Alternatively, take a look at 'Move Your Desk' on page 42.

Quick Desktop Refresh

Actions such as creating files or folders on the Desktop or making certain changes in the Registry sometimes take a while to register, and may even seem not to have happened at all. To refresh the Desktop quickly, click on it once to 'select' it, and press *F5*.

To force Windows to automate the 'refresh' process, go to 'More Refreshing!' on page 80.

Tip

Refresh Without Restart

Some operations (such as changes to Policy Editor settings, system folders or the Registry) won't take effect until you close all running applications and restart Windows. Here's a quicker method of refreshing the system:

Screen 2.2 – **The Close Program dialog**

I   Press *Ctrl + Alt + Del* to bring up the **Close Program** dialog (Screen 2.2).

2   Select Explorer and click **End Task**.

3   A window pops up to ask if you want to shut down the computer. Click **No**.

4   After a few seconds' pause, another window appears to ask if you want to close Explorer (Screen 2.3). Click on **End Task**.

5   Explorer will shut down briefly – taking the Taskbar and Desktop icons with it – and then immediately reload when *Windows95* realizes it can't run without Explorer. As it reloads, the system is refreshed to take account of the changes you made.

Screen 2.3 – **The 'End Task' screen**

This operation shouldn't have any effect on other applications running at the time, but it will remove icons from the Tray. The applications they represent are still running nonetheless – you can check this by pressing *Ctrl + Alt + Del* for a list of current apps (but make sure you use **Cancel** to close this window!).

System Folders On The Desktop

You can recreate system folders such as **Printers, Dial-Up Networking** and **Control Panel** on the Desktop for easier access. Just drag the folders from **My Computer** with either mouse-button – a shortcut will always be created.

Tip

Desktop Duality

Sometimes it can be useful (or aesthetically pleasing) to have a different Desktop; perhaps one associated with work and another for leisure. Many of the tips in this chapter suggest shortcut candidates for your Desktop: to use them all would result in an unorganized mess but having, for example, a Desktop dedicated to the Internet smothered with URL shortcuts and another especially for word-processing and accounts allows you to select different layouts to suit different types of Windows session.

Windows95 doesn't inherently allow for multiple Desktops, but its support for *multiple-users'* preferences gives an easy way to achieve them:

1   Open **Control Panel** and double-click **Passwords**.

2   Select the **Users can customize their preferences...** radio button.

3   Put a mark in the checkbox for **Include Desktop icons...** (and for **Include Start Menu...** if you'd like to create a different Start Menu to go with the new Desktop). Click **OK**.

Screen 2.4 – **The Passwords applet in single-user mode**

4   At the 'You must restart the computer' dialog, click **OK**.

5   As Windows restarts, you'll see a 'Welcome to Windows' dialog
(shown in Screen 2.5). Type a new name or nickname in the User
Name box. If you want this Desktop to be password protected, enter a
password in the second box; otherwise leave it blank (see 'Insecurity'
on page 39). Click **OK**.

Screen 2.5 – **Windows'
log-on screen for multiple
users**

6   Now you'll see a 'Please confirm the password you entered' dialog: if
you entered one, enter it again and click **OK**. If you didn't, just click
OK.

7   The last dialog asks whether you want Windows to remember your
settings: you do (or you'd be wasting your time changing them!) so
click **Yes**.

8   Finally the Desktop will appear, looking very like your other one, with
the possible exception of icon layout. You can now customize this
Desktop to suit your needs, including system sounds, wallpaper,
Desktop shortcuts, colours – just about anything.

9   Now select **Shut Down** from the Start Menu. You'll see an extra option
– **Close programs and log on as a different user**. Select this option; the
Taskbar and icons will vanish and be replaced a moment later by the
'Welcome to Windows' dialog again. Follow steps 5–8 again to create
your second Desktop. (You can keep creating more in the same way.)

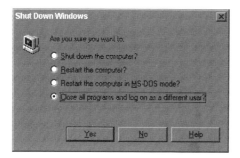

Screen 2.6 – **The 'Shut Down' dialog
with its new addition**

To toggle between the two Desktops, just select **Shut Down / Close Programs and log on as a different user**. Windows will remember the last user-name to gain access and will default to this name next time access is required: to log on with this name again you can simply press *Return* (unless you opted to use a password which you will need to enter).

To return at any time to your 'single Desktop mode', return to **Control Panel / Passwords** ('Passwords' has since grown an extra page to allow users to change their log-on password), select the **User Profiles** tab and click 'All users of this PC use the same preferences'. Click **OK** to restart Windows as before. The Desktop you used before creating 'multiple users' will reappear.

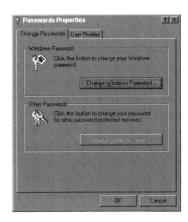

Screen 2.7 – **The 'Passwords' applet in multiple-user mode**

 (i) The first time you set up the computer for more than a single user, a subfolder named **Profiles** is created in the Windows folder, and a further folder created in **Profiles** corresponding to each user name. Since complete copies of all Desktop and Start Menu items, preferences and so on must be kept here, these folders can be pretty hefty – don't be surprised to see the odd megabyte of disk-space vanish into the ether.

(ii) Each 'user' also has his own **Recent** folder inside his **Profiles** folder as a security measure, so if you created a batch-file to clear your Documents menu ('Zap The Docs' on page 8) make sure you substitute this new path.

 Read 'Which User Am I?' on page 215 to check the impact this will have on your Registry-editing.

For more information about where and how these different layouts are stored, take a look at 'Where Is It?' on page 211.

Insecurity

To keep young children or the easily intimidated out of your system, a password-protected Desktop may be of some use. Bear in mind, however, that anyone can enter a new name during the log-on procedure and gain access as easily as you did, or indeed, just click **Cancel** or hit *Esc*. The password, therefore, provides no security at all against someone who knows the system or has enough active brain-cells to think of trying this manoeuvre.

Tip

Warnings & Threats

If you opt to use different user-names to access multiple Desktops, you can use Policy Editor to add a warning to the log-on procedure. And, best of all, you can decide exactly what this warning should read: you might choose to greet trespassing colleagues with threats of torture, or give yourself a friendly welcome every time you log on . . .

I   Run **Policy Editor** and select **File / Open Registry**.

2   Double-click on the **Local Computer** icon.

3   Expand **Network**, then **Logon** and check the **Logon Banner** box.

4   At the bottom of the page you can type a caption and a message of your own after deleting the defaults.

5   Click **OK**, select **File / Save** and close Policy Editor

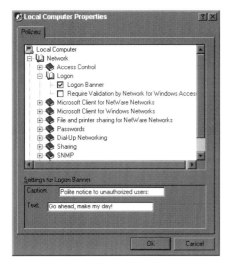

Screen 2.8 – **Add a friendly welcome to unexpected visitors**

Tip

Protect Your Desktop Settings #1

A major irritation in *Windows95* is the 'rearranged Desktop syndrome' – you can spend a few minutes carefully organizing the sizes and positions of your folder windows, selecting the view you want, arranging the icons to your taste, only to find a short time later that these settings have all reverted to some kind of arbitrary default.

The official line on this is that you should hold *Ctrl* when closing a window to protect its settings, but this makes no demonstrable long-term difference. The true solution can be found in Policy Editor. (If you don't have this little gem on your system, take a look at 'Installing Policy Editor' on page 227 for details.)

Before running Policy Editor, first set up everything just as you want it: this includes positions of folders and icons on your Desktop; positions and sizes of single-pane and dual-pane windows; View preferences (whether particular windows should show a List or Details view for example); Toolbar and Status Bar on or off for specific windows, and so on. Hold *Ctrl* as you close each window to ensure the settings are retained at least temporarily whilst setting up the rest. (Read 'Forward Planning' on page 42 for a layout tip.)

As soon as everything is set to your taste, select **Shut Down / Restart the computer** – Windows will save these settings as it shuts down. (To restart quickly, after clicking the radio button for **Restart the computer** press *Shift* as you click on **Yes** – this will restart Windows rather than the entire system.)

Now use Policy Editor to ensure that these settings are retained:

1   Start **Policy Editor**, and select **File / Open Registry**.

2   Double-click the **Local User** icon.

3   Expand **Shell**, then **Restrictions**, and click the checkbox for **Don't save settings at exit**.

4   Click **OK**, select **File / Save**, and close Policy Editor.

The settings are now safely stored and can't be changed until you clear the **Don't save...** checkbox: this is something you'll want to do from time to time as you add new items to your Desktop or want to change a particular folder's view.

In fact, the settings are now so safe that if you open a folder, change some aspect of its view preferences, close it and then re-open it, it will have immediately reverted to its last saved settings. So to purposely alter settings and resave them, you need to disable **Don't save settings at exit** *before* trying to make the changes.

If you're using multiple Desktops (as covered in the 'Desktop Duality' tip on page 36), you'll need to go through the whole 'setting-up + restarting + editing Policy Editor' experience for every 'user' as if each Desktop were an entirely separate computer.

Protect Your Desktop Settings #2

If you don't have Policy Editor installed, or don't have the *Windows95* CD-ROM, or just don't want the hassle of installing it, you can make the same edit directly into the Registry. It's not as handy as using Policy Editor, since you'll probably need to disable and re-enable the setting from time to time and this is a slower and more cumbersome way of doing so, but it works.

Follow the same initial procedure covered in the previous tip to set up your preferences, and save them by restarting Windows.

1   Start the Registry Editor (type **regedit** on the **Run** command-line).

2   Expand **HKEY_CURRENT_USER** and open \ **Software** \ **Microsoft** \ **Windows** \ **CurrentVersion** \ **Policies**.

3   Click on the **Explorer** key below **Policies** and look in the right pane. You should see a string named **NoSaveSettings**. Double-click it, and a dialog-box will pop up with the cursor flashing in the correct position.

4   Press *Delete* once, and then type **01** (i.e., zero, one). Click **OK**. The **NoSaveSettings** entry should now have a value that reads **01 00 00 00**.

5   Press *F5* to refresh the Registry settings, and close the Registry Editor.

6   Next time you exit Windows, your settings will not be saved.

If you want to change your settings and resave them, you must first follow these instructions again but type **00** when you get to step 4 (the result being **00 00 00 00**). You can then make the changes you want to the Desktop and exit or restart Windows. Don't forget to restore step 4's value to **01** next time you run Windows to ensure that you keep your new settings.

There is a way to speed up this process by exporting branches of the Registry – take a look at 'Working With Reg' on page 217.

Forward Planning

When you're deciding on sizes and positions of Explorer-windows and placement of Desktop icons in preparation for the two previous tips, bear in mind that you might want to drag items from a window to a printer-shortcut, Recycle Bin, floppy-drive icon and so on. Make sure these won't be covered by the window!

You might also want to set up the windows for your hard- and floppy-drives to open side-by-side for easy drag & drop.

Desktop Icons

Clear Your Desk

Want to see an uncluttered Desktop? Try this to remove every item:

I   Start **Policy Editor** (see page 227 for details on installing this program from the *Windows95* CD-ROM if you haven't already done so).

2   Select **File / Open Registry**.

3   Double-click the **Local User** icon.

4   Select **Shell** then **Restrictions** and click **Hide all items on Desktop**.

5   Click **OK**, click the **Close** button, and hit *Return* to save the settings.

6   Restart Windows, sit back, and gaze at your wallpaper!

To get your icons back, follow the same routine but clear the **Hide all items** checkbox.

This has the curious side-effect of turning off the Autoplay function of your CD-ROM drive.

 If you don't have Policy Editor you can still hide all the Desktop icons using the Registry. Follow the tip 'Remove Run From The Registry' on page 12, but call the new DWORD value **NoDesktop**.

Move Your Desk

If you follow the tip above, of course, you immediately lose access to all your Desktop icons. The trick is to *move* your desk to the Start Menu. You've probably already got shortcuts to most of the applications and documents you need here already – if you haven't, right-click on the Start button, create a folder called **Desktop** and move or copy the missing shortcuts into it.

Now open **My Computer**, select every item and drag shortcuts to them into your new folder, together with Recycle Bin, InBox and any other system-icons. You can now follow the tip above and still keep everything within easy reach.

Tidy Your Desk

Right-clicking on the Desktop gives you two arrangement options: **Arrange Icons** (with a sub-menu containing the 'sort-by' choices), or **Line up Icons**. Using **Arrange** will place your icons in columns from top-left to bottom-right (see Screen 2.9). If you like to do the basic arrangement yourself, perhaps in separate groups around the Desktop, use **Line Up** just to straighten the rows and columns afterwards.

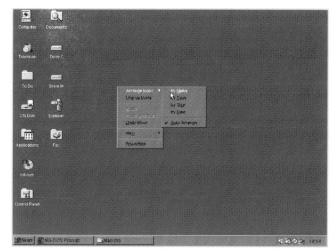

Screen 2.9 – **The result of 'Arrange Icons'**

Once you've used either option, you can use the left mouse-button to draw an expanding selection-box around a group of neatly arranged icons and drag them elsewhere.

Keyboard Navigation

When you have a clear Desktop view (i.e., any open windows are minimized), press *Tab* repeatedly until a Desktop icon is highlighted. You can then use the arrow keys to move from icon to icon, and *Enter* or *Return* to run an application or open a folder.

A quicker method is to press the key of an item's initial letter to select it (and press it repeatedly until the required item is highlighted if several have the same initial). Once again, use *Enter* or *Return* to carry out the item's default action.

Keyboard Right-Click

While cruising the Desktop in the manner above, you can also use *Shift + F10* to perform a right-click on any item with the 'focus' on it. To select an option from the resulting context-menu, press the underlined letter in the option's name (for example, to access the **Properties** of a highlighted item, press *Shift + F10* followed by *R*).

Screen 2.10 – **Place apps & drives on My Computer's context-menu**

Registry Tip

Quick Start

If you're tired of searching the Start Menu for the apps you use regularly, here's a trick to place application-shortcuts on **My Computer's** context-menu, as shown in Screen 2.10. Let's try it with Control Panel:

1   Open the Registry Editor and navigate to **HKEY_CLASSES_ROOT \ CLSID \ {20D04FE0-3AEA-1069-A2D8-08002B30309D} \ Shell**.

2   Right-click on **Shell** and choose **New** and **Key**. Name the new key **ControlPanel** (the choice of name here doesn't matter so choose something you'll recognize another time).

3   In the right pane, double-click on (**Default**) and type **Control Panel** (this is the name that will appear on the context-menu itself).

4   Now right-click on **ControlPanel** in the left pane and create another new key called **command** (and this name *does* matter!).

5 Double-click on (**Default**) in the right pane, and type **C:\Windows\ Control.exe** (see Screen 2.11). Press *F5* to refresh, right-click on **My Computer** and select your new Control Panel entry to check it out.

To save opening My Computer to access drives, you could create entries for them on this context-menu. For example, choose obvious names in steps 2 & 3, and in step 5 type **C:\Windows\Explorer.exe /n, /e, C:** (leave out the **/e**, switch for a single-pane view). Remember you can only create entries here for executable and batch (**.exe** and **.bat/.pif**) files.

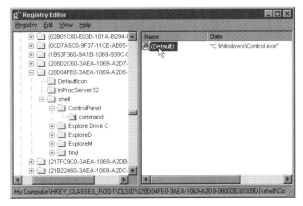

Screen 2.11 – **The new keys in Regedit**

Rename My Computer

If you haven't already (and for most *Windows95* users it's the first job!), click the icon, then click the label and type in a new name. Any name – it can only be an improvement.

After renaming it, giving it a better icon has to come a close second . . .

Registry
Tip

Change Desktop Icons

To change some of those less-than-inspiring Desktop icons takes a delve into the Registry, so start **Regedit**. If you followed 'Cascading System Folders' on page 5, you're about to meet those hex-codes again.

I   Expand **HKEY_CLASSES_ROOT**.

2   Scroll down the list (or type *cls*) to find the key **CLSID** and expand it.

3   Choose one of the following icons to change and find its corresponding hex-code in the left pane (see Screen 2.12):

❑   **My Computer:** {20D04FE0-3AEA-1069-A2D8-08002B30309D}

❑   **Network Neighborhood:** {208D2C60-3AEA-1069-A2D7-08002B30309D}

❑   **Inbox:** {00020D75-0000-0000-C000-000000000046}

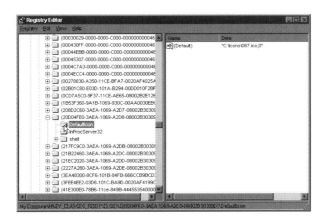

Screen 2.12 – **Changing My Computer's icon in Regedit**

4   When you've located the hex-code for the item you want to change, expand it and click on the **DefaultIcon** key.

5   In the right pane, double-click on (**Default**) and enter the path to the new icon. This may be a single icon-file (***.ico**) or one of the icons from a **.dll** file.

Make sure you specify the number of the icon from the **.dll** file: these are numbered from 0, so to choose the 14th icon from **shell32.dll** (the globe) you'll refer to it as '13'. Your full entry for this icon would be:

C:\Windows\System\Shell32.dll,13

If you've selected a single **.ico** file, the entry might be something like:

C:\Artwork\Icons\Binicon.ico,0

(For an **.ico** file, the icon-number will always be zero.)

❑ **Recycle Bin:** {645FF040-5081-101B-9F08-00AA002F954E}

The Recycle Bin functions in a slightly different way in that two icons are required: 'full' and 'empty'.

❑ **Folders:** Go to **HKEY_CLASSES_ROOT**, scroll down the list to find and expand the **Folder** key, and click on **DefaultIcon**. Double-click (**Default**) in the right pane and select a new icon as you did for the above items.

(i) *Plus!* pack users can, and should, use the **Plus!** tab in the **Display Properties** applet to change icons for **My Computer**, the **Recycle Bin** and **Network Neighborhood**.

(ii) If you've renamed My Computer or Network Neighborhood (and since restarted Windows), the names are now stored in the Registry. Instead of searching for the abominable hex-codes above, use the 'Find' option to locate the correct Registry-key.

Finding Network Properties

For quicker access to Network Properties than opening Control Panel and double-clicking the **Network** applet, just right-click the **Network Neighborhood** on your Desktop and select **Properties**.

Lose The Network Neighborhood Icon

On a stand-alone computer, the Network Neighborhood icon is just cluttering up the Desktop. To get rid of it:

1 Start **Policy Editor** (if you don't have this program on your system, see page 227 for installation details).

2 Select **File / Open Registry**.

3 Double-click the **Local User** icon.

4 Expand **Shell** then **Restrictions** and click **Hide Network Neighborhood**.

5 Click **OK**, click the **Close** button and hit *Return* to save the settings.

6 To get the icon back, follow the same steps but clear the checkbox.

If you don't have Policy Editor you can still remove the **Network Neighborhood** icon by using the Registry. Follow the tip 'Remove Run From The Registry' on page 12, but call the new DWORD value **NoNetHood**.

Recycle Bin

 ### Delete or Recycle?

When you 'delete' a file or a shortcut in the normal way, rather than vanishing from your system it's moved into the hidden folder C:\Windows\Recycled, making the Recycle Bin a possible security concern on a shared computer.

To immediately and permanently delete a file, hold down the *Shift* key while hitting *Delete* on the keyboard, selecting **Delete** from the context-menu or dragging the file onto the Recycle Bin.

Recycle Without Confirmation

To send files to the Recycle Bin immediately without the annoying confirmation prompts, right-click on the Recycle Bin, select **Properties** and clear the **Display delete confirmation dialog** checkbox.

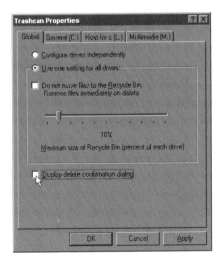

Screen 2.13 – **Recycle Bin's properties page**

 ### Bypass The Recycle Bin

If you like to live dangerously, right-click the Recycle Bin, select **Properties** and **Do not move files to the Recycle Bin**. All deleted files will be removed permanently, though you will always be presented with the confirmation dialog.

Undelete

Double-clicking any Recycle Bin icon will display the files you 'deleted'. To undelete a file, right-click it and choose **Restore** – the file will be resurrected in the folder from which it was deleted (recreating the folder if that was deleted as well). You can undelete multiple files by selecting them while holding *Ctrl* or *Shift* in the usual way and right-clicking on any one of them.

If you can't remember the original location of the file (and, therefore, where it will be restored to), just double-click it to bring up its **Properties** page and look at the 'Origin' entry. You can also see the date of deletion on this page.

Undelete To Here

You can undelete by drag & drop if you want the item restored to somewhere other than its original location. Just drag the item with the right mouse-button from Recycle Bin's window to wherever you want to restore it, and choose **Move Here** from the context-menu.

Customized Delete

By selecting Recycle Bin's **Properties** page and clicking **Configure drives independently** you can make settings for immediate deletion and maximum size for each drive individually – useful if you keep one drive for sensitive work-related files.

The Other Option . . .

If you prefer to work in 'immediate delete' mode, bypassing the Recycle Bin, you have no safety-net: either you delete a file or you don't. If you'd still like the option of a temporary holding place occasionally, try this:

I   Rename your Recycle Bin to **Shredder** following the steps in 'Trash The Bin' on page 50. You could apply a suitable icon as well to complete the analogy (see 'Change Desktop Icons', page 45).

2   Create a folder somewhere convenient called **Bin**. Create a shortcut to **Bin** on your Desktop and give it a suitable icon. (See Screen 2.17 on page 58 for alternatives.)

3   Create shortcuts to both **Shredder** and **Bin** in your **Send To** folder (C:\Windows\Sendto).

From now on, use the context-menu's **Send To** option to delete a file: send it to **Shredder** for immediate delete or to **Bin** to put it somewhere you can retrieve it from later if necessary.

The Desktop-icons give you the same options via drag & drop. You can double-click on **Bin** to sort through your rubbish and 'shred' any items you're sure you don't need.

Too Comfortable?

By using the Recycle Bin as Microsoft clearly intended, it's easy to be lulled into a false sense of security – all manner of files are trashed in the happy belief that you can get them back if you need them. But bear in mind that files deleted from floppy disks are gone for good, as are files deleted in MS-DOS.

Oops!

Ever deleted a file and immediately thought better of it? Provided this was your last action, you can undo the deletion simply by pressing *Ctrl+Z*.

 Remember that even 'undo' can't retrieve a file deleted using *Shift+Del* though.

 For more on the 'Undo' function, read 'Using Undo' and 'Power-Using Undo' on page 69.

Registry
Tip

Trash The Bin

If you find 'Recycle Bin' grates on you almost as much as 'My Computer', you've probably tried to change it to something better (Dumpster, Trashcan, Black Hole, etc.). For some unfathomable reason this is discouraged: it takes a Registry hack to do the job.

1   Start **Regedit**, hit *F3* ('Search'), type **recycle bin**, and hit *Return*. There will be several references to it and since Regedit has no 'search & replace' facility you'll have to enter the new name each time. The quickest method is as follows:

2   When the search finds the first instance of 'Recycle Bin', double-click on the highlighted entry in the right pane and type your new name in the dialog-box.

3   Then swipe the mouse over the name you just typed to highlight it and press *Ctrl+C* to copy it to the clipboard.

4   Click on **OK** to finalize the name-change and press *F3* again to find the next instance.

5   Once again, double-click the highlighted text on the right, but this time just press *Ctrl + V* to paste the name into the box (apart from being quicker, this method ensures you get the same name with no typos.) Click **OK**, then *F3* to continue searching.

6   Keep repeating step 4 every time an instance is found, until you reach the end of the Registry – click the **OK** button to close the dialog telling you so.

7   Right-click on the Desktop and press *F5* – almost immediately you should see your Bin change name.

You might feel tempted at this point to rename the 'Recycled' folder (the hidden C:\Recycled). Don't do it! Windows needs a folder called Recycled, and will just create another one. If you've done it already, you have to open a DOS-window and use the **rd** ('remove directory') command to get rid of it, making sure you've *undeleted* any files you need first.

If you've followed this tip to rename the Recycle Bin, you'll almost certainly want to change its icon too. Check out 'Change Desktop Icons' on page 45.

Remove The Recycle Bin

If you've got the Bin's properties set for immediate-deletion, you don't need its icon cluttering up your Desktop. You can get rid of it by deleting a key in the Registry. (Before carrying out step 3 you might want to export this key as a file in case you ever want to put it back.)

1   Start **Regedit**, and go to **HKEY_LOCAL_MACHINE \ SOFTWARE \ Microsoft \ Windows \ CurrentVersion \ Explorer \ Desktop \ NameSpace**.

2   Below the **NameSpace** key, you'll see a subkey whose name begins {**645FF040**... This is the Recycle Bin's CLSID number – if you click on the key you should see 'Recycle Bin' as the value-data.)

3   Click once on this CLSID key and hit Delete.

You might have several other keys here, such as one for Internet Explorer, whose function is to create an 'undeletable' icon on your Desktop. You can delete those in the same way.

Shortcuts

Bi-Directionality

It's easy to think of shortcuts to folders as being the equivalent of one-way streets; in other words, you double-click them just to view or launch items that are already in the target-folder.

The other aspect of folder-shortcuts (as well as shortcuts to drives) is that you can use them to *put* items in the target-folder, whether by dragging & dropping an item onto the shortcut's icon, or by double-clicking the shortcut and creating a new item inside it.

Shortcuts For Everything

Keep in mind that you can create shortcuts to almost anything – drives, printers, folders, Control Panel applets, Dial-Up Networking connections, Internet websites... Whatever it is, use the right mouse-button to drag it to where you want it, and choose **Create Shortcut(s) Here** from the context-menu.

Shortcut Anonymity

Any shortcut can be renamed to anything you want, and can be assigned any icon from its **Properties / Shortcut** page. There's no particular reason why the name or look of a shortcut should bear any resemblance at all to the item it links to.

Shortcut Creation

In true *Windows95* style, there are countless ways to create shortcuts. The one you'll probably use most is to drag an item with the right mouse-button and choose **Create Shortcut(s) Here** from the context-menu. Or you might use the Shortcut Wizard by right-clicking and choosing **New** and **Shortcut**, then filling in the details.

One often-overlooked method is to use the context-menu: right-click on any item and choose **Create Shortcut**. The shortcut will be created in the same folder. Right-click it and choose **Cut** (or select it and hit *Ctrl + X*), go to the folder where you want to place it, right-click and choose **Paste** (or hit *Ctrl + V*). This method has the benefit of letting you put the same shortcut in several places if you want to by repeatedly 'Pasting'.

Quicker Shortcut Creation

If you're a big fan of the mighty context-menu, there's an even quicker method than the one above. When you right-click files and folders, there's a **Copy** option on the menu. Choose it! This saves the hassle of finding and 'Cutting' the shortcut file. When you've decided where you want to put a shortcut, right-click and choose the **Paste Shortcut** option instead of **Paste**.

This is also one to remember if you started out by wanting to copy the file elsewhere, and then belatedly decided a shortcut would do.

Guaranteed Shortcuts Every Time

If all this 'right mouse-button' stuff seems too uncomfortable, try this method of working instead: use the left button to drag & drop a file while holding down *Ctrl + Shift* to force a shortcut rather than a Copy or Move.

Remove The 'Shortcut To'

A tip from Microsoft themselves – you can teach *Windows95* to leave out the words 'Shortcut To' that prefix every shortcut you create.

Immediately after creating a shortcut by drag & drop, remove the words 'Shortcut to'. After doing this about 6 times, Windows will get the message and stop inserting them.

Unfortunately, this only holds true during your current Windows session: next time you boot up, Windows will be inserting them again!

 Among its other handy features, Microsoft's add-on applet 'TweakUI' permanently removes the prefix – find out more about it on page 328.

Personalize Your Folders

If you'd prefer to have different icons for all of your Desktop folders, make them shortcuts instead! Open Explorer and create a folder somewhere called 'Desktop Folders' (for example, C:\Desktop Folders) and move the folders on your Desktop into this one by dragging them with the right mouse-button and selecting **Move Here** from the context-menu.

Now draw a box around these folders with the left button to highlight them. Right-click on any one of them and drag them back onto the Desktop, this time selecting **Create Shortcut(s) Here** from the pop-up context-menu.

You can now assign an icon to each folder individually by right-clicking it, selecting **Properties**, clicking the **Shortcut** tab and selecting **Change Icon**.

Apart from the chance to choose your own icons for desktop folders, using shortcuts means that your can also use hotkey-combinations to open them fast. See 'The Hotkey To Success' on page 55.

Fake Control Panel

The Windows Control Panel has always been an irritating animal for its lack of editability – it's the ideal home for the myriad system accessories that computer-users tend to accumulate (not to mention 'built-in' utilities such as Backup and DriveSpace, system folders like Printers and Dial-Up Networking, batch files *et al.*). If this sounds like your kind of Control Panel, fake it . . .

Following on from the previous tip, create a new folder within 'Desktop Folders' called Control Panel and double-click to open it. Next open **My Computer** and the 'real' Control Panel and drag all the icons into your custom version using the right mouse-button and selecting **Create Shortcut(s) Here** from the context-menu.

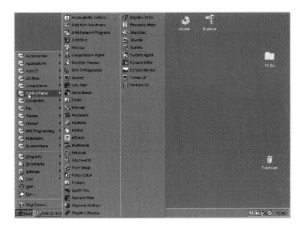

Screen 2.14 – **'Fake' Control Panel on the Start Menu**

Now close your customized folder in Explorer (by pressing *Backspace* to move up one level) and drag it onto the Desktop with the right mouse-button, once again selecting **Create Shortcut(s) Here**.

Finally, to create the fake, right-click the shortcut, select **Properties / Shortcut / Change Icon** and choose the Control Panel icon (a folder with a hammer and screwdriver on it) from approximately halfway through the **Shell32.dll** list.

To this folder, unlike the 'real' Control Panel, you can add shortcuts to any useful applet or system accessory you like and have them all in one place. Other useful additions are suggested in 'Keep 'Em Together' on page 251.

For extra-quick access to all these applets and accessories, create the 'Control Panel' folder in **C:\Windows\Start Menu** instead. You can then drag a shortcut to the Desktop in the same way, with the bonus of a cascading Start Menu list too (as demonstrated in Screen 2.14). You can simply add new accessories to C:\Windows\Start Menu\Control Panel which will be immediately available from both the Start Menu and the 'fake' on the Desktop.

Screen 2.15 – **It's a fake Control Panel. Or is it?**

Of course the fake doesn't look too convincing with that black-and-white shortcut arrow attached to it; take a look at 'Fire The Arrows!' on page 56 to find out how to get rid of those pesky little fellows.

The Hotkey To Success

You can assign a hotkey combination to any shortcut on the Start Menu or Desktop for the ultimate quick launch. The beauty of hotkeys is that you can use them at any time, and from whichever application you happen to be using.

Screen 2.16 – **Setting up hotkeys on the 'Properties' page**

Right-click the shortcut's icon and select **Properties**. Click the **Shortcut** tab and click once inside the box marked **Shortcut key**. Now type in the hotkey combo you want to use. Typing just a single letter or number will default to a hotkey combo of *Ctrl + Alt + the selected key*. If you'd prefer to use a different combination such as *Shift + Alt* you must press these keys too.

 Make the most of the punctuation-keys since applications tend not to use these for their own internal keystrokes.

Reheated Keys?

You can also use the same hotkey combos to switch to an application or window already opened, whether in the background or minimized.

If you assigned a hotkey to a *document* shortcut, however, and its associated application is already running, you can't use the hotkey to load that document into the application or to open a *second* instance of the app. In other words, the hotkey is a command to start the program and then load the document: if the program is *already* running, *Windows95* will regard the job as done and go no further.

 For more methods of task-switching, see pages 82–3.

Use Alt Gr

If you find the *Ctrl + Alt* key-combo awkward, use the *Alt Gr* key to replace it. See 'Awkward Keystrokes' on page 182 for another method of simplifying hotkey combinations.

Registry
Tip

Fire The Arrows!

Every time you create a shortcut somewhere, you get an ugly black & white arrow added to its icon. Follow this Registry trick to remove the arrows from all your existing shortcuts and any you create in the future:

I   Start the **Registry Editor**.

2   Expand **HKEY_CLASSES_ROOT**.

3   Scroll down the list to find the entry **lnkfile** and click on it. In the
right pane you'll see a string named **IsShortcut** – click on it and press
Delete, then click **OK** when prompted.

4   Carry on scrolling down the list to find the entry **piffile**. This has the
same **IsShortcut** string which should be deleted in the same way.

5   Click on the Desktop and press *F5* to refresh; you should see your
shortcut-arrows vanish as you do it.

Remember that, without these arrows, a shortcut's icon will look no
different to the icon for a file or an application: ugly as they are, these little
guys are there to help, so only remove them if you're sure you can remember
what's 'real' and what's not.

 If you're using **Internet Explorer** from the *Plus!* pack, you'll notice the
arrows on your internet shortcuts are still there after following this tip.
Read 'Arrow Goodbye' on page 198 to get rid of those too.

Immediate Screensaver

Create a Desktop shortcut to your favourite password-protected screensaver (or
create a folder containing shortcuts to all your **.scr** files and choose a different
one each time). A quick double-click, and your computer is secure while you're
away from your desk . . .

 . . . or rather, it's more secure than it would have been. Take a look at
'Screensaver Insecurities' on page 177.

 Create your own screensaver using an **.avi** video file – see page 315.

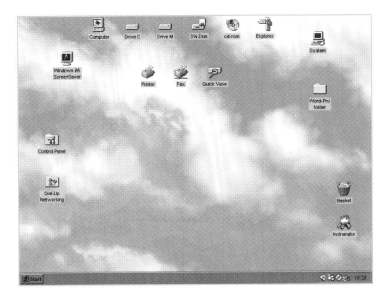

Screen 2.17 – **A few Desktop shortcut candidates**

Localized Pane

Make your files and folders more accessible: for a quick'n'easy single-pane view of each of your computer's drives, open **My Computer**, drag each of the drive-icons onto the Desktop or Start Menu. (Use either mouse-button – it's impossible to create anything but a shortcut). You can rename these and change their icons as with any other shortcut.

 If you're manic about fast access, you can also create hotkeys to open these windows: see 'The Hotkey To Success' on page 55.

Icons Unlimited

Remember that shortcuts are quite separate entities from the files they represent and can therefore have different icons. Right-click the icon, select **Properties** and **Shortcut** then click the **Change Icon** button.

In addition to the default icon file (**Shell32.dll**), C:\Windows\System offers a couple of other useful collections. **Pifmgr.dll** (Screen 2.18) is the icon-library you're offered when you want to pick a new icon for a shortcut to a DOS program; you'll also find a few extras in **Cool.dll**. **Progman.exe** and **Moricons.dll** are still in C:\Windows for that bit of *3.x* nostalgia. Click on the **Browse** button to locate one of these files.

Many applications (**.exe** files) also contain icons. After clicking the **Browse** button, select **Programs** in the 'Files of type' list-box and double-click the application whose icons you want to filch.

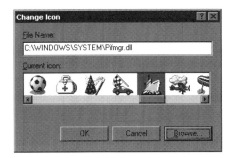

Screen 2.18 – **Pifmgr.dll shows off its iconic offerings**

Desktop Printing

Open **My Computer** and the **Printers** folder, grab your printer icon and drag it onto the Desktop as above. You can then use our two friends Drag & Drop to print files without opening the application first (provided the file-type has **Print** listed as an action – see 'Right-Click & Print' on page 258).

 For another method of quick printing, put a printer-shortcut in your Send To folder. See page 118 for more on the Send To function.

Drag'n'Launch

If you drag a file (or a shortcut to a file) and drop it onto an application shortcut, the app will start and load the file automatically if it can. This can be a handy way to open a file in an application other than the one to which the file-type is registered.

If the application is already open, just drag the file shortcut onto its title-bar.

Quick-Launch Control Panel Applets

If you find yourself accessing the same Control Panel applets frequently, why not drag them onto the Desktop to create more accessible shortcuts? Use either mouse-button for this – a shortcut will always be created.

Quick-Launch Internet Sites

For users of the optional *Plus!* pack, try doing the same thing with any often-used web-sites. Select the **Run** command from the Start Menu and type **Favorites** to open the **.url** files' folder. Drag any sites that you use regularly onto the Desktop with the right mouse-button and select **Copy Here** from the context-menu (these are shortcuts already so we don't want to create shortcuts *to* them).

Double-clicking one of these will launch **Internet Explorer** and catapult you to the chosen site. And, of course, you can rename these shortcuts and change their icons.

 Take a look at 'Move Your Favorites' on page 196 for a couple more ways to keep your Internet shortcuts close at hand.

Keeping Tabs?

If you're a MIDI-user, do you find it irritating that you can't get straight to the **MIDI** tab in the **Multimedia** applet? Want to view **Device Manager** without seeing the **General** tab first in the **System** applet? Here's how to avoid the extra mouse-clicks, taking those two as examples . . .

Right-click on the Desktop or in a folder window and choose **New** and **Shortcut**. In the 'Command line' box, type one of the following:

> **C:\Windows\System\Mmsys.cpl Multimedia,2**

> **C:\Windows\System\Sysdm.cpl System,1**

(Note the space after **.cpl**, the comma, and that there's no space before the digit. Capitalization has only been included here for clarity.) Enter a name for the shortcut on the next page and you're done.

You can do the same for most of the tabbed Control Panel applets. The C:\Windows\System\ remains a constant and is followed by the three items we'll refer to as CPL Name, Applet Name, and Tab Number.

The Tab Number can be easily found just by running the applet. The tabs are numbered left to right from zero (although entering **0** on the command-line would give the same result as just running the applet unaltered of course!).

Figure 2.1 details the Control Panel applets that are prepared to submit to this sort of indignity, and their corresponding CPL Names. (Make sure you include the spaces and backslashes in the Applet Name as applicable.)

Fig. 2.1

Applet Name	CPL Name
Accessibility Options*	Access.cpl
Add/Remove Programs	Appwiz.cpl
Date/Time	Timedate.cpl
Display	Desk.cpl
Keyboard	Main.cpl
Regional Settings	Intl.cpl
Multimedia	Mmsys.cpl
System	Sysdm.cpl

* Note – This applet counts from 1, not 0.

Easy Install

If you frequently install new software from floppy-disk, create two new shortcuts somewhere accessible with the command-lines **A:\Setup** and **A:\Install**. Since most software uses one of these two filenames to begin its installation procedure you can just double-click the appropriate shortcut instead of searching the drive.

 And, of course, you can do the same for your CD-ROM drive by creating **D:\Setup** and **D:\Install**.

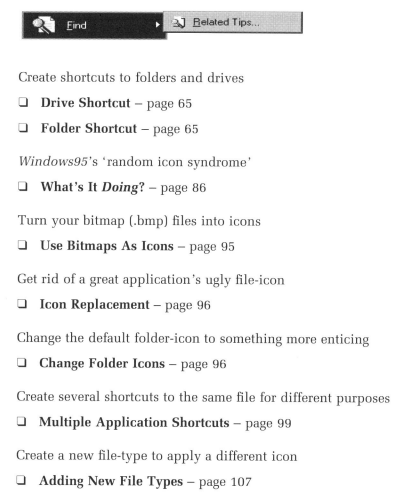

Create shortcuts to folders and drives

❏ **Drive Shortcut** – page 65

❏ **Folder Shortcut** – page 65

Windows95's 'random icon syndrome'

❏ **What's It *Doing*?** – page 86

Turn your bitmap (.bmp) files into icons

❏ **Use Bitmaps As Icons** – page 95

Get rid of a great application's ugly file-icon

❏ **Icon Replacement** – page 96

Change the default folder-icon to something more enticing

❏ **Change Folder Icons** – page 96

Create several shortcuts to the same file for different purposes

❏ **Multiple Application Shortcuts** – page 99

Create a new file-type to apply a different icon

❏ **Adding New File Types** – page 107

Organize and protect your fonts by using shortcuts

Create custom icons

Shortcuts to MS-DOS programs

Set the Run properties for shortcuts

Change the look of the Desktop

3

Explorer & Windows

Explorer Views

Know Your Views

Throughout *Windows95* there are two ways of looking at the folders and files on your system, both supplied by the **Explorer.exe** program: the **single-pane view**, showing just the items contained in a single folder (such as the My Computer window), and the **dual-pane view**, displaying a single folder's contents in the right pane and the tree structure of the drive(s) in the left pane.

The two-pane window is sometimes referred to as the 'Explorer-view' and the single-pane window the 'Open' view. These names correspond neatly with the options you find on the context-menus for drives and folders, but aren't as intuitive. For the purposes of this book, both windows are termed 'Explorer windows' and described specifically as single- or dual-pane should a distinction be necessary.

Change Your Views

Creating a shortcut to Explorer by entering the command-line **C:\Windows\ Explorer.exe** opens a window with the default settings: a single-pane view of your Windows folder.

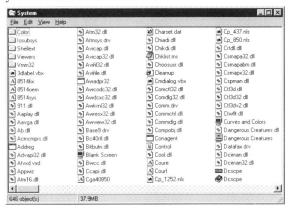

Screen 3.1 – **C:\Windows\Explorer.exe**
C:\Windows\System

63

Using **switches** within the command-line lets you tailor the view to your own requirements (and, of course, you can create as many shortcuts to Explorer.exe as you need, each with their own parameters). The following switches can be used:

❏ **/n,** forces Explorer to use a new window rather than using one that's already open (useful if you like to open two instances of Explorer to drag files between them)

❏ **/e,** for a dual-pane view

❏ **/select,** (followed by a file, folder or drive, including the path if necessary) will open the Explorer window with that item highlighted.

❏ **/root,** used in combination with the **/e,** switch, this forces the left pane to display only the object folder and its subfolders, rather than the full tree-structure of the drive.

❏ **object** the name (and path if necessary) of the folder you want Explorer to display, or the item to be 'selected'. In Screen 3.2 the object is "**C:\Windows\Resource Kit**".

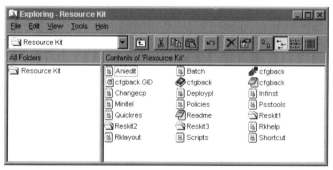

Screen 3.2 – **The 'rooted' view, using the command-line**
C:\Windows\Explorer.exe /n, /e, /root, "**C:\Windows\Resource Kit**"

The 'root' switch does just what it says: a rooted view of a particular folder allows access to folders and files below it, but moving above the 'root' is impossible.

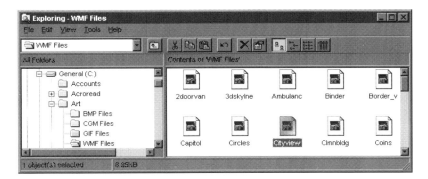

Screen 3.3 – **The 'select' switch in action: C:\Windows\Explorer.exe /n, /e, /select,** "**C:\Art\WMF Files\Cityview.wmf**"

The simplest type of Explorer shortcut to a particular folder could look something like: **C:\Windows\Explorer.exe C:\Windows\System** which would give the single-pane view of the System folder shown in Screen 3.1.

Drive Shortcut

The quickest method of creating a shortcut to display the contents of a drive is to ignore Explorer.exe and its switches completely. Right-click on the Desktop (or wherever you want the shortcut created), select **New** and **Shortcut**. In the command-line box type **C:** and select a name for the shortcut in the next dialog. Double-clicking this new icon will present a single-pane view of your 'C' drive's contents.

Folder Shortcut

Of course, the same method works with all folders (since C:\ is just another folder itself). Type **C:\Windows\System** on the command-line to create a shortcut to this folder, giving an identical result to that in Screen 3.1. (Remember to use the "quotes" for any folder using long filenames.)

Exploring Folders #1

If you create shortcuts to folders using the method above, double-clicking them will give you a single-pane view of their contents. If you prefer a dual-pane view, click the icon once to select it, then hold down *Shift* while double-clicking. A second option (for folders themselves, but not shortcuts to them) is to right-click the folder and select **Explore**.

Exploring Folders #2

You can 'explore' folders with a simple double-click if you prefer this view.

Go to **My Computer / View / Options** and click the **File Types** tab. Choose **Folder** from the list and click on the **Edit** button. In the **Actions** box, choose 'explore' and then click the **Set Default** button ('explore' will now be displayed in bold type as shown in Screen 3.4). Next time you double-click on a folder, you'll automatically get a dual-pane view of its contents.

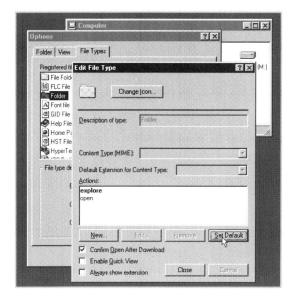

Screen 3.4 – **The file actions for folders**

No Explore Option For Folders?

If you don't have the 'explore' option listed for folders it's easy to add it. Click on the **New...** button shown in Screen 3.4.

In the 'Action' box type **&Explore** (the ampersand makes the following letter the keyboard-hotkey for the option).

In the box below it labelled 'Application used to perform action', type **c:\windows\explorer.exe /n, /e, %1** taking care to include the commas and spaces. Click **OK** and set this as the default by clicking the **Set Default** button.

Explore My Computer

When you double-click on **My Computer**, would you rather have a two-pane window open than the default single-pane view? Run the Registry Editor and walk this way...

1 Expand **HKEY_CLASSES_ROOT** and find the **CLSID** key by scrolling about halfway down the pane (or by typing *cls*).

2 Expand **CLSID** and find the key labelled {**20D04FE0-3AEA-1069-A2D8-08002B30309D**} (These keys are in numerical order so tracking it down shouldn't be difficult.) When you've found this key, expand it.

3 Right-click on **Shell** and choose **New** and **Key**. Name the key **Open**.

4 Right-click on **Open** and choose **New** and **Key**. Name the key **Command**.

5 Make sure **Command** is highlighted and double-click on (**Default**) in the right pane. In the dialog-box, type **explorer.exe /n, /e, /select, c:** (taking care to observe the spaces and commas) and click **OK**.

6 Close the Registry, click on the Desktop and press *F5* to refresh, then double-click the **My Computer** icon to see the result.

Open Folders From DOS

If you're working in an MS-DOS Prompt window, you can 'explore' the folder indicated by the prompt by typing **start .** (note the space after 'start') – Explorer will launch a single-pane view of the folder.

To explore a different folder, type **start** followed by the path and folder name. If the path is already specified in a PATH=line in your **Autoexec.bat** you can just type the folder name, such as **start system** to open the Windows\System folder.

 For a few tips on how to 'speak DOS', turn to page 285.

 Read 'Stating A Path' on page 265 for details on the PATH=line.

Double Vision

If you find that you often copy or move files between the same two folders, it makes sense to create a shortcut to both of them, double-click both icons and then select one of the **Tile** options by right-clicking the Taskbar. If you use Policy Editor to save your settings (see 'Protect Your Desktop Settings #1' on page 40) you can force these windows to open tiled whenever you select them.

To remove the tedium of all that double-clicking to get started, create a batch (**.bat**) file instead to open the two instances of Explorer for you with one double-click. Open **Notepad** and type:

```
@echo off
c:\windows\explorer.exe c:\notes
c:\windows\explorer.exe c:\oldnotes
```

(replacing these object-folders with your own and inserting any switches you need before them), and save the file with a **.bat** extension to a convenient folder. Create a shortcut on your Desktop or Start Menu to the **.bat** file, right-click it and select **Properties**. Click the **Program** tab, select **Minimized** in the **Run** box, check the **Close on exit** box, and click **OK**.

Explorer Turbo

Running Explorer

When the focus is on a dual-pane Explorer-window (i.e., its title-bar is highlighted) you can access a version of the Start Menu's **Run** command to move between folders quickly. Just press *Ctrl + G* for the **Go To** folder dialog (see Screen 3.5). Either type in a path to the folder or select a recently used one from the drop-down list imported from **Run**.

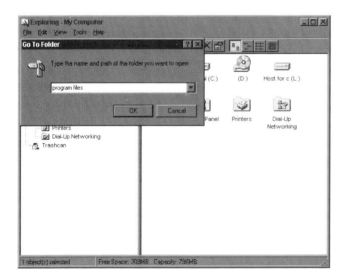

Screen 3.5 – **Ctrl + G: Exploring** with a bullet

To use **Go To** and **Run** most effectively, make sure you've included your most frequently travelled paths in your **Autoexec.bat**. See page 265 to find out what 'paths' are all about.

'Go To' Oddity

If you open a 'rooted' Explorer-view using, for example, the switch **/root**, **C:\Windows**, you'd expect to be restricted to working within the Windows folder and its subfolders. In most cases you are, but a 'feature' of the **Go To** command is that you can bypass the root completely. Type in a folder name such as **program files** and hit *Return* and you'll get a second dual-pane window, with your computer's whole drive- and folder-tree structure displayed, open and ready for business.

Use Find In Explorer Too

Pressing *F3* (or choosing the **Find** option from the Tools menu in a dual-pane window) will bring up the **Find** command. By default, the **Look In** box will automatically be rooted to the folder displayed in the Explorer window. Or right-click on a folder and choose **Find** for a search rooted to that folder.

Using Undo

To undo your last action in Explorer, click the ⟲ button on the toolbar or press *Ctrl + Z*. Holding your mouse pointer over the button will display a tooltip to tell you what action you're about to undo (such as 'Undo Rename' or 'Undo Delete'). In some cases, multiple levels of Undo are possible.

Power-Using Undo

The problem with the 'Undo' button, for all its tooltip-help, is that you can't always be sure exactly *which* action is going to be undone: after a few minutes' work, you might remember moving a few files but you can't remember which was the *last* you moved.

This trick relies on having the Status-Bar visible so select it from the **View** menu if it isn't. Next, click on the Undo button but keep the mouse-button depressed – if you look on the Status-Bar, you'll see the filename(s) and the action about to be undone. If you want to go ahead and undo the action, release the mouse-button in the normal way; if you don't want it undone, move the pointer away from the Undo button (as if you were dragging it) before you release the mouse-button.

Going Up

To move from the current folder to its parent folder, click on the ⬆ button or press the *Backspace* key. You can also use either method in **Open** and **Save As...** application dialogs.

If you're using a 'rooted' Explorer view, you can only move up as far as the folder specified as the root.

Invert It !

If you have a folder chock-full of files and you want to delete, cut or copy all of them except one or two, select those that you want to *keep* and then choose **Invert Selection** from Explorer's **Edit** menu: the highlight will shift to all the items you *didn't* select ready for you to carry out the required action.

Boxing Clever

In an Explorer-window, or on the Desktop, you can draw an expanding box around a group of items with either mouse-button to select them, instead of clicking on each one individually. Place the pointer above and to one side of an icon, press the button and start dragging diagonally to enclose all the items you want.

Screen 3.6 – **Drag a box around items to select them**

Selective Deselection

There is a multitude of ways to select files: hold *Ctrl* and click on individual files; click the first item in a list and hold *Shift* while selecting the last required item to include all those in between; press *Ctrl*+*A* to select all files; draw a selection-box around a group of items... but how do you *deselect* an item from a group?

Whichever of these methods you've used to highlight a batch of files or folders, just press and hold *Ctrl* while clicking on any item(s) that you want to remove from the selection.

You Want Properties?

There are seemingly endless ways to get at the properties of a selected file, folder or shortcut. In an Explorer-window, one of the obvious methods is to click the 🖳 button on the toolbar. The other options – both here and on the Desktop – are to right-click the icon and select **Properties** from the context-menu; hold down *Alt* while double-clicking the icon; or highlight the icon and press *Alt*+*Enter*.

Going For A Drive

To quickly select a drive to display in an Explorer-window (provided **View / Toolbar** is checked), press *F4* to drop down the drive-list and click on the drive's icon to select it.

The same key also expands the **Open** box in **Run**; the **Named** box in **Find**; the **Look in** and **Save in** boxes in the 'Open' and 'Save As' dialogs of 32-bit applications – the drop-down list is a feature of the interface that appears frequently, and it's often easier to hit *F4* than to click the little arrow-button.

A second method of selecting items from drop-down lists is to use the arrow-keys: in Explorer-windows this also drops the list; in most other situations it scrolls through the items one by one.

Open or Expand?

In a single-pane Explorer window, opening a folder requires a double-click. This is also the case in the right pane of a two-pane view. In the left pane, however, a single click will open a folder and a double-click will open the folder whilst also expanding the tree beneath it.

And don't forget the boxed-crosses in the left pane: they correspond to the + & − keys on the numeric-keypad (with *NumLock* on). Use 'add' to show all subfolders of an expandable branch and 'subtract' to retract a collapsible branch.

Letter Getter

To navigate an Explorer window quickly, don't use the mouse and scrollbar to locate the file or folder you need: just press the first letter of its name on the keyboard. Windows will automatically select the first item it finds in the window with that initial: in a large folder such as C:\Windows this is a quick way to get somewhere near the file you want.

Pressing the letter again will move the focus to the next, and so on. (In a two-pane view, this applies to the pane that currently has the focus. To change the focus to the other pane, press *F6*.)

If there are two or more items with the same initial, type the first two or three letters of the name to make sure the correct one is selected.

For example, beneath C:\Windows you have Command and Config folders: hitting 'C' takes you to Command; typing 'CO' does the same; 'CON' takes you to Config. (You have to type reasonably quickly or Windows thinks the next letter is the initial of a new item instead – if you like this method of file-finding, get into the habit of always typing the first three letters of the name in quick succession.)

You can use the same method to select items in the **File Types** and **Open With** dialogs, **Regedit**, and almost any other list or tree-view you find.

Getting To The Bottom Of It

To get to the top or bottom of an Explorer-window, use the *Home* and *End* keys. The focus toggles between the first and last item in the folder. Once again, the same keys work in tree-views, **File Types** and **Find** lists, you name it!

Refreshing Explorer

Changes you make in Explorer, such as creating or deleting an item, often don't register correctly until the next time you open the window: make Explorer recognize these changes by pressing *F5* afterwards.

 To force Windows to automate the 'refresh' process, read 'More Refreshing!' on page 80.

Refreshing The Floppy View

If you put a disk in the floppy drive, double-click the drive-icon to see its contents and then insert a different disk, there's no need to close the window and double-click the icon again to see the new disk's contents: just press *F5* and Windows will take another look at the drive and update the window.

Using Details View

When you select **View / Details** or press the button on Explorer's toolbar, the entries in the right pane are grouped in columns under bars headed Name, Size, Type and Modified. Clicking one of these bars sorts the files alphabetically by name or type, in order of size from smallest to largest, or in order of modification from the most recent. Pressing the bar a second time reverses the order: for example, pressing 'Name' twice will sort the files counter-alphabetically.

Remember it's not just Explorer that offers **Details** view: you have the same option in **Find**, **Exchange**, 'Open' and 'Save As' dialogs, and a variety of other applications and accessories.

 Are your columns all the wrong size? Take a look at 'The Wicked Width' on page 87 for a quick solution.

Selection By Extension

Explorer has no inherent method of allowing you to mask files with a particular extension, to show only **.gif** files for example. One way around this is to use **Details** view, sort files by **Type**, and scroll down to where the appropriate files are now gathered together, but this still sorts by *type* not *extension* so you may not get the results you expect.

To isolate files with a particular extension, such as **.gif**, press *F3* to bring up the **Find** dialog (which will be automatically rooted to the current folder) and type ***.gif** in the 'Named' box – the resulting list will display all files with this extension ready for selection.

You can mask files in MS-DOS, however. Open a prompt-window for the required folder and type **dir *.gif**.

Bear in mind that file-types are different from file-extensions: read 'Searching For File Types' on page 16 to make sure you get the results you want.

Masking In File Manager

Another method of masking files with a particular extension is to use **File Manager** (Winfile.exe in your Windows folder). Choose **By File Type...** from the **View** menu and type an extension into the 'Name' box such as ***.txt**. (To return to the default view, return to this dialog and type ***.*.**)

Bear in mind that your options are limited in File Manager when you've masked the files: long filenames and the right mouse-button aren't supported. And File Manager can only display files from one folder at a time, compared with **Find**'s ability to show files matching your criteria from any number of folders in a single window.

Scrolling Panes

If you move or copy files in a single- or dual-pane window by dragging and dropping them, you can force the window to scroll upwards or downwards by dragging the file to the topmost or bottommost edge of the window and holding it there. (The 'hot-spot' for this is narrow, so it takes a little practice to position the pointer correctly.) When the desired target comes into view you can then drop the file onto it.

It's amusing to watch, but why would you want to work that way? Take a look at the next tip, for dual-pane windows only, and at 'Quick Cut, Copy, Paste' on page 105.

Advanced Scrolling

Copying, moving, and creating shortcuts to items by drag-and-drop is faster and easier in a dual-pane window: open the folder containing the items you want to move, then scroll through the left pane until the target folder comes into view. You can then simply select the items from the right pane in the usual way and use the right mouse-button to drag and drop them onto the target folder in the left pane (making the choice between Move, Copy or Create Shortcut from the context-menu).

Missing Windows 3.x?

Pine no more – the Windows folder still contains the *Win3.x* Program Manager and File Manager. Select **Run** and type **progman** or **winfile** on the command-line. The appearance of both apps has been altered a little (particularly in the case of Progman) and neither supports long filenames or the right mouse-button, but both are perfectly usable. Screen 3.7 shows Progman and File Manager running cheerfully together.

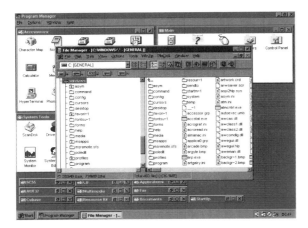

Screen 3.7 – **Progman & Fileman come out of retirement**

Want a real nostalgia trip? Why not use progman as your shell? (Answers on a postcard please...) See 'New Light Through Old Windows' on page 283 to find out how.

Working With Windows

Open New Windows?

If you go to **My Computer / View / Options** you have the choice between opening each new folder in a separate window or reusing the same window. Whichever of these you choose for your regular browsing, if you hold down *Ctrl* as you double-click on a folder you'll get the opposite result.

Screen 3.8 – **Here's where you do your 'window-shopping'**

It's A Pane

If there's one word that springs to mind working in *Windows95*, it's 'choice'. For just about anything you want to do there are usually several methods giving a variety of options. Opening folders is a case in point: the result you get depends upon:

❑ whether you're in a single- or a dual-pane window

❑ which setting you chose in **My Computer / View / Options / Folder**

❑ whether you double-click, or right-click and use the context-menu

❑ whether you're holding *Ctrl* as you double-click

All this can be a tad confusing. Let's clarify:

Single Panes

Right-click on a folder in a single-pane window and you'll see that the default-action (bold-type) for a double-click is **Open**. The 'Open' action will always result in a single-pane window: whether it's the same window or a new one can be set in **My Computer / View / Options / Folder**.

You also have the option to 'Explore' from the context-menu: this will open a new *dual-pane* window.

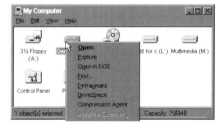

Screen 3.9 – **The 'Open' default for single-pane window items**

Dual Panes

If you right-click on a folder in a dual-pane window, you'll see the default-action for a double-click is **Explore**. A double-click will always result in the same window adjusting to show that folder's contents.

You can also 'open' the folder from the context-menu: if you opted to always re-use the same window this will give you a new large single-pane window.

If you opted to use a new window for each folder, you'll get a new *neatly sized* single pane (try it with a folder containing about half-a-dozen items!).

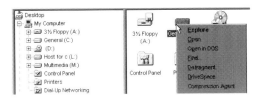

Screen 3.10 – **Double-click in a dual-pane window to 'Explore'**

Choose Your Views

If you don't care about the view as long as you can always see the folders' contents *somehow*, all well and good. But if you'd like a little more consistency, first select **Browse folders by using a single window in My Computer / View / Options**, then decide whether you prefer single- or dual-panes.

- ❏ To view everything in dual-panes, follow the instructions in the tips 'Exploring Folders #2' and 'Explore My Computer' on pages 65–7.

- ❏ To view everything in single-panes, edit all your Explorer shortcuts to remove the **/e**, and **/root**, switches.

Whichever of the above you've chosen, follow the steps in 'Open New Windows Easily' below to create a **New Window** entry on your context-menu. (Dual-pane fans should follow the 'Option' paragraph at the end; single-paners should ignore it.)

Registry Tip

Open New Windows Easily

Most users opt for opening folders in the same window to prevent the Desktop becoming unnecessarily cluttered with windows. If you like to work this way, but want quicker access to a new window when you need one, follow these steps to put the option on the context-menu:

1   Open the **Registry Editor**.

2   Expand **HKEY_CLASSES_ROOT** and scroll down to the **Folder** key.

3   Expand **Folder** and right-click on **shell**. Select **New** and **Key** and name the new key **opennew**. In the right pane, double-click on (**Default**) and type New &Window. (This is the text that will appear on the menu; the ampersand specifies that the next character will be the hotkey for the command.)

4 Right-click on **opennew** and select **New** and **Key**. Call this key **command**.

5 Double-click on (**Default**) and type **explorer /n, %1**

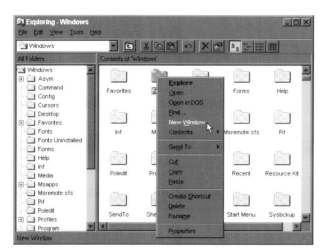

Screen 3.11 – **An optional 'New Window'**

Now you can open a new window for a folder by right-clicking on it and selecting **New Window** (or by pressing *Shift+F10* then *W*). You'll also find the same option available on the context-menu for drives, useful if you have two hard-disks or multiple partitions or compressed drives. If you'd prefer not to have the option on the drives' menus, use the **Directory** key instead in steps 2 & 3. (Don't use both – you'll end up with the option listed twice on your menus!)

The only untidy detail about this trick is that right-clicking on *any* Desktop-folder (or the Start-button) will give you the option to open a *new* window for it, even if there's none open yet!

Option

Following the tip above will let you open a new *single-pane* window for the folder you right-click on; if you'd rather have a dual-pane window just type **explorer /n, /e, %1** when you get to step 5.

Doubled-Up

If you like to work with a *separate* window for each folder, but would prefer each one to be a dual-pane view, the previous tip is the ideal starting-point.

When you've added the entry to the context-menu as above, following the *Option* paragraph as well, go to **My Computer / View / Options / File Types**, find the **Folders** entry and click on **Edit**. In the Actions box, select the 'New Window' entry and click on **Set Default**. Now every time you double-click a folder you'll get a new dual-pane window.

To return to the previous mode of working, edit the **Folders** entry again, select 'New Window' and again click on **Set Default** – 'New Window' will revert to being a context-option (shown in normal-type) rather than the bold-type default.

Organize Windows

No matter how many windows or applications you have open, right-click on the Taskbar and select one of the 'arrangement' options: **Cascade, Tile Horizontally**, or **Tile Vertically**. You'll find it ridiculously easy to drag & drop files between windows. (Only open windows are included; minimized windows will stay minimized.) If you open or close a new window, just select the same option again and Windows will re-sort things to slot it in with the rest.

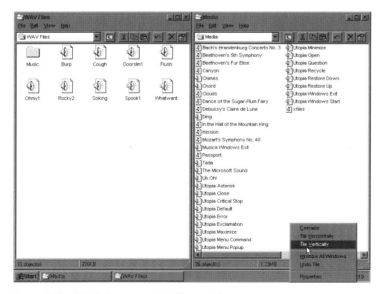

Screen 3.12 – **Whole lotta vertical tiling goin' on**

To go back to your original view, right-click the Taskbar again and take the new **Undo Tile** option.

Registry
Tip

More Refreshing!

You'll probably have noticed that whenever you make a change to the Registry, or you move, copy and paste items in folders and Explorer windows, you have to click on the Desktop and press *F5* to refresh the layout. This trick makes the view refresh automatically:

1   Open the **Registry Editor**.

2   Go to **HKEY_LOCAL_MACHINE \ System \ CurrentControlSet \ Control**.

3   Expand **Control** and click on **Update**.

4   In the right pane, double-click on **UpdateMode**.

5   In the pop-up dialog-box, type **0** (i.e., zero) and click **OK** (see Screen 3.12).

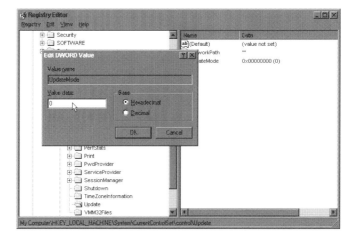

Screen 3.13 – **The DWORD dialog**

6   Close **Regedit**. This setting won't take effect until you restart *Windows95*.

The Control Menu

The small icon in the top left corner of every application and window holds its own secrets: you can click on it to access the **Control Menu** which contains the useful commands **Maximize** (*Alt + Spacebar*, *X*), **Minimize** (*Alt + Spacebar*, *N*) and **Restore** (*Alt + Spacebar*, *R*). If you've got something against the great *Alt + F4*, you can use *Alt + Spacebar, C* to close the window or application.

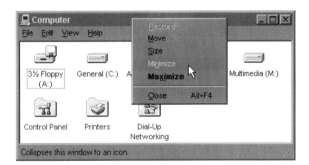

Screen 3.14 – **The Control Menu from the title-bar**

If you find aiming the mouse at the icon too troublesome, right-clicking the title-bar opens the Control Menu too.

Mouse Control

The entries given in **bold** type on the Control Menu (in keeping with all other menus) indicate the effect of double-clicking: a double-click on the title-bar will toggle the window between the **Maximized** and **Restored** states, while a double-click on the Control-icon itself gives a quick way to exit an application or close a window.

Running Behind

In normal circumstances, when you double-click a file or application to run it, it opens in the foreground covering the Explorer-window you were looking at. Most of the time this is what you want, but it is possible to have the application open *behind* any currently open windows instead – just make sure no icons are highlighted, hold *Ctrl* and double-click the icon you want.

Multiple Instances

One of the easiest ways to copy information between two documents of the same type is to open two instances of the application side by side. *Windows95* applications (such as **WordPad**, **Paint** and **Notepad**) support this.

To do it, you could double-click on, for example, a **.bmp** file, wait for **Paint** to open, then minimize it and double-click on another. The quickest method, however, is to select multiple files (by holding *Ctrl* and clicking each individually or *Shift* to select a contiguous group of files) then hold *Ctrl + Shift* while you double-click on any one of the selected files. Each file will open in its own instance of **Paint** ready for you to tile them and start copying.

Opening Multiple Folders

Want to open two or more folders in separate windows in one operation? Press *Ctrl* and click once on each folder you want to open to highlight them. Then press *Ctrl + Shift* and double-click on any one of them – hey presto, a separate Explorer window for each folder. Just tile them and start dragging your files around.

Quick Close

There are three quick ways to close any window: click the ▣ button in the top right corner; double-click the control-icon in the top left corner; or press *Alt + F4*. A slower method, on windows with a menu-bar, is to select **File / Exit** or **Quit**.

Closing Multiple Windows

If you've opted to open folders in new windows, you can end up with quite a stack after a few double-clicks. Rather than close each one individually, hold *Shift* while you close the top window: its parent-windows beneath will be closed along with it.

Task Switching

There are several possible ways of moving between applications and open windows in *Windows95*: the more obvious ones are to click the corresponding button on the Taskbar or to click on the window itself if you can see any of it.

Aside from these there are three methods, each of which will be familiar to hardened *Windows 3.x* users:

Option #1

Hold *Alt*, and press *Tab* to see an iconized list of currently open windows. Pressing *Tab* repeatedly toggles the focus from icon to icon – release both keys when the icon for the desired application or window is highlighted and you'll be switched to that app. By default, the last window you were using is first in the list, so if you're toggling repeatedly between the same two windows don't bother waiting for the list of icons to pop up, just press *Alt + Tab* and release them immediately.

Option #2

A similar approach is *Alt + Esc*: holding *Alt* and repeatedly pressing *Esc* switches between the open windows themselves, rather than iconized views of them.

Option #3

An advanced version of *Alt + Tab* called **Taskman**, shown in Screen 3.15. Select the **Run** command from the Start Menu and type **taskman**. This works rather like the Taskbar with the difference that you can close multiple apps and windows in one go: hold *Ctrl*, click the desired icon-bars and select **Windows / End Task**.

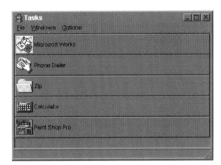

Screen 3.15 – **Taskman**

Power Switch

The problem with **Taskman** and the *Alt + Tab* combination is that only *applications* are shown: items such as Control Panel applets or the **Open With...** dialog are excluded from the list. Rather than minimize your open applications and windows to see what else is lurking behind them, use *Alt + Esc*: this combination switches through all currently open items of any description (although nothing is perfect − *Alt + Esc* ignores any minimized items).

Hot Switch

In addition to the methods of switching between windows covered in 'Task Switching' above, if you assigned hotkey-combinations to any of your currently open (or minimized) folders or applications, you can use the same key-combo to make this the active window.

For more on hotkey-combos, see 'The Hotkey To Success' on page 55.

Button Trouble?

If you're working on a high-resolution screen, do you find yourself aiming at the minimize, maximize or close buttons on a window's title-bar and missing completely, or hitting the wrong one? When you re-size the title-bar these buttons are re-sized as well.

Right-click on the Desktop, select **Properties** and click the **Appearance** tab. In the **Item** box find either Active Title Bar or Caption Buttons, and then increase the value in the size box beside it. (Changing the font size in the lower box will have the same effect as a by-product.)

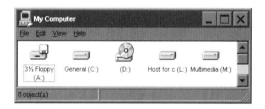

Screen 3.16 – **Adding 10 to the caption-buttons sure makes 'em visible!**

Another possible candidate for a size-increase is the Scrollbar item if you find that your mouse pointer keeps 'slipping off' the arrow buttons.

Registry
Tip

Turn Off Window Animation

On a fast system, the animated window-zooming that accompanies a maximizing, minimizing or restoring manoeuvre looks sharp and effective. If you have a slower video-card or a lower boredom threshold you might find that it's either slowing you down or winding you up. If you want to turn it off:

1   Start the **Registry Editor**.

2   Expand **HKEY_CURRENT_USER**, and go to **Control Panel \ Desktop \ WindowMetrics**.

3   In the right pane, find **MinAnimate** and double-click it.

4   In the pop-up dialog, type **0** (i.e., zero) and click **OK**.

5   Close **Regedit**. This trick needs *Windows95* to be restarted before it'll take effect.

MinAnimate is a binary-value: it will understand only two possible value-settings, **1** and **0**. If you want to turn window-animation back on in the future, follow the same steps and type **1** in the dialog.

What's This?

While navigating through tabbed pages, dialog-boxes and other features of the interface, right-click on anything you don't understand and a little menu containing the words **What's this?** will appear. Click on it to get a pop-up description. When you've finished reading it, just click it to make it vanish.

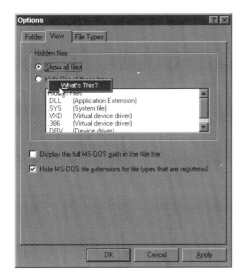

Screen 3.17 – **What's this? It's a very small context-menu.**

As an alternative, on pages and windows with a question-mark icon in the top-right corner, you can click the button and then click on the item you're uncertain about to get the same pop-up.

ALT Shortcuts

The underlined letters in menus and on menu-bars are keyboard shortcuts. To select a menu-bar shortcut, press *Alt + underlined letter*. To select a menu item, press just the underlined letter. Therefore, to access the oft-used **View / Options** item in **My Computer**, press *Alt + V* followed by *O*.

 An alternative is to press *F10* to highlight the first menu-bar item and then use the arrow keys to move around, *Enter* to select, and *Esc* to cancel.

Working With MDIs

Some Windows-compatible applications have MDIs (Multiple Document Interfaces): you can open more than one document at a time within the application, each in its own window, and work with each as if they were separate apps. Keystrokes and menu options act on the document with the focus.

Each document window has its own **Control Menu**, accessed by the keystroke *Alt + −* (minus-sign), containing similar options to the application's Control Menu, plus a useful addition: to move between the open documents, select **Next** from the menu or press *Ctrl + F6*.

To close a single document within a MDI application, press *Ctrl + F4* or choose **Close** from the **File** menu.

Tabbing Between Tabs

A new addition to the Windows interface is tabbed pages, as in the **View / Options** item mentioned above. To move between tabs from the keyboard, hold *Ctrl* while pressing *Tab*. (You can also move backwards through the tabs by holding *Ctrl + Shift* while pressing *Tab*, but you might find it more comfortable just to keep going forwards and wait until the tab you wanted comes around again!)

Alternatively, press *Ctrl + Tab* once, then keep pressing *Tab* until one of the page-tabs is selected (i.e., it has a dotted line around it). You can then use the arrow-keys to move between tabs freely.

What's It Doing?

Once in a while you might open Explorer, Control Panel, or your Start Menu, and see that your My Computer icon or your applet icons have changed: don't worry, and don't bother trying to put them right – this is just Windows being

Windows. They'll sort themselves out again next time you start up. In the meantime, they'll still function exactly as normal.

Cover Story

Occasionally the edge of an application's window disappears under the Taskbar (and/or the Shortcut Bar if you have **Office95** installed). If this happens, check the application is maximized. Some applications do this in 'restored' position, but when maximized they resize themselves to fit.

Another problem you might come across is the maximized application that grabs the whole screen for itself and covers the Taskbar. This is a quirk of the application's construction rather than *Windows95* – to get around it, you'll have to click the Restore button and then enlarge the window manually by dragging.

The Wicked Width

When you use **Details** view in Explorer, Find, Exchange, Backup, and elsewhere, the information is presented in columns, each with a bar at the top. The width of these columns seems subject to random variation, the only common rule being that either the information you want to see is truncated with an ellipsis or it's vanished off the right side of the window! Of course, you can resize these columns by grabbing the right-edge of each bar and dragging it, but there's a quicker and much neater way.

Go to the right-edge of a bar as usual, so that the pointer turns into a vertical bar straddled by a double-headed arrow, but don't drag – double-click! The column will automatically resize itself so that it's the perfect width to display its contents.

The 'Find' results window

❑ **Using Find Results** – page 18

The Recycle Bin window

❑ **Undelete To Here** – page 49

Viewing hidden files & folders

❏   **Show Me** – page 91

❏   **Open Hidden Folders** – page 91

Pre-defining window-sizes in shortcuts

❏   **Run Properties** – page 97

Copying and moving files between Explorer windows

❏   **Quick Cut, Copy, Paste** – page 105

Editing a window's display characteristics

❏   **Display Solutions** – page 174

❏   **Let's Get Personal** – page 175

Explorer's Fonts folder

❏   **'FONTS & FONT FILES'** – page 115

4

Files & Folders

Names, Icons & Sizes

Quick Rename

There are several ways to rename a file, folder or shortcut in *Windows95*; in order of speed from slowest to fastest, these are:

❑ Right-click on the icon and select **Rename**.

❑ Left-click the icon and press *F2*.

❑ Left click the icon and then the label itself (but avoid double-clicking!).

Show File Extensions

You may have many different file-types associated with the same application and therefore having the same icon, such as a variety of image files that all open with Paint Shop Pro for example. Without seeing the file-extensions, it's impossible to tell one image-format from another.

To show the DOS-extensions (such as **.gif**, **.jpg** etc.) for all files, select **View / Options** from Explorer's menu-bar and clear the checkbox beside **Hide MS-DOS file extensions for file types that are registered**.

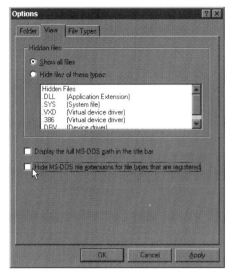

Screen 4.1 – **Clear the box and extend your filenames**

Change File Extensions

If you want to change a file's extension, you need to see it displayed as part of the file-name. Unless you've opted to always show the extension for files of this type (see 'What's The Extension? – part two' on page 92), this entails temporarily showing all extensions, making the change, and then hiding all extensions again.

Aversion Therapy

Whenever you change a file extension, *Windows95* threatens that the file may become unusable. In fact, the worst that can happen is that you give it an extension that isn't registered to an application, or you give it no extension at all.

In either of these cases, the file is still there and still visible, and when you double-click to try and launch it you'll be presented with the **Open With...** dialog to choose the correct application (or to try a few if you've forgotten which app it belonged to!). Whatever happens, you can always add or replace the extension if you need to.

 This doesn't apply to system files – never change the extensions of these unless you know exactly what you're doing!

Show Me

By default, certain files and folders installed by *Windows95* are hidden: this is to prevent them being accidentally erased or altered. To show these files and folders, check the radio-button for **Show all files** on Explorer's **View / Options** page.

Provided that you don't delete your Windows folder or any of its subfolders (or the contents of any of these folders, unless you have an extremely good reason and even better backups), this will give a clearer view of the contents of C:\ and C:\Windows.

Open Hidden Folders

Within your Windows folder, the subfolders Inf, NetHood, Pif, Recent, ShellNew, Spool and Sysbckup are hidden. If you choose to keep them that way, you can still view their contents when you need to: just type the path (such as C:\Windows\ShellNew) on the **Run** or **Go To** command-line.

Private Treatment

You can hide any files or folders on your system that you choose if you want to keep them away from prying eyes – another user would have to know of the existence, the exact name, and the whereabouts of the item to access it. (You must have selected **Hide files of these types** on Explorer's **View / Options** page to hide the items.)

❏ Hide a single folder or file – Right click on the file or folder and select **Properties**. Check the box marked **Hidden** and click **OK**.

❏ Hide multiple items – While holding *Ctrl*, select each item required. Then right-click on any selected item and carry out the same procedure as above.

Once hidden, these items can only be accessed from the **Run** command, Explorer's **Go To** command, or the MS-DOS prompt by typing in their full path and name. You can also open hidden files (or files in hidden folders) by typing the full path into an application's **File / Open** dialog.

If the folder containing the hidden items (or a hidden folder itself) is specified in the PATH= line of your **Autoexec.bat** you need only enter the required filename. The **Find** command won't search hidden folders or locate hidden files.

To remove the hidden attribute from an item, select **Show all files** so that you can then right-click the item and access its **Properties** page to remove the checkmark.

See 'Stating A Path' on page 265 for more details about the Path statement in **Autoexec.bat**.

What's The File Extension? – part one

Here are three quick methods to find the MS-DOS extension of a particular file:

❑ Right-click its icon and choose Properties (or press *Alt + Enter* or *Alt +* double-click): the full MS-DOS name is shown halfway down the page.

❑ Start the **Run** applet from the Start Menu, and drag & drop the file onto the command-line.

❑ Drag & drop the file into an MS-DOS Prompt window.

The last two options will also display the full path of the file, though the DOS-prompt version will truncate long filenames to the DOS 8.3 naming system.

What's The File Extension? – part two

Certain file types may have different extensions but may all be associated with the same application, and may therefore have the same icon, making it impossible to tell them apart. Good examples are files with the extensions **.txt, .ini, .sys, .gid** (and perhaps a good many more), all of which are probably associated with Notepad and have Notepad's icon.

To make Windows display the DOS extensions for specific file types:

I Open **My Computer** and select **View / Options / File Types**.

2 Scroll down the list and select a file type such as **INI File**.

3 Click on **Edit** and check the **Always show extension** box.

4 Click **OK**.

5 Repeats steps 2–4 for all the necessary types.

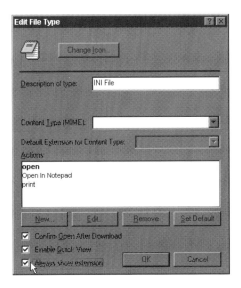

Screen 4.2 – **Choose which extensions you want to see**

This provides a handy middle ground between the 'all or nothing' options provided in Explorer's **View / Options** page.

 An alternative is to give each file-type its own individual icon. See 'Icon Replacement' on page 96.

A Dotty Solution

You can now use dots anywhere in long filenames, not just to separate the name from the extension. (The extension will automatically become the text following the last dot.)

This can be used as a quick solution to the problem of having, for example, the same picture in two different image-formats associated with the same application: just include the extension in the name. Save one as **My Dog.gif.gif** and the other as **My Dog.jpg.jpg**. In this way, you can avoid showing extensions for *all* **.gif** and **.jpg** files but still tell these two apart.

A quicker way to tell one file-type from another is by selecting different icons for them. In order to do this you'll often need to create at least one new file-type. See 'Adding New File Types' on page 107 for details.

Exact File Size

One backward step from the days of *Windows3.x* is the vagueness of file-sizes displayed in Explorer's status-bar. If you need a precise size to the nearest byte, you have to look at the **Properties** page for the selected file.

Exact Folder Size

To make up for this shortcoming, you can now do the same with a folder. There are two options:

❏   If you click on a folder in the left pane of a dual-pane window you'll see the total size of the folder's contents, excluding its subfolders, in the status bar (provided you've checked the **Status Bar** option on the **View** menu).

❏   By right-clicking a folder anywhere and selecting **Properties**, you can find the exact size of the folder *and* its subfolders – try it with your Windows folder for a disturbing insight into where all that disk space went!

You can also find the total size of a group of files or folders. Either hold *Ctrl* while selecting each individually and then right-click on one, or draw a selection-box around the required items with the right mouse-button. Select Properties from the context-menu as above.

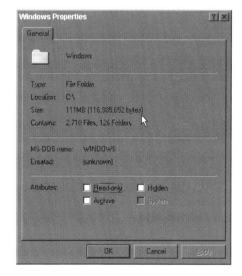

Screen 4.3 – **An exact folder-size. Perhaps a little too exact . . .**

Use Bitmaps As Icons

By simply changing the **.bmp** extension of a bitmap file to **.ico**, you can use the same file as an icon. Windows will resize it and convert it to 16 colours but it should still be recognizable.

Registry
Tip

Iconized Bitmaps

When you open C:\Windows\Cursors you see each cursor or animated-cursor file displayed as an icon of itself. This is a trick to force Windows to do the same with bitmap (**.bmp**) files, allowing you to preview the image without opening an application:

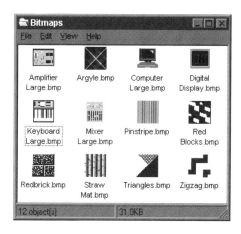

Screen 4.4 – **No more anonymous .bmp files**

I   Start the **Registry Editor**.

2   Expand **HKEY_CLASSES_ROOT** and scroll way down to **PAINT.PICTURE** (or just type **pai** quickly).

3   Expand **PAINT.PICTURE** and click on **DefaultIcon**.

4   In the right pane, double-click on (**Default**); in the dialog-box that pops up replace the entry with **%1**.

5   Click on the Desktop and press *F5* to refresh, then open any folder containing bitmap files and check 'em out (choose **Large Icons** from the **View** menu for best effect).

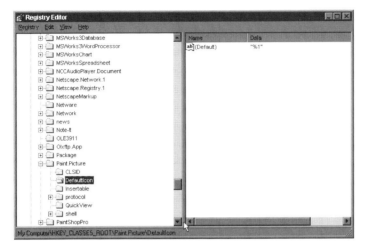

Screen 4.5 – **The PAINT.PICTURE key and %1 value**

Icon Replacement

Sometimes a great application carries with it an extremely ugly icon which gets applied to all its associated files. If you can't bear to see these any longer, here's how to change them:

1   Open **My Computer** and select **View / Options**.

2   Click the **File Types** tab.

3   Scroll down the list until you find the offending file type and click it.

4   Click on the **Edit** button.

5   Click on **Change Icon** and browse for an acceptable replacement.

6   Click **OK** to close each successive dialog.

This also gives a neat way of telling the difference between file-types that are all associated with the same program, such as **.txt**, **.ini** and **.sys** which are usually associated with Notepad and therefore all have Notepad's icon.

Change Folder Icons

Had enough of those golden folder icons? Change them all to something else:

I   Open **My Computer** and select **View / Options...**

2   Click the **File Types** tab.

3   Scroll down the list to find **Folder**, select it and click the **Edit** button.

4   Now click on **Change Icon** and select a new one.

On Location

To find the full path of an object, right-click it and select **Properties** from the context-menu. Hold the mouse-pointer over the **Location** entry for a few seconds and the item's full path will appear in a tooltip.

Running Applications

Run Properties

By right-clicking on the shortcut to a file or application and selecting **Properties / Shortcut**, you can choose how the application (or the application *associated with the file*) should be run: Maximized, Minimized or Normal.

❑   **Maximized** will present a full-screen view of the app.

❑   **Minimized** will open it as a button on the Taskbar.

❑   **Normal** will open it with the default (or last-saved) window size and position.

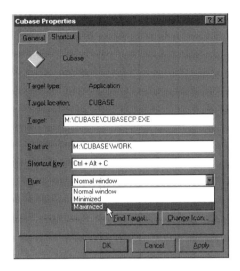

Screen 4.6 – **The 'Run' and 'Start in' boxes**

Of course, at most times if you double-click a shortcut you'd normally want to see the application-window immediately rather than just a button. This option really comes into its own when used with shortcuts in the **StartUp** folder.

For example, if you'd like Windows to load with Explorer available to you at the click of a Taskbar button rather than in a window, select **Minimized**. On the other hand, if you don't like the idea of working from a Desktop, select **Maximized** and Windows will automatically start with Explorer filling the screen (rather like using **File Manager** as the shell under *Windows 3.x*).

The Run Solution

Aside from their value in the **StartUp** folder, the Run options can be used to solve niggles with some of your applications. If a certain application opens by default with a particularly small window, or a badly positioned window, and you can do nothing but change it manually each time, select the **Maximized** option.

Start Here

Another useful option on the **Shortcut / Properties** page is the 'Start In' command-line box (see Screen 4.6 above). Here you can specify which folder the application should display in its **Open** and **Save As** windows.

For example, if you regularly create and use word-processor files in a folder called C:\Wordpro\Docs, type this into your word-processor shortcut's 'Start In' box. When you start the word-processor from this shortcut, this folder will automatically be presented when you want to open a file or save a new one.

This applies only to shortcuts to the application itself. If you start the app from a file-icon or a file's shortcut, the application will default to using the path of that file in its Open/Save As dialogs.

Never Run Applications

From a point of view of speed, running an application by clicking on its icon (or a shortcut to the **.exe**) is a total no-hoper: when you get there, you've still got to track down and open the file you need.

Make sure you've got shortcuts to regularly used files no more than a click away from the Desktop or Start Menu and that all the file-types you work with are associated with the applications you actually use.

There's No File!

Sometimes, of course, there *is* no file: you're starting the application to create a new one. There's still a quicker way though: right-click on the Desktop or in a folder, and select **New** followed by the file-type from the sub-menu. Type a name for the file, double-click the icon and there's the application!

Of course, this relies on having the correct file-type in your **New** sub-menu - even some of the newer applications built specifically for *Windows95* don't add their file-types to this menu. Fortunately you can add them yourself: see 'Adding To The "New" Sub-Menu' on page 108 for details.

Multiple Application Shortcuts

There's another way to start an application with a particular file automatically opened in it that has nothing to do with file-associations: add the filename as an 'argument' to the application's path in its shortcut.

This can be especially useful with generic formats such as **.txt**, **.rtf** or **.bmp**. These are probably associated with one particular program, so double-clicking the file automatically runs that program. If you like to open the file in various applications at different times this is the neatest way to do it (and still requires only one copy of the file on your system!).

Create a shortcut somewhere convenient to each of the applications in the usual way. Then, one by one, go to the **Properties / Shortcut** page of each and add the path to the file after the path to the app (making sure you leave a space between the two paths). For example:

> "C:\Program Files\Accessories\WordPad.exe" C:\Reports\1995.rtf

Give each shortcut a suitable name (e.g., '1995 Report In WordPad'). Now, even if your **.rtf** files are associated with a different program, double-clicking this shortcut will open the file in WordPad.

File Associations

What Are They?

Windows95 is a document-oriented operating-system: instead of starting an application and then tracking down the file you want to view or edit, you can 'run' the file itself which will launch the required application.

This is handled by means of *associations*: file-types are listed in the Registry as 'belonging to' particular applications so that when you double-click on a file's icon (or a shortcut to the file), Windows checks the Registry to see which application should be run to open it.

The two required elements, therefore, are the **file-types** themselves (which Windows distinguishes by their MS-DOS extensions, with all registered types listed on the **My Computer / View / Options / File Types** page), and their **associated applications** (see 'Open With...' and 'Changing File Associations' on pages 101–2).

Viewing .CAB Files

If you double-click on a **.cab** (Cabinet) file such as those found on the *Windows95* CD-ROM or the beautifully named **Mini.cab** in the System folder, the **Open With** dialog will appear (see Screen 4.8). Click on **Other**, navigate to **Extract.exe** in C:\Windows\Command and double-click it. You'll then be returned to the **Open With** dialog with Extract.exe added to the list and selected. Click **OK**. The file will then be opened in an MS-DOS window to let you see its contents. Type **exit** at the command prompt to close the DOS box.

Screen 4.7 – **Mini.cab, stripped down**

To save the aggravation of navigating the **Open With** menu every time you want to view a **.cab**'s contents, check the box marked **Always use this program to open this type of file** before clicking **OK**; this creates an *association* between **.cab** files and **Extract.exe**.

 If you want to extract files from a Cabinet file, see 'Opening Cabinets' on page 131.

Fixed Associations

Tip

There are a few file types for which *Windows95* won't let you change the association. If you're sure you want to change it anyway, run **File Manager** (Winfile.exe in your Windows folder), select **File / Associate...** and make the changes there instead.

Open With . . .

By default, a particular file-type is associated with a single application. The default action for that file-type is usually **Open**, so that double-clicking the file's icon starts the app and opens that file in it.

For some types of file there are times when you want to use a different application to open them. The solution is simple: click once on the file's icon to highlight it, then *Shift*+right-click it and you'll see that an **Open With...** option has been added to the pop-up context-menu. Selecting this option takes you to the **Open With** dialog from which you can choose an application from the list or select **Other** and browse for an unlisted app.

Screen 4.8 – **The 'Open With' list of apps with registered file-types**

Changing File Associations

You can use the **Open With** dialog to change a file-type's association permanently if you want to: after choosing the target application from the list as in
the previous tip, just check the box marked **Always use this program...** to fix
it as the default application.

Multiple Associations

The above suggestion is okay as long as the situation arises only occasionally,
but what if you want to regularly use different applications for a file type?
Perhaps you want to open **.txt** files in Notepad, WordPad or Word at different
times? One solution is to include these options on the context-menu. Using
this example, here's how to do it:

1   Go to **My Computer / View / Options / File Types**.

2   Find the **TXT File** entry, select it and click on **Edit**.

3   Highlight **Open** in the Actions box, click **Remove** and **OK**.

4   Now click on **New**. In the Action box type **Open in Notepad**.

5   In the Application box below it type **c:\windows\notepad.exe**

6   Click **OK**.

7   Repeat steps 4–6 for WordPad and Word, substituting the correct
     name for the Action and the correct path to the Application for each.

8   Decide which of these three applications should be the default app
     for text files (usually Notepad), click on its entry in the Actions box
     and click **Set Default**. Then click **OK** to finalize.

According to this example, whenever you double-click on a **.txt** file it will automatically open in Notepad, but if you right-click it instead you'll have the added options on the context-menu of 'Open in WordPad' and 'Open in Word'.

 A different method of achieving the same result is to create shortcuts to WordPad and Word in your Send To folder (see 'Send To An Application' on page 118).

View Any File Type

Once in a while, you come across a text-based file (maybe a system or word-processor file) that you'd like to have a quick look at to get a rough idea of what it contains. **Quick View** may be one solution (see page 136); another is to add a context-menu option that lets you view any file in **Notepad**. With a small Registry hack, you can do this without having to edit every single file-type on your system:

1   Run **Regedit**, and expand the **HKEY_CLASSES_ROOT** key. Right-click on the * (asterisk) key at the top of the 'tree' and choose **New** and **Binary value**. Name this new value **EditFlags**.

2   Double-click **EditFlags** and type **02 00 00 00** (don't type the spaces: Regedit will insert these automatically).

3   Press *F5* to refresh, and close the Registry Editor.

4   Now go to **My Computer / View / Options / File Types**. You'll find a new entry at the top of the list named "*" (asterisk): this is a new 'file-type' for which you can create actions that will affect all the other file-types. Highlight it, and click the **Edit** button. In the **Description** box, replace the asterisk by typing **All File Types** to make this new entry easier to recognize.

5   Now click the **New** button. In the 'Action' box, type **View As &Text**; in the 'Application used to perform action' box type **C:\Windows\Notepad.exe**. Click **OK** twice to confirm and shut the dialogs.

Now when you right-click on any file, you'll see a **View As Text** option allowing you to see the file's contents in Notepad. (Clearly non-text based files, such as graphics files, will be unrecognizable in Notepad though.)

 If you're going to follow this tip, you can use it to add the **Quick View** option to all file types too, producing exactly the same result as in

'Quick View All File Types #3' on page 137. Before clicking **OK** the second time in step 5, check the box marked **Enable Quick View**.

File Management

Drag & Drop Problems

Copying and moving files and creating shortcuts by 'drag & drop' is a priceless feature of Windows, but its implementation is hardly intuitive: the result you get depends upon what you drag and where you drag it to.

If you use the left mouse-button (which is usually the more comfortable), dragging a file between drives creates a copy, whereas dragging it elsewhere on the *same* drive will move it – this is okay as long as you're always consciously aware of your system's geography. But, more confusingly still, if you drag an **.exe** file anywhere at all this creates a shortcut rather than a copy or move. There are two methods of adding a little certainty to the process:

> ❑   Holding *Ctrl* while dragging will force a copy anywhere; holding *Shift* will force a move; holding *Ctrl + Shift* will force a shortcut.

> ❑   Always drag with the right mouse-button instead: when you drop, the context- menu will give you the option to Move, Copy or Create Shortcut.

The first option has the attraction of (usually) having no confirmation/option dialogs; the second allows you to be sure you've done what you wanted, and is a lot easier to remember!

One extra tip for drag'n'droppers: when you start dragging, a small icon is added to the base of the pointer to indicate the result (or the *default* result if you're using the right button) – a small + sign denotes a copy, a curved arrow a shortcut. No icon indicates a move. You'll see the icon change as you drag over different drive or document windows, or onto the Start button.

Don't Tile Windows!

When you drag and drop from one window to another, it isn't always necessary to tile them or have them side by side. If one folder window is partially obscuring another you can still drag from the lower one provided you can see the item you want to drag. If you do it correctly, you won't find that the upper window vanishes underneath when you click the item ...

The trick is to click and drag in one manoeuvre: as you click on the item in the lower window it won't become highlighted but it *is* selected, so drag it without 'letting go'. The focus doesn't actually shift to the bottom folder when you click, but when you *unclick* (i.e., release the mouse-button).

Drag & Drop To The Taskbar

Dragging & dropping an item onto a minimized button on the Taskbar just gets Windows annoyed. Instead, drag the item to the button and hold it there for a moment: the window will re-open, letting you drop the item into it. (The same method can be used if the window or application you want to 'drop' to is hidden behind a stack of other open windows – in this case, hovering over its button will bring the window to the front.)

Drag & Drop To Floppy

You've probably got a shortcut to your floppy-disk drive in your **Send To** folder, giving a quick method of copying files to floppy disk. A speedy competitor is to keep a shortcut to **A:** on your desktop (by dragging its icon from **My Computer**): items dropped onto this shortcut will be automatically copied to the floppy-disk.

You can use the same method in a dual-pane Explorer window provided you make sure the floppy-drive's icon is visible in the left pane before you start dragging from the right.

If you want to *move* files to floppy (i.e., delete them from your hard-disk at the same time), drag with the right mouse-button and choose **Move Here** from the context-menu.

Drag & Drop To An Application

With most applications, it's possible to drag a file from the Desktop or an Explorer-window and drop it into the application's window to open it – but beware! In applications that support OLE the dropped file will become a linked object in the currently open document (if there is one) instead of opening. To make sure this doesn't happen, always drop the file at the top of the application-window in the title-bar/menu-bar/toolbar area.

On Second Thoughts . . .

If you're halfway through a drag & drop manoeuvre and change your mind, simply click the other mouse-button or hit *Esc* to cancel the action.

Quick Cut, Copy, Paste

In addition to Explorer's Toolbar buttons for Cut, Copy & Paste, and the same three options on the context-menu, keyboard fanatics can now use the old favourites *Ctrl+X, Ctrl+C & Ctrl+V* for file management, thus eliminating some of that 'drag & drop' head-scratching.

Drop It In A Folder

When you want to drag & drop a file into a different folder (whether it's for a copy, a move or a shortcut operation) you don't need the target folder to be open. As long as you can see the folder-icon you can just drop the file(s) onto that, saving you the trouble of opening and tiling two windows.

Creating A Twin

If you want to make a duplicate of a file in the same folder as the original (perhaps as a backup), select the file's icon, hit *Ctrl+C* followed by *Ctrl+V*. You'll now have a new file named 'Copy of...'.

 Alternatively, right-click and drag the file to a clear area in the window, drop it and select **Copy Here** from the context-menu.

'Open' & 'Save As' Dialogs

The new **Open** and **Save As** dialogs in *Windows95* (and 32-bit applications built for it) have a bunch of handy features.

❏   If you're just about to save a new file and realize that you haven't created the folder you wanted to save it to, click the toolbar-button with the shiny new folder on it.

❏   You can use the two buttons on the right of the Toolbar to toggle between List and Details views of the window's contents.

❏   Alternatively, right-click on an empty area of the window to access the remaining View options (Large or Small Icons), add new folders and blank files or check an item's properties.

❏   You can even carry out complete file-management tasks here without ever leaving your application – right-clicking on an item in the window gives you all the usual Rename, Delete, Copy, Paste and Send To options.

❏   To drop down the **Look in** or **Save in** boxes quickly, just hit *F4*.

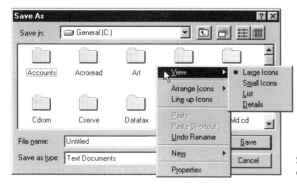

Screen 4.9 – **Context-menus in file dialogs**

Save With A New Extension

Whenever you save a new file by typing a name in the **Save As** dialog, the application's default file-extension is automatically applied (e.g., **.bmp** in Paint, or **.txt** in Notepad). Nevertheless, you can specify a different one by typing it in along with the name. The problem comes when you try to save with an extension that hasn't been registered in the **File Types** list: the default extension will then be added on the end. For example, trying to save a Paint file as **My Picture.zzz** will result in a file called **My Picture.zzz.bmp**. The obvious way to avoid this is to first create a new file-type for files with a **.zzz** extension (see the following tip). If you don't want to do this, just enclose the full name in quotes (″) when you type it into the dialog.

Adding New File Types

Occasionally you want to register a new file-type so that double-clicking the file's icon will automatically launch it in the selected application – for example, you might want to create a collection of text-file documents about Sheep Farming with the extension **.shp**, and still have them open in Notepad:

1   Click your way to **My Computer / View / Options/ File Types**.

2   Click the **New Type...** button.

3   Type a description (such as Sheep Doc) in the first box.

4   Type the extension (.shp) in the second box.

5   Now click on the **New** button at the bottom of the page.

6   In the next dialog that pops up, type **open** on the 'Action' line.

7   Type C:\Windows\Notepad.exe on the 'Application used to perform action' line and click OK.

8   Click **Close** on the previous page to finalize.

Of course, you could just save the files with the .txt extension, but one great advantage to creating new extensions and file-types is that you can add a different icon to them. In the example above, the .shp files would still have the default Notepad icon making them indistinguishable from any other file with a Notepad association. Before carrying out step 3, click the Change Icon box and browse for a different icon – perhaps one with a sheep connotation?

Quick File Type Selection

Instead of using the scroll-box (or, worse still, the scroll-arrows) to find the entry you're looking for in the File Types dialog, just type the first two or three letters of its name to go straight to it. You can use the same trick to select items in Explorer-windows, Registry Editor, the file/folder windows of 'Open' and 'Save As' dialogs, the Open With dialog – almost any listing you come across.

Registry
Tip

Adding To The 'New' Sub-Menu

Right-clicking on the Desktop, or within a window or **Open/Save As** dialog, gives you the option to place a file there from the **New** sub-menu and give it a name. Double-clicking the file's icon runs its associated application with this file ready loaded. This tip describes how to add a *template* file to the sub-menu (i.e., a file that already contains data, such as a letterhead or a preset spreadsheet).

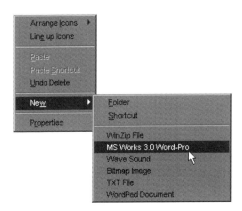

Screen 4.10 – **A new addition to the 'New' sub-menu**

I   Run the application for which you want to create a **New** sub-menu item and choose its **File / New** or equivalent. Set up this document as a template with all the preferences you would usually set, such as page-size, margins, default font and so on. You might also want to add text to create, for example, a letter-template with your address at the top. When the document is complete, save it somewhere convenient.

2   Open Explorer and copy the new file (not a shortcut) to the hidden folder **C:\Windows\ShellNew**. (Make sure you've selected **Show all files** from Explorer's **View / Options** page to make this folder visible.)

3   Now run the Registry Editor and expand **HKEY_CLASSES_ROOT**.

4   Scroll down the left pane until you find the extension for the file-type that you just created. Right-click on it, choose **New** and **Key** and name the new key **ShellNew**.

5   Now right-click on **ShellNew** and choose **New** and **String Value**. The new string will appear in the right pane.

6   Type the name **FileName** for this new string, and press *Enter*.

7   Double-click on **FileName**, and in the dialog-box type the name of the file you created – don't include any path details as Windows knows to look in the ShellNew folder, but you must include the extension.

8   Click once on the Desktop and press *F5* to refresh, then right-click on the Desktop and choose **New** from the context-menu: you should see your new file-type gazing back at you.

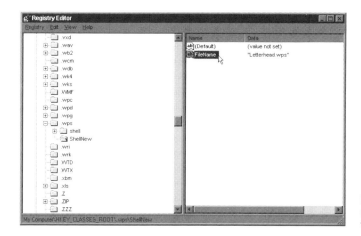

Screen 4.11 – **Find the extension, type the filename**

The Alternative

Rather than create a template file, you could instead opt to use a *nullfile*: this is a 'blank' file, the equivalent of what you get when you click **File / New** in the target application to start a fresh piece of work.

Using a nullfile is quicker: there's no template file to create first. Under **HKEY_CLASSES_ROOT**, find the extension for the file-type for which you want a nullfile. Right-click on it, choose **New** and **Key** and name the new key

ShellNew. Next, right-click on **ShellNew**, choose **New** and **String Value**, then name the new string **nullfile** and press *Enter*. Now follow step 8 above to check it out.

An optional extra

The document-description on the sub-menu itself may not be to your taste: as an example, 'Microsoft Works 3.0 Word-Processor' is hardly snappy, and more than doubles the width of the menu. The description can be changed, but bear in mind that whatever you call it will be carried through to the Explorer description of all files with this extension too:

1   Continue scrolling down the left pane of Registry Editor from your current position. Following the tree-list of file-extensions comes a similar list of file *types*. Search for the correct file-type that matches your file's extension (in the case of the above example it's 'MSWorks3WordProcessor').

2   Click on the file-type. In the right pane you'll see the same description listed for the (**Default**) string as you found on your sub-menu. Double-click on (**Default**) and type into the dialog-box the description you'd like to see.

3   Once again, click the Desktop, press *F5* and take another look at your **New** sub-menu.

For some applications the contents of this tip may need some tweaking to make them work if they register their entries differently; indeed, one or both of the operations may not work at all. Take careful note of what keys and strings you add or modify so that you can restore the Registry by deleting additions and reversing modifications.

Registry
Tip

Streamline The 'New' Sub-Menu

If you find that your 'New' sub-menu contains a collection of file-types that you never use, they're easily removable: start the Registry Editor, hit *F3* and type **shellnew** to find the file-types with a 'New' entry one at a time. For any that you don't want, just delete the **ShellNew** key and click on **OK** to confirm.

You might prefer to first backup any Registry settings that you're going to delete by exporting the branch as a **.reg** file. See 'Working With Reg' on page 217 for details.

Add Options To Disk Drives

Windows95 considers disk drives to be a File Type – you can add commands to their context-menus just as you can with a file or folder. Useful actions to add might be 'Defragment', 'Backup', or 'Run DriveSpace'.

1   Navigate to **My Computer / View / Options / File Types**, select the **Drive** entry from the list of file-types and click the **Edit** button.

2   Click the **New** button on the Edit page.

3   Type a name for the action, such as **Defragment** in the first box.

4   Type the application path in the second box **(C:\Windows\Defrag.exe)**.

5   Click **OK** to add this new action to the list.

6   Repeat steps 2–5 for any other actions you'd like to add.

You can also reach these options from the drive-icons' **Properties** page. Here you'll find tabbed pages from which you can run Scandisk, Backup, Defrag and DriveSpace, and find other useful details about the drive which will be missing from shortcuts.

Registry Tip

Personalize Windows Folders

There's a little bunch of folders that *Windows95* creates, names, and places by default in the Windows folder. These are folders that the *Windows95* interface relies upon, such as **Desktop**, **Start Menu** and **SendTo**. You can't easily delete these folders, and you usually have no need to, but you might want to move them or rename them: you can do that with Registry Editor. To take an example, let's say we want to move the Desktop folder into a folder called **C:\Emily\Play** and rename it **Front Desk**:

First, open an Explorer window and find your **Desktop** folder. Right-click on it and choose **Cut**. Now navigate to and open the **C:\Emily\Play** folder. Right click on a blank space inside this window and choose **Paste**. Your **Desktop** folder should appear. Click on its label and type **Front Desk** as the new name.

Now fire up the Registry Editor (**Regedit.exe**).

I   Expand **HKEY_CURRENT_USER \ Software \ Microsoft \ Windows \ CurrentVersion \ Explorer**.

2   Click on the key named **Shell Folders**.

3   In the right pane, you'll see the list of well-known folder names as string- values with their paths and names as value-data. Check this list to see if your folder-move has been updated automatically in the Registry. If it has, shut the Registry – you've finished! If it hasn't, go to step 4.

4   Double-click the entry named **Desktop**. Look at the dialog-box that pops up: the new folder position and name might be listed here. If it is, just click **OK** and shut the Registry. If it isn't, carry on with step 5.

5   In the dialog-box type: **C:\Emily\Play\Front Desk** (making sure you enter the *full* path and correct spelling), click on **OK**, and shut the Registry.

Long Filenames

What Are They?

Previous versions of Windows and MS-DOS have restricted the length of filenames to an eight-character name plus a three-character extension, all uppercase and separated by a period, in the form **FILENAME.EXT** (referred to as an '8.3' name or 'MS-DOS' name). Certain special characters could be included in the name: **$ % ' – _ @ ~ ' ! ( ) # &**

Under *Windows95*, filenames can consist of up to 255 characters, using upper- and lowercase letters, more than one period, spaces, and the additional special characters **+ , ; = [ ]**. The extension becomes the characters following the final period in the name.

For backwards compatibility, *Windows95* still assigns an 8.3 name to all files (shown on the file's **Properties** page): names using more than eight characters and/or spaces and the additional special characters are truncated to their first six legal characters followed by '**~**' (tilde) and a number. If the name consists of no more than eight characters, which are all legal, the name will be retained but converted to uppercase. Extensions are derived from the text following the final period, with four or more characters being reduced to three.

Figure 4.1 shows a few examples of files with long names, all in the same folder, with their corresponding 8.3 names:

Fig. 4.1

Long Filename	Short Filename
Accounts for 1993.doc	ACCOUN ~ 1.DOC
Accounts for 1994.doc	ACCOUN ~ 2.DOC
Appendix.01	APPENDIX.01
Projected Unit.Cost.Report	PROJEC ~ 1.REP

LFN Dilemmas

To illustrate the kind of problems that long filenames (LFNs) can cause, let's take the first two examples in Fig. 4.1. On your own *Windows95* system, you can easily spot the difference between 'Accounts for 1993' and 'Accounts for 1994'. This is fine, as long as they stay on a *Win95* system.

If you now copy '1994' to floppy disk, Windows realizes there is no other file on the floppy beginning ACCOUN, so changes its 8.3 name to ACCOUN ~ 1.DOC. Do the same now with '1993' and it becomes ACCOUN ~ 2.DOC – in other words, the 8.3 filenames have been reversed. Since *you* can still see the LFNs there is no apparent problem, but if you now give this floppy disk to someone using *Windows 3.x* or MS-DOS it's a recipe for confusion. And, worse still, if your colleague saves these files again from a 16-bit application the long filenames will vanish for good, causing even more problems if you then want to copy the files back to your own system. And, since the LFN and the 8.3 names have both changed, shortcuts to these files won't work either.

If you expect to share files with non-*Windows95* users, use one of these three options to prevent this sort of chaos:

❑ Name the files with legal 8.3 names such as ACC-1993.DOC

❑ Put variable elements of the name at the start (1993 Accounts.doc)

❑ Prefix the LFN with an 8.3 name (1993Acc-Accounts for 1993.doc)

Avoid The Tilde

If you're still using *Windows 3.x* applications under *Windows95*, you probably rename the files you create, replacing them with long filenames for easier identification in Explorer. After you do this, the application will display these files with 6-character names followed by ~**1**. A quick method of making sure files saved from 16-bit applications use the full eight characters is to do the following:

1   Before saving the file in the *3.x* application, decide what your *long* filename should be. For this example, we'll choose 'New Product Preview.zzz'.

2   Save your file using the first eight characters of the desired name (i.e., newprodu.zzz) and close the program or document.

3   Now find the file in Explorer and rename it with the chosen long filename.

4   When you return to your application and select **File / Open**, you should see your new file still represented as 'newprodu.zzz' rather than the slightly less meaningful 'newpro ~ 1.zzz'.

(i) It's worth noting that if the folder contains more than one file beginning with the same eight characters, the tilde suffixes will be called back into play.

(ii) The suffixes will only be removed from *subsequently created* files – if you're really determined to lose them for good, you'll have to rename all existing files and folders using them.

Registry
Tip

Kill The Tilde

If you want a permanent method of removing the tilde-suffix in *3.x* filenames, here's a Registry trick that will do the job:

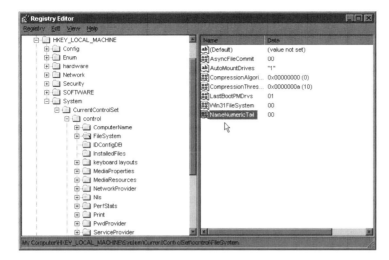

1   Open the Registry Editor.

2   Expand **HKEY_LOCAL_MACHINE** and go to \ **System** \
CurrentControlSet \ **control**.

3   Expand **control** and right-click on **FileSystem**. From the context-
menu, choose **New** and **Binary value**. Name this new value
NameNumericTail.

4   Double-click on the new **NameNumericTail** value, press *Delete* once
and type **0** (i.e., 'zero'). The value-data should now read **00**.

5   Click on **OK**, close the Registry Editor, and restart *Windows95* for the
change to take effect.

Your short filenames will now always be the first 8 characters of the long
filename (spaces being removed automatically by Windows), but still with the
unavoidable exceptions noted for the previous tip.

Fonts & Font Files

The Fonts Folder

It's worth noting that the **Fonts** folder (C:\Windows\Fonts) is a special folder:
Windows reads the fontname from the file-header and displays it. If you put
these files in a different folder they will be displayed with their own filename,
which may bear little or no resemblance to the fontname. This can make it
tricky to reinstall fonts via drag & drop or cut & paste.

Sorting Fonts

Explorer offers several different views of the Fonts folder, including the facility to compare fonts by similarity with each other and to hide font variants (such as bold). If you choose **Details** view, each font's filename is shown alongside the font-name.

Installing Fonts

To install new fonts (or reinstall fonts that you'd previously removed in a manner that lets you see the correct font-name), take the following steps:

I   Open Explorer and go to the Windows\Fonts folder, or choose **Fonts** from Control Panel.

2   Select **File / Install New Font**.

3   In the Folders box, find the folder containing the fonts and click it. Windows will load and display the font-names it finds in that folder.

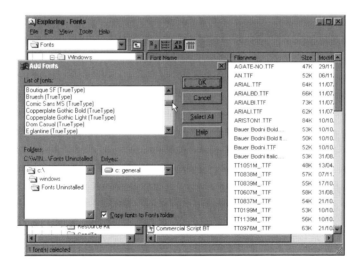

Screen 4.13 – **The Fonts folder and Add Fonts dialog**

4   To install all of them, click on **Select All**. To select specific fonts, hold *Ctrl* and click each font you require.

5   Uncheck the **Copy fonts to Fonts folder** if you want to create shortcuts to the fonts instead (see the next tip). Click **OK** to install.

In contrast with *Win3, Windows95* stores its font details in the Registry, so you can have as many fonts installed as you want to without your system showing any ill-effects.

If you previously installed a particular font and later removed it, there's no need to use the **Install New Font** procedure if you want to install it again: you can just drag it into the Fonts folder using the right mouse-button or use Cut/Copy/Paste.

Font Shortcuts

When installing fonts from the **Install New Font** menu-option, you can uncheck the box marked **Copy fonts to Fonts folder**. If you do so, a *shortcut* to the font will be placed in the **Fonts** folder (indicated by the customary shortcut-arrow, even if you've removed these from all your other shortcuts). To use fonts represented by shortcuts, the original font-file must of course be on an accessible (i.e., non-removable) drive.

By the same token, you can drag a font-file to the **Fonts** folder using the right mouse-button and choose **Create Shortcut(s) Here** to achieve the same result if you've had the font properly installed on your system at some time in the past. Of course, you need to know which fonts are which so that you can decide whether to install them or not – see 'Quick Font Identification' below.

Uninstalling Fonts

Fonts are removed by manually deleting them from the **Fonts** folder (or by moving them to a different folder).

Shortcuts to fonts can, of course, be deleted in complete safety – you still have the original font-file somewhere on your system. If the original font-file is in your **Fonts** folder, and only there, you need to be sure you'll really never need it again before hitting that *Delete* key!

Font Suggestion #1

If the font-selection boxes in your applications are getting so full that you can't easily find the one you want, create a new folder called 'Spare Fonts' and move any of the rarely used fonts here.

Windows has a useful partial-solution to the same problem: if you only ever use TrueType fonts, go to **View / Options / TrueType** and check the box to hide non-TrueType fonts in applications.

Font Suggestion #2

To prevent the possibility of 'uninstalling' a font and later regretting it, select every font file in **Fonts** (and any others on your system) and move them to a folder called 'Master Font Files' or something similar. Then use **Install New Font** to install any of these you need in *shortcut* form, following the previous tips and making sure **Copy fonts to Fonts folder** isn't checked.

Quick Font Identification

You can use **File / Install New Font** just to identify the font-names in your Spare Fonts folder or elsewhere on your system. However, *Windows95* long filenames give you a much neater option: simply rename these files to replace the anonymous 8-character filename with the font-name itself.

Another quick method is just to double-click the font-file: the **FontView** applet will open to show the fontname and a preview of the font at various sizes, with the option to print out the preview for reference.

The 'Send To' Folder

How Does It Work?

Sendto is an ordinary folder located within your Windows folder. You can add application shortcuts, folder shortcuts and even subfolders to it, all of which will appear beside the **Send To** option on your context-menu. In effect, it's a fast version of the Cut/Paste combination.

Send To An Application

Placing shortcuts to applications in the **Send To** folder gives the same result as *Shift+Right-clicking* on a file and choosing from the **Open With** list. Just right-click on the file, select **Send To** and pick the application you'd like to use. The app will start with the file opened in it.

Useful 'Send To' Shortcuts

Here's a few good candidates for inclusion in your Send To folder:

- ❏ **Notepad** – for opening text-based files with unusual file-extensions
- ❏ **Quick View** – for similar reasons
- ❏ **Zip/Compression Software** – decompress files with a single click

❏   **Fax Software** – for one-click faxing

❏   **Uuencoding software** – encoding and decoding of email attachments

❏   **Floppy, Tape & Zip drives** – for immediate backup of new work

❏   **Network drive** – to quickly send files to colleagues

❏   **Printers** – for fuss-free printing

❏   **Folders** – for moving files around your own system fast.

Send To A Folder

One of the most useful aspects of the **Send To** option is the ability to move files around your system at will by adding shortcuts to frequently accessed folders. For example, you might have work folders titled 'This Week', 'Next Week', 'Sometime' and 'Never' – create shortcuts to each of these in Sendto to easily prioritize your working files.

When you send an item to a folder, the result follows the same defaults as a drag & drop operation with the left mouse-button (see 'Drag & Drop Problems' on page 104) – if you send an item to a folder on the same drive it will move; send it to a different drive and it'll be copied. If you try to send an **.exe** file to a folder anywhere, you'll only be offered the opportunity to send a shortcut.

An easy way to create shortcuts to folders in the Send To folder is to open two instances of Explorer and drag folders from one to the other using the right mouse-button. Alternatively, right-click on a folder and choose **Copy**, then right-click on or in your Send To folder and choose **Paste Shortcut**. Here's a few folder suggestions:

❏   Create a shortcut to your **Desktop** folder (C:\Windows\Desktop) to group together all the files you need to work on this session.

❏   The **Send To** folder itself (C:\Windows\Sendto) to let you easily add new items to the Send To sub-menu as you stumble across them.

❏   Adding a shortcut to the **Start Menu** (C:\Windows\Start Menu) lets you add new items to the Start button quickly.

❏   If you're in a workgroup, add shortcuts to your colleagues' **shared folders**.

Folders Within Folders

You can create new subfolders in the Sendto folder in the normal way, and move shortcuts to these to make a cascading context sub-menu similar to the

Start Menu. If you find you're creating shortcuts to just about every folder on the system this is a handy way to organize them.

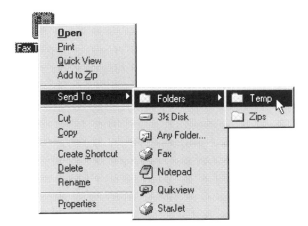

Screen 4.14 – **A 'Send To' sub-menu with ambition**

In Screen 4.14 a new subfolder imaginatively named 'Folders' has been created under C:\Windows\Sendto and shortcuts to folders named 'Temp' and 'Zips' placed in it.

'Send To' Alternative

If you regularly move files from one folder to another (for example from a 'Work In Progress' folder to a 'Work Completed' folder), create a shortcut to the target folder inside 'Work In Progress': you can then just drag files onto its icon to move them rather than cluttering up your **Send To** sub-menu.

If the whole idea of shortcuts to folders gets you confused about what's 'real' and what isn't, change the shortcut's icon to something less folder-like and give it an un-foldery name such as 'Move It!'.

Using folders in DOS

❑   **Open Folders from DOS** – page 67

❑   **Open In A DOS Window** – page 295

Alternative collections of icons

❑   **Icons Unlimited** – page 58

Viewing font files

❏ **Preview Fonts** – page 130

Working with document-scraps

❏ **Desktop Scraps** – page 144

Using OLE

❏ **'WORDPAD TIPS'** – page 140
❏ **Copying from Media Player** – page 164

Specifying paths in Autoexec.bat

❏ **Stating A Path** – page 265

Previewing files

❏ **'QUICK VIEW'** – page 135

Working with media files

❏ **'MULTIMEDIA PROPERTIES'** – page 159

Working with CD Audio and CD-ROM files

❏ **'CD AUDIO & AUTOPLAY'** – page 166

5

Applets & Accessories

Install & Uninstall

Missing The Goodies?

If you selected **Typical Install** during *Windows95* setup you may be missing out on some of the tasty morsels it shipped with. This chapter gives a few tips and suggestions concerning the more ubiquitous apps, but it's worth running **Add/Remove Programs** from the Control Panel, clicking the **Windows Setup** tab and taking a closer look at what else is available if you haven't already done so.

 Take a look below for details on using Add/Remove Programs to install new software on your computer.

Getting The Goodies

If you installed *Windows95* from floppy-disks, you won't have access to a bundle of additional files that were included on the CD-ROM, including accessories such as **Character Map** and **Quick View**. Either ask your retailer how to get the 'fulfilment disks' containing the extra files on the *Windows95* CD-ROM, or download them free from Microsoft's website (see the URL headed *Windows95 Software Library* on page 205). The collection is well worth getting for **Quick View** alone.

If you opted for the 'Typical' *Windows95* setup, or installed from floppy-disks, what you're missing is shown in Fig. 5.1

Fig. 5.1

Windows95 Component	Included in Typical Setup	Included on Floppy Disk
Accessibility Options	X	X
Character Map	X	X
Clipboard Viewer	X	X
NetWatcher	X	X
Dial-Up Networking	X	√
Direct Cable Connection	X	√
Microsoft Exchange	X	√
Microsoft Fax	X	√
Internet Mail	X	√
CompuServe Mail	X	√
System Monitor	X	X
Disk Compression	X	√
Multi-Language Support	X	X
Video Compression	√	X
Sound Schemes	X	X
Screensavers	X	X
Extra Cursors	X	X
Games	X	X
Quick View	X	X
Sound & Video Clips	X	X
Windows95 Tour	X	X
Online User's Guide	X	X

Add & Remove Windows Components

Always use **Add/Remove Programs** to install or remove files from the *Windows95* installation disk(s). Choose the **Windows Setup** tab, highlight the group containing the component you want to add or remove and click **Details**.

Check or uncheck the boxes beside any components to be installed or removed (respectively) and click **OK**. If you want to add or remove elements from another group, carry out the same procedure for that group.

Finally, click **OK**. Windows will then compare its own list of installed elements with your newly edited setup and install and/or remove elements accordingly.

Change Setup Path

When you install *Windows95*, the drive you install from is logged. So if you installed from CD-ROM and later needed to add or remove components from floppy-disks for some reason, Windows would still be looking for the CD. There are two solutions – the first is suited to a permanent change of installation media; the second requires no Registry editing and lets you pick and choose your path.

Option One

Open the Registry and go to **HKEY_LOCAL_MACHINE \ SOFTWARE \ Microsoft \ Windows \ CurrentVersion \ Setup**. In the right pane you'll find the value-name **SourcePath**. Double-click it and type in the required new path (such as **A:** or **D:\Win95**).

Option Two

When you try to install a component from the Windows Setup tab in Add/Remove Programs without the correct disk in the drive, you'll be prompted to insert it and click **OK**. If you can't insert it, click **OK** anyway. You'll then get a file dialog into which you can type a different location for the files.

For slightly speedier access than CD-ROM (and a huge time-saving for floppy-disk users!) you can copy the contents of the disk(s) to a folder on your hard-disk and redirect Setup to that folder. Provided you have the disk-space, this is an option to keep in mind whenever you have to install or reinstall software spanning several disks.

Add & Remove *Plus!* Components

Microsoft *Plus!* has its own version of the Add/Remove dialog: run **Setup.exe** from your **Program Files \ Plus! \ Setup** folder and click the **Add/Remove** button.

Two entries ('Desktop Themes' and 'Visual Enhancements') are groups: by selecting one of these and clicking the **Change Option** button, you can refine your choice of elements to be installed or uninstalled (such as removing a particular Theme). Click **Continue** to update the installation or **Cancel** to exit.

Installing New Software

Use the **Add/Remove Programs** applet whenever possible to install new software on your system. *Windows95*-aware programs will automatically add themselves to the Add/Remove list allowing you to uninstall them quickly and thoroughly in the future if you want to.

To use **Add/Remove** to install a new program:

1   Click the **Install** button on the Install/Uninstall page. Insert the software's floppy or CD-ROM (if it has one) and hit *Return*.

2   Type in the path and filename of the software's setup program and click **Finish**; or click **Browse** and go look for it, then click **OK** and **Finish**.

3   Leave the rest to Windows. If the new software is *Windows95*-aware, its name will be added to the list on the Install/Uninstall page; if not, it will still be installed but you'll have to handle any uninstallation yourself.

Is It Really Necessary?

Actually, no. If your new software is *Windows95*-aware, it'll log itself correctly even if you just click its **Setup.exe** or **Install.exe** file in Explorer. But the Add/Remove dialog is a great habit to get into because of its *uninstallation* abilities.

If you can equate 'stuff to do with software' with 'the add/remove programs thing' you're more likely to look here first when you want to kiss an application goodbye. If you just delete the app's folder, you might be leaving bunches of Help files, **.dlls**, **.inis**, Registry-keys, file-associations, and so on, scattered all over your hard-disk. In addition, if the software *was* 95-aware, you'll still have its entry on the Add/Remove list, and you can't get rid of it by clicking the **Add/Remove** button.

Registry
Tip

Edit The Add/Remove List

The list in the **Add/Remove Programs** box shows you which programs were added to the Registry on installation: removing the program is a simple job of selecting the program's name from the list and clicking the **Add/Remove** button. But if you get into the predicament mentioned above, and you want to remove the item itself (the *reference* to the program) from the list, here's how to do it:

1   Open the **Registry Editor**.

2   Expand **HKEY_LOCAL_MACHINE**, then **SOFTWARE, Microsoft, Windows, CurrentVersion, Uninstall**.

3   With **Uninstall** expanded, you'll see a separate key (folder-icon) for each of the installed programs. Simply delete the key for the item(s) you want removed from the list.

Other Install/Uninstall Possibilities

Of course, not all the software you install will be *Windows95*-aware to the point of logging itself in the Registry. There could be many reasons for this. The most obvious is that the software predates *Windows95*. Of the recent software, if it doesn't come with an install routine there's nothing to log – some software just asks you to create a new folder and copy files into it, so 'uninstallation' would consist of dragging the folder to Recycle Bin.

If your software does have a setup/install program, but doesn't log itself into **Add/Remove Programs**, you'll usually find that re-running the setup program will give you the option of uninstalling. This is preferable by far to just deleting the application folder as it should locate all those scattered files, but it may still leave some clearing-up to be done manually – one frequent result is the empty application-folder still residing on your hard-disk. When you try to delete this, Windows often says this may 'impact one or more registered programs'. Don't be fazed by this: the folder is empty, so how much more impact can it have?

Accessories

Welcome!

Remember the 'Welcome Screen' that greeted you when you first installed Windows? The one you probably regarded as an 'unwelcome screen' and disabled immediately (even before renaming 'My Computer'). This is a program called **Welcome.exe** in the Windows folder. To take another look at it, and scroll through its hints and tips, type **welcome** on the **Run** command line.

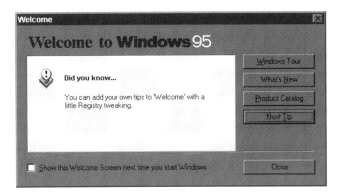

Screen 5.1 – **Welcome back to Welcome!**

 Use the checkbox labelled **Show this Welcome Screen...** to choose whether you want to see it next time you start Windows.

 Make **Welcome** worthwhile – customize it to add your own tips, jokes or friendly startup greetings. Take a look at the page 311 for details.

Using Character Map

Use **Character Map** to locate specialized characters and symbols such as ©, $\frac{1}{2}$ and $\pm$ for pasting into your word-processor document. Select the desired font from the drop-down menu, and click on the required character. There are two methods of importing the character into your document:

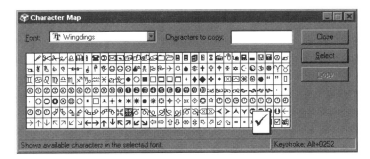

Screen 5.2 – **WingDings' useful offerings**

Method One
After clicking the character you need, click on **Select**. If you need other characters, do the same for each – they will all be added to the **Characters to**

copy box. When you've selected all you want, click **Copy**. Return to your document and select **Paste** from the **Edit** menu, or press *Ctrl + V*. The characters will be pasted at the cursor position. You can then delete the characters you don't want in that particular position. (Provided you don't subsequently Cut or Copy anything else, these characters will remain on the clipboard to be pasted again.)

Method Two

After clicking the required character, note the **Keystroke** in the lower right corner of the window (eg. the copyright symbol is *Alt + 0169*). Return to your document and position the cursor where you want to insert the symbol. Making sure *Num Lock* is on, hold *Alt* and type *0169* on the numeric keypad.

Large View In Character Map

To examine the various characters in a magnified view, click anywhere on the map, and then move around using the arrow-keys (see Screen 5.2).

Easy Connection

Every time you fire up **HyperTerminal** by double-clicking its icon, you're prompted to choose a name and icon for the connection you're about to make. Making the same connection in future is as easy as just double-clicking its icon. To access a connection quickly, drag a shortcut to it somewhere convenient.

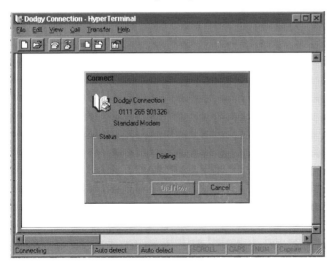

Screen 5.3 – **HyperTerminal**

Check Back

Once you make (and save) a connection in **HyperTerminal**, the on-screen text is logged and saved. If you double-click the same connection-icon again (and cancel the dial-out) you can scroll back to review the previous online-session.

Whose Crazy Idea . . . ?

For some reason, the *Windows95* setup creates a *shortcut* to your **Hyper-Terminal** folder in Start Menu / Programs. This is hardly a quick way of getting at your connections or at HyperTerminal itself. To speed things up, try this:

1   Right click on Start and choose **Open**.

2   Navigate to the HyperTerminal folder-shortcut and delete it.

3   Right-click and select **New** and **Folder**. Give the folder a name ('HyperTerminal' would seem the obvious choice here).

4   Double-click the new folder to open it.

5   Open Explorer and go to C:\Program Files\Accessories\Hyperterminal.

6   Holding *Ctrl*, select **Hypertrm** and any connection icons you want by clicking them. Then right-click on any selected icon, drag them to your newly created Start Menu folder, and select **Create Shortcut(s) Here** from the context-menu.

You now have the usual cascading folder, with all your connections and the terminal itself a single-click away. As you create new connections, drag shortcuts to them into this folder.

Alternative
The alternative solution is not to use shortcuts at all. Simply *move* your Hyperterminal folder out of **Program Files\Accessories** and put it in **Windows\Start Menu\Programs**. Any new connections you make will then automatically be saved into this folder and immediately be shown on the cascading Start Menu.

Make Compatible

The vast majority of *Windows 3.x* programs work perfectly under *Windows95*. A few, however, suffer slight performance glitches or other behavioural defects. 'Make Compatible' (**Mkcompat.exe** in the Windows\System folder) is a little utility aimed at solving these problems.

To have a go at improving a program's *Windows95* compatibility, type **mkcompat** on the **Run** command-line. Select **File / Choose Program...** and locate the **.exe** file you want to work with. Select **File / Advanced** to give yourself more parameters to play with if the default parameters don't seem to do the trick.

There is no text-support at all for **Mkcompat.exe** so trial-and-error is the only way to go for most users. Just check some of the likely looking boxes and see if they have any effect when you run the application. (Remember to hit **File / Save** to apply the settings before testing the app.)

Preview Fonts

Font collections often include several hundred or more fonts. In *Windows 3.x* you had to install each font-file before you were able to look at it and decide whether or not to keep it. *Windows95* includes a useful applet called Fontview which displays a preview of the font when you double-click on the font file's icon (see Screen 5.5). The file in question can be anywhere on your system.

A useful feature of **Fontview** is the ability print a sample file of the chosen font: this can be handy as a means of auditioning its suitability for a particular project, or to create your own quick-reference 'catalogue' of the fonts on your system.

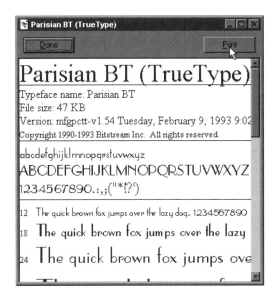

Screen 5.5 – **Audition and print new fonts at a double-click**

Tip

Opening Cabinets

Cabinet (**.cab**) files are the compressed archives on the *Windows95* installation disks, and intimate poking is usually unnecessary since the Add/Remove Programs dialog can help you deinstall and reinstall a problematic program. But if you accidentally delete a vital **.dll** file for example, you may not know which application to reinstall to get it back again. The answer is to use **Extract.exe** in an MS-DOS window.

If you type **extract** and *Enter* at the DOS-prompt you'll get the usual rather cryptic command-set. Here's a few example operations to make for less painful extractions. (If you installed from floppies, replace the path **d:\win95** with **a:**)

❑ View the contents of Win95_02.cab:
  extract d:\win95\win95_02.cab

❑ View only the **.dll** files in that archive:
  extract /d d:\win95\win95_02.cab *.dll

❑ Extract **enable.dll** to the folder specified by the command-prompt:
  extract d:\win95\win95_02.cab enable.dll

❑ Extract **enable.dll** to your System folder:
  extract d:\win95\win95_02.cab /l c:\windows\system enable.dll

❑ Extract the contents of the cabinet to a folder named C:\Temp:
  extract /e d:\win95\win95_02.cab /l c:\temp

Clipboard Viewer

The **Clipboard Viewer** is a handy accessory installed from Windows Setup. It handles the basic task of displaying the contents of the clipboard after a Cut or Copy operation. Additionally, you can save the contents of the clipboard to file (though long filenames are not supported), and reload them as required to paste into another document. You can even clear the contents of the clipboard by pressing *Del*.

 If you haven't yet installed this accessory, first read the next tip: the Clipbook Viewer is small but perfectly formed, and acts as a replacement to Clipboard Viewer.

Clipbook Viewer

Microsoft have kept remarkably quiet about this one, despite its superiority to the **Clipboard Viewer**. This handles precisely the same functions, but with one extremely useful extra: an item on the clipboard can be copied to a so-called *clipbook* – a sort of database of clips – which is automatically loaded and available whenever you run the **Clipbook Viewer**. This is a MDI application, presenting one window for the clipboard and another for the clipbook.

To install the app, run **Add/Remove Programs**, click the **Windows Setup** tab and the **Have Disk** button. Click the **Browse** button and navigate to D:\Other\Clipbook – you should see **Clipbook.inf** selected in the 'File Name' window. Click **OK** and the **Have Disk** dialog will appear. Check the box beside 'Clipbook Viewer', and click on **Install** to proceed.

Screen 5.6 – **Clipbook Viewer's dual windows**

The installation process tends to get confused, asking for a disk labelled 'Distribution Media'. If this occurs, use the **Browse** button to redirect it to D:\Other\Clipbook again. After installation, you'll need to restart the computer; *Windows95* will add a shortcut to the program in Start / Programs / Accessories (or update an existing shortcut to Clipboard Viewer).

Since the online Help supplied is typically minimal, here's a few pointers:

❑ To save an item on the clipboard, go to **File / Save As** and type a filename in the usual way; the file will be saved with the default **.clp** extension. (This is a 16-bit application, restricted to the old DOS 8.3 filenames.)

❑ To add the item currently on the clipboard to your Clipbook, make the Clipbook window active and press *Ctrl+V* ('paste'). A dialog will prompt you to enter a descriptive name for your own recognition purposes. Networking users can choose whether a particular clip should be available to other users as well.

❑ Items in the Clipbook are saved automatically by Windows after you enter a description for them, and the list of descriptions automatically loaded when you run the accessory. To view one of the clips, just double-click it.

❑ From the **View** menu (when the focus is on the Clipbook window), you can choose whether to view the clips as a Table Of Contents (i.e., descriptions only), or as thumbnail representations.

❑ To transfer a clip back to the clipboard ready for pasting into a document, either click or double-click the required clip, and press *Ctrl+C.*

Floppy Briefcase

The **Briefcase** accessory seems to be largely dismissed by Microsoft as only being of use to folk with portable computers. In fact it's perfectly usable (and useful) with floppy-disks. If you have an office PC and a home PC but no portable to act as go-between, or you co-author documents with others, Briefcases are a handy way to organize files.

To install Briefcase go to Add/Remove Programs / Windows Setup / Accessories. For a short explanation of its usage with floppies, start Windows Help, click the **Find** tab and type **reinsert** – the relevant heading will be shown below. Here's a few details not covered in Help:

To copy files into Briefcase, just drag with the left-button: a copy is always created. To move the Briefcase to your floppy-disk, either drag it in the same way or use Send To: the Briefcase is always moved. On your second computer, after inserting the floppy-disk, either edit the files by opening the Briefcase and double-clicking them, or copy them to your hard-disk – *don't move the Briefcase off the floppy-disk or the synchronization will be lost*!

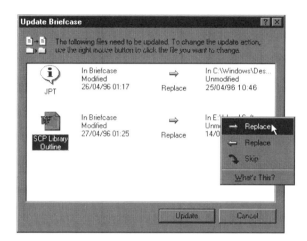

Screen 5.7 – **Updating file versions in Briefcase**

If you copied the files to hard-disk, open the Briefcase and choose **Update All** or **Update Selection** when you've finished editing. When you return to your first computer, you can leave the Briefcase on the floppy, or move it back to the hard-disk, and choose one of the **Update** options again. You'll be presented with a graphic dialog of contents and suggested actions like the one shown in Screen 5.7 – right-click on an item to change actions or get extra help.

Briefcase works by comparing the date/time stamp on different versions of the same file. Fundamental to its success is that all the computers you use are synchronized!

Briefcases Unlimited

You can have as many Briefcases as you want, create them where you want them and call them whatever you like. Once Briefcase is installed, right-click in any folder and choose **New** and **Briefcase**. If you deal with various categories of file, or different projects and clients, it's worth keeping a permanent Briefcase for each in the relevant folders and updating them when needed.

Briefcases Limited

There is one major limitation in the implementation of **Briefcase** with floppy-disks: for some unexplained reason, disk-spanning is not supported. If the total size of your Briefcase exceeds the capacity of your floppy-disk, you'll be prompted to insert a second disk, but the files placed on it will have no synchronization, the result being precisely as if you'd copied the files directly to disk instead. (In addition, of course, you can't use Briefcase for files larger than the floppy-disk's capacity.)

Quick View Tips

Where Is It?

Quick View is a handy accessory that attaches itself to the context-menu of certain file-types to let you view them without having to open their associated application. If you decide you want to edit the file, clicking the icon on the left of the toolbar will open the registered application and load the file.

If you haven't got Quick View installed already (it resides in C:\Windows\System\Viewers as **Quikview.exe**), pop your *Windows95* installation CD-ROM in the drive and go get it now!

1   Run **Add/Remove Programs** from the **Control Panel**.

2   Click the **Windows Setup** tab.

3   Click **Accessories** followed by the **Details** button (see Screen 5.8).

4   Scroll down the list of Accessories to find the **Quick View** entry, check its box and click **OK** twice to install it.

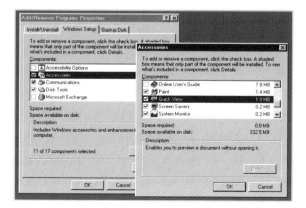

Screen 5.8 – **Installing Quick View via Add/Remove Programs**

For file-types that **Quick View** is capable of previewing, you'll get the same result by right-clicking on a *shortcut* to the file as by clicking on the file itself.

 If you installed *Windows95* from floppy-disks, you'll be noticeably lacking in the **Quick View** department. Your retailer should be able to supply a set of 'fulfilment disks' containing this and the other missing files. If you have Internet access, you can download them from the URL headed *Windows95* Software Library on page 205).

Quick View Any File Type

On installation, **Quick View** is added as an option to a limited range of file-types. But adding it to others is easy:

1   Open **My Computer** and go to **View / Options / File Types**.

2   Scroll down the list to find the file-type for which you want to add the option.

3   Click on the file-type and choose **Edit**.

4   Place a checkmark in the **Enable Quick View** box and click **OK**.

5   Repeat steps 2–4 for any other file-types required.

 Bear in mind that Quick View isn't able to read *all* possible file-types so some of these efforts may be wasted.

Quick View All File Types #1

A quick cheat to ensure the **Quick View** option is available for any file-type is to just create or drag a shortcut to Quikview.exe into your **Send To** folder and rename it **Quick View**. Keeping a shortcut to **Notepad** here too will ensure that most files can be viewed reasonably quickly and will be recognizable in one or both.

Quick View All File Types #2

Create or drag a shortcut to Quikview.exe onto your **Desktop** – this way you can drag & drop files onto its icon to be viewed.

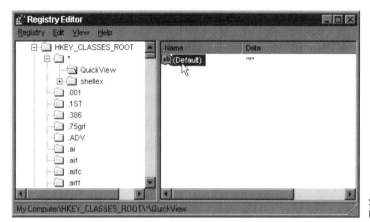

Screen 5.9 – **The asterisk
key under ROOT**

Registry
Tip

Quick View All File Types #3

With this Registry hack, you can make the **Quick View** option available on the menu for any file you right-click on:

1   Start the Registry Editor.

2   Expand **HKEY_CLASSES_ROOT**.

3   The first key immediately below it should be * (i.e., 'asterisk'). If it isn't there, you'll need to create it: right-click on **HKEY_CLASSES_ ROOT** and choose **New** then **Key**. When the new key appears, type * and press *Enter*.

4   Now right-click on * and select **New** then **Key**. Name this key **QuickView**.

5   In the right pane, double-click on (**Default**) and type * in the dialog-box.

(i) Even though the **Quick View** option will now appear for files of all types, bear in mind that Quick View doesn't have the necessary viewers to cope with *all* possible file-types thrown at it, so on occasions selecting the option may have no result.

(ii) There is a slightly untidy by-product of this trick: on the context-menus for folders and drives you'll find the **Quick View** option but it will have no effect; on the context menus for *shortcuts* to files you'll find *two* **Quick View** entries.

There's a second method of producing this result, combined with another handy context-menu option: read 'View Any File Type' on page 103.

Quick View Tricks #1

Try sending a **.dll** file to Quick View – this can often give an insight into which application(s) need it. If it belongs to a previously deleted app, you might be able to regain some disk space by deleting it. (A word of caution though: some **.dlls** are used by a whole host of programs, so try moving or renaming it and leaving it a few weeks just in case you were wrong!)

Conversely, you can also 'Quick View' an **.exe** file to find the version number and a list of the **.dll** files it uses: look at the 'Imported-Name Table'.

Quick View Tricks #2

If there's a particular document that you regularly want to refer to for information, but rarely need to edit, create a shortcut to it that opens in Quick View. Create a file-shortcut as usual, right-click on it and select **Properties / Shortcut**. In the **Target** box, click once to remove the highlight, position the cursor at the far left and type:

   C:\Windows\System\Viewers\Quikview.exe

so that it's placed immediately before the path to the file. Make sure you leave a space between the two entries. The **Target** entry could look like this:

   C:\Windows\System\Viewers\Quikview.exe C:\Docs\Work.txt

❏ If you find the Quick View window too small, use the Run box on the **Properties / Shortcut** page to select **Maximized**.

❏ When you add **Quick View** to the command-line in the **Target** box, the shortcut-icon will change to reflect this. Go to **Properties / Shortcut / Change Icon** to select the file's original icon, or a different one.

Notepad Tips

Mark Time

Pressing *F5* in **Notepad** will insert the current time and date at the cursor position.

Bohemian Wrap

While viewing files in **Notepad**, you'll often turn on Word Wrap (on the **Edit** menu) to force the text to remain within the boundaries of the current window-size. When you come to close the file, Windows informs you that the file has been altered and prompts you to save it.

There's a slight anomaly here since Notepad won't actually include the Word Wrap layout when it saves – if you've made no other changes, you're saving an unchanged file. The only way to retain this view is to input carriage returns manually.

If the word-wrap business grinds you down, why not associate **.txt** files with **WordPad** instead? This way, you can set WordPad's Textfile option to word-wrap for you automatically (see 'Having Options' below). Alternatively, add the **Open In WordPad** option to your context-menu (see 'Multiple Associations' on page 102) and give yourself the choice.

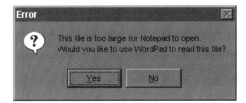

Screen 5.10 – **A new variation on an old theme**

Too Large For Notepad?

Windows 3.x users will remember the 'File is too large for Notepad' pop-up you sometimes got when double-clicking a text-file, and the ritual trek back to Program Manager to run **Write** and track down the file again from the File Open dialog. Fortunately, *Windows95* has got it licked: if you double-click a file that **Notepad** can't cope with, Windows will offer to open it for you in **WordPad** instead.

Find Text In Notepad

To search for a particular word or phrase in a **Notepad** document, you have to use the mouse and the **Search** menu to bring up the dialog. The *F3* key is just a shortcut key to **Find Next**. However, if this is your first search since opening Notepad, pressing *F3* will bring up the **Search** dialog anyway because it has nothing to search for yet!

After typing in the text-string to be found, press *Return*. The dialog remains on the screen and you can keep pressing *Return* to search for further instances of the specified text.

If you find the dialog is getting in the way, close its box and use *F3* instead to continue searching.

Word Work

To select a word in **Notepad** (to delete, copy or overtype), don't waste time swiping it with the pointer to highlight it – just double-click it!

As an alternative to swiping a *section* of text to select it, click where you want the selection to start, then hold *Shift* and click where the selection should end.

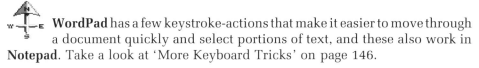 **WordPad** has a few keystroke-actions that make it easier to move through a document quickly and select portions of text, and these also work in **Notepad**. Take a look at 'More Keyboard Tricks' on page 146.

WordPad Tips

Find Text In WordPad

Finding a specific text-string in **WordPad** is done in a similar way to **Notepad** with the difference that there is a shortcut-keystroke to the initial *Find* dialog, *Ctrl+F*. Alternatively, you can click the Binoculars button on the Toolbar. Unusually, *F3* can't be used to start a new search as it can in **Notepad** and **Registry Editor**. To run a 'search & replace', press *Ctrl+H*.

Having Options

The **View / Options** menu lets you choose specific options for the different file-types **WordPad** is capable of working with, such as Word-Wrap and Toolbar view. These options are automatically saved as you exit.

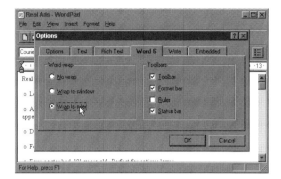

Screen 5.11 – **WordPad's multi-format option setting page**

Computer Dating

WordPad has a similar date/time option to **Notepad**. Choose **Date and Time** from the **Insert** menu or Toolbar and you're given a list of different formats. Double-click one to place it at the insertion-point using the currently selected font and size.

Marginally Useful

As well as having **Notepad's** features for text-selection (see 'Word Work' on page 140), **WordPad** has another trick up its sleeve: if you move your mouse pointer into the left margin you'll see it turn into a right-slanted arrow. Once you get used to positioning it, this is a great way to select text. Click once to select a single line, double-click to select the whole paragraph, or hold *Ctrl* and click to select the entire document. To select several lines, move the pointer into the margin in the same way, click, and drag upwards or downwards.

Introducing . . . The Triple-Click!

The *triple*-click has finally made an appearance, used in **WordPad** and **Word** amongst others. Triple-clicking anywhere in a paragraph will select the whole paragraph for editing. If you move the pointer into the margin, as in the previous tip, and triple-click, you'll select the whole document (equivalent to the *Select All* command).

WordPad OLE

One of the powerful features of **WordPad** is the ability to **link** or **embed** files in a document. These might be graphics used to illustrate points made in the text, media-clips used to form a prototype or economy-sized presentation, or other documents and files on your system for quick comparison or reference.

From the **Insert / Object** menu, you can opt to create a new file by selecting a file-type from the list and clicking **OK**. The relevant application (known as a 'server') will open to let you create the file.

Alternatively, click **Create from File** and **Browse** for an existing file to import. The **Display As Icon** box lets you decide how the object should be displayed in the document – either by the file's contents or with an icon. For file-types such as **Wave Sound** and **MIDI Sequence** the files' contents are meaningless when displayed, so the icon-view is required; for a **Bitmap Image**, however, you would usually want to display the picture. Double-clicking an iconized object will carry out the command associated with it ('play' for media files, 'open' for documents and so on). The first three objects in Screen 5.12 show these three file-types in a WordPad document.

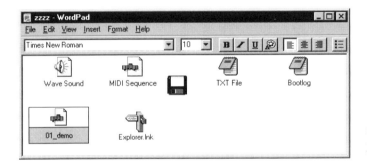

Screen 5.12 – **Linked & embedded objects in WordPad**

The other choice to make is whether to **link** or **embed** the object. An **embedded** object is a copy of the original as it was when you imported it – editing an embedded object will have no effect on the original, and vice-versa. A **linked** object is, in effect, a shortcut to the original file – any change you make to one will be reflected in the other.

When you embed an object, its icon is given an anonymous name (as with the **TXT File** object shown in Screen 5.12), whereas a linked object is displayed with the original filename (**Bootlog**).

Bear in mind that an embedded object will be saved as part of your WordPad document – if you embed a wave file, for instance, you could end up with a pretty large document, but you could give this document to someone else and he could double-click the icon to hear the file. A linked object, being just a shortcut, will hardly affect the file-size, but if you give the resulting document to someone the link won't work – the file in question is still on your hard-disk! You'd have to also hand over the file and specify the full path required for it.

Linking is also known as Dynamic Data Exchange (DDE), because the information you see in the document is automatically (*dynamically*) updated whenever you edit the original file to which the link points.

Quick OLE

In addition to using the **Insert / Object** menu, you can drag & drop files into a **WordPad** document, automatically creating an **embedded** object. Right-clicking on the icon gives access to Cut, Copy, Paste options and the ability to change properties.

The final two icons in Screen 5.12 were inserted by dragging them into the WordPad window; double-clicking the MIDI Sequence will play it; double-clicking the Explorer shortcut will launch Explorer.

Paste Special

WordPad, along with other OLE 2.0-compatible applications, has an extra Paste command on its Edit menu, **Paste Special**, providing another method of linking or embedding files (or sections of them) into a document. Copy a file to the clipboard from Explorer, or a section of a document from an application, using *Ctrl + C*, then return to WordPad and select the **Paste Special** option. In the resulting dialog you can choose to embed the contents of the clipboard (the default), or create a link to the original document. The dialog also provides a few options concerning the format you'd like to use for the data (such as pasting formatted text from a word-processor as plain text) – the first option is usually the one you'll want to take.

 If you want to embed the clipboard's contents, you can avoid the Paste Special option entirely by just pressing *Ctrl + V* in WordPad.

 For more on the Paste Special option, see 'Copying From Media Player' on page 164.

Dragging Text

A useful day-to-day facility in **WordPad** is text-drag: rather than using Cut, Copy & Paste to move sections of text or graphics around, you can simply highlight the desired area then click and drag it to the position you want it. To create a copy of the selection, hold *Ctrl* while dragging.

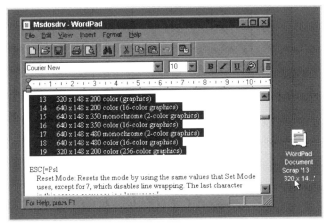

Screen 5.13 – **Dragging text to the Desktop as a scrap**

Desktop Scraps

You can even drag a section of selected text or graphic onto the Desktop or an Explorer-window from **WordPad** or any OLE 2.0-compliant application. This will create a **Scrap** document which can later be double-clicked to launch the same application or dragged back into any OLE application when you're ready for it.

This makes a useful alternative to the Clipboard when planning a long document – compose your paragraphs in any order, drag each to the Desktop as a 'scrap' and, when you're ready, drag them back one by one in the required order.

There are two methods of creating Scraps: if you use the **Edit / Copy** command (or *Ctrl+C*) to copy the selection, then right-click on the Desktop and choose **Paste**, you'll get something called just **Scrap**. Do it again and you'll get **Scrap (2)** and so on. But if you drag & drop the selection with the left mouse-button you'll get something called **Document Scrap (???)** where the **???** represents the first sixteen characters of the text you dragged. So if you intend to use several scraps at once, it's worth making sure you can see enough of your Desktop to use the drag & drop method.

Document Shortcuts

Document Shortcuts are a great *Windows95* feature for OLE2-compliant apps, but WordPad doesn't support them. The tip is included here for its possible relevance to other word-processing applications you may be using such as **Word**.

Select a small amount of text, drag it to the Desktop (or elsewhere) with the right-mouse button and choose **Create Document Shortcut Here**. The result is an icon titled **Document Shortcut** plus the first 16 characters of your selected text.

This works as a bookmark: double-clicking the shortcut will take you to that point in the document. Best of all, if the document isn't open, the shortcut will run the application, open the document, *and* find your place for you! Creating a collection of these representing all the headings in a long document or a collection of documents could be a real timesaver.

As with Scraps, mentioned above, you can use **Edit / Copy** or *Ctrl + C* to copy the selection, then right-click the Desktop and choose **Paste Shortcut**. And, once again, you'll end up with the anonymous **Document Shortcut, Document Shortcut (2)** style of naming.

If you have an application that does support Document Shortcuts, always use the right mouse-button to get all the choices under the sun: **Create Scrap Here, Move Scrap Here, Create Document Shortcut Here**, and the ever-popular **Cancel**.

WordPad Shortcuts

Speed up document formatting by using keyboard-shortcuts instead of sending your rodent off to the Toolbar: use *Ctrl + B, Ctrl + I* and *Ctrl + U* to toggle Bold, Italic and Underline on and off.

You can set paragraph-alignment using *Ctrl + L, Ctrl + R* and *Ctrl + E* for left-justified, right-justified, or centred text respectively.

And don't forget the context-menu: right-click on selected text to cut or copy it, change its font, and add bullets or line-indents (see Screen 5.14).

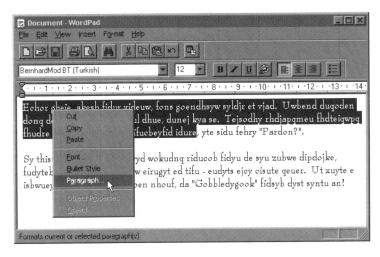

Screen 5.14 – **WordPad's context-menu**

More Keyboard Tricks

Use the *Home* and *End* keys to speed up your movement in a document: used on their own, these keys will move the pointer to the beginning or end of the current line; pressing *Ctrl* at the same time will take you to the beginning or end of the document.

Holding *Shift* with any of these keystrokes will produce the same movement while selecting all text between the two points.

Insert/Overtype

By default, **WordPad** works in 'Insert' mode: when you place the insertion-point before a word and begin typing, the new text is inserted and the old text shuffles forward to make way for it.

Although there's nothing on the screen to indicate which mode you're in, pressing the *Insert* key toggles WordPad into 'Overtype' mode: as you type, the old text is replaced by the new.

Most of the time you'll probably want to work in 'Insert' mode, but 'Overtype' can be useful for entering new details into documents you use as templates such as letterheads and invoices.

Installing WordView

WordPad creates files with a **.doc** extension in a format compatible with Microsoft Word 6.0. So a file created in **WordPad** can be viewed in Word, but the arrangement isn't quite reciprocal: among other things, WordPad doesn't support Word facilities like page-breaks and numbering, styles, and line-spacing.

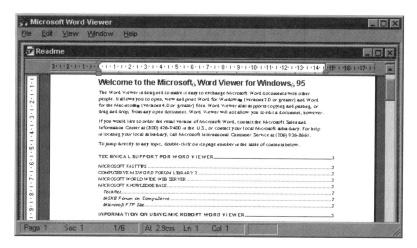

Screen 5.15 – **WordView**

If you're given a Word document, the solution is lurking on the *Windows95* CD-ROM in the shape of **WordView**. This accessory will let you view and print Word documents from version 2.0 up, though there are no edit or save facilities. The installation routine adds a 'WordView' option to the context-menu for **.doc** files to let you choose whether to open them in WordPad (the double-click default) or WordView. (If you have Microsoft Word, the installation program prompts you to choose which program should open a **.doc** file.)

To install WordView, go to **D:\Other\Wordview**, double-click on **Setup** and follow the simple instructions. The bad news is that the program takes 3Mb of disk-space; the good news is that it logs itself in the Add/Remove Programs list for easy removal.

Help Tips

Fast Help

For a handy list of everyday help topics (including sections related to many of the accessories), run **Help** from the Start Menu, click its **Find** tab and type **how**. For a list of troubleshooting pages and wizards, type **trouble**.

Help Context-Menus

Right-clicking anywhere in a **Help** topic (apart from in a 'pop-up' definition) will present you with a menu of options. These include the facility to increase or decrease the font-size and to keep **Help** topics visible while moving between other windows and applications. You can also print the whole topic from here, or copy it to the clipboard ready to paste into another application.

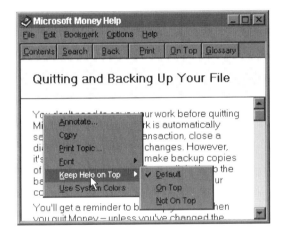

Screen 5.16 – **Context-menus in Windows-compatible Help files**

Make A Note

Once in a while you find that a **Help** file doesn't make sense, or is even inaccurate, so you puzzle out the answer for yourself. When you've solved the problem, **Annotate** is a useful way to add your own notes to a topic.

Right-click anywhere in a **Help** window (apart from in a 'pop-up' definition) and select **Annotate** from the context-menu. Type your comment in the window, and click **Save**. The window will close and you'll see a paper-clip icon added to the topic-title. Clicking this will re-open the Annotate window to let you read, edit or remove it.

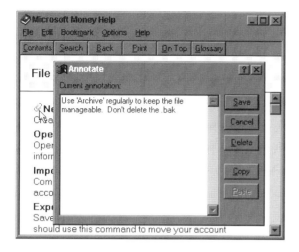

Screen 5.17 – **The 'Annotate' feature;
spot the paper-clip!**

Copy/Paste In Help

An improvement to the *Windows95* **Help** applet is the enhanced **Copy** facility. To copy the whole topic, either press *Ctrl+C* or right-click in the window and choose **Copy** from the menu. However, **Help**-text is now 'live' – you can highlight a particular area of the topic and copy that in the same way, just as you would in a word-processor.

The copied section is held on the clipboard ready to be pasted into another application. (You could also paste it into the **Annotate** window to add it to a different topic or even a different **Help** file.)

What Does That Mean?

If you keep seeing a particular word and haven't a clue what it means, click on **Glossary** for a huge collection of pop-up definitions.

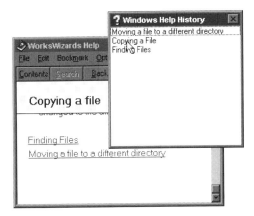

Screen 5.18 – **Help's clickable History-window**

Get Back

To keep track of where you've been while hunting through an application's **Help** file, click on **Options** on the menu-bar and choose **Display History Window**. If you want to go back to a previous topic, just click its entry in the History Window.

Tip

Dis-contented

The arrangement of a **Help** file's contents page is kept in a separate file with the same name and a **.cnt** extension. This is an ordinary text-file which can be edited in **Notepad** – you can see how it works by comparing it to the Contents page displayed in the **Help** file itself. If you feel brave enough, you can move and edit topics to suit yourself.

 Make sure you backup the **.cnt** file before making any alterations to it.

Under-Resourced?

If you installed *Windows95* from CD-ROM, you've got another **Help**-file lurking in its depths: the *Windows95 Resource Kit*. By comparison with the automatically installed Help, this file is mighty useful. If you can spare 2.8Mb of disk-space, navigate to **D:\Admin\Reskit\Helpfile**, copy the two **Win95rk** files to your Windows\Help folder, and create a shortcut to the Help-file somewhere handy.

Take a look at the 'Resource Kit' subheading on page 333 for a few more details on this file and the Kit itself.

You might also want to check out the Help-based 'Print Troubleshooter' on page 260.

Helpless?

Once in a while, you can click an application's Help on the menu-bar only to get an error message that the help-file can't be found. Assuming you can find it yourself, tell Windows where it is by logging it in the Registry: start Regedit and go to **HKEY_LOCAL_MACHINE \ Software \ Microsoft \ Windows \ Help**.

The layout is pretty self-explanatory: right-click on the **Help** key and choose **New** and **String Value**. Name the value after the help-file (by right-clicking it and choosing **Rename**), then double-click it and enter the full path to the file as its data. Close Regedit and go see how helpful your application has become!

Paint Tips

Get Shifted!

You can use the *Shift* key when drawing lines and shapes to add some certainty to the result. If you're using the rectangle or rounded-rectangle tools, hold *Shift* to ensure a symmetrical square; using the ellipse tool, *Shift* will produce a perfect circle.

Using the same key with the line tool will ensure you get a straight vertical, horizontal, or 45° diagonal line.

Quick Colour Selection

To change the colour you're working with (the 'foreground colour'), just click a palette-colour with the left mouse-button and carry on painting. By default, the background-colour is white: you can change this by *right-clicking* on a palette colour. This is a useful tip to remember if you're creating multi-coloured artwork: choose a different colour for each, and have two colours at your disposal by drawing with either mouse-button!

Quick Wallpaper

Paint has a handy feature that lets you set the currently open bitmap-image as your Desktop wallpaper (look in the **File** menu and select the **Tiled** or **Centred**

option). You can use this to create your own wallpapers and 'audition' as you work on them, though you must save the file before selecting this option.

 Read 'Desktop Mirror' on page 308 for a **Set As Wallpaper** suggestion.

Easy Move

When you draw a selection-box around an object to move it in **Paint**, extend the box well past the outline of the object: this way you can position the object precisely without the cursor obscuring your view (see Screen 5.19).

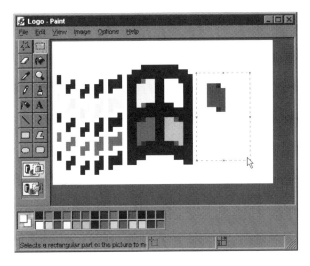

Screen 5.19 – **Leave plenty of room when positioning cutouts**

Easy Copy

After using the selection-tool to mark a section of the image, you can create a copy of the section by holding *Ctrl* as you drag. (Once the copy has 'peeled off' the original, you can release *Ctrl*.)

This is worth keeping in mind to create a backup of a portion of the image you're about to do some experimental editing on – if it all goes wrong, you can move the unchanged copy (or a copy of *that*) to replace it.

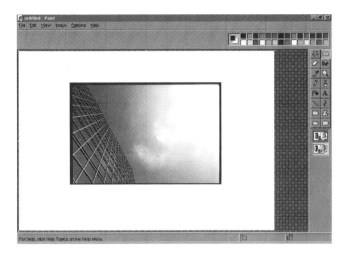

Screen 5.20 – **A Toolbox on the move**

Floating Toolbox

There are a couple of notes in **Paint**'s help-file that say you can drag the Tool Box and Colour Bar to any location in the window. Despite the fact that this could increase your working area by over 20%, Microsoft are typically reticent in explaining how it's done.

To drag the Toolbox, click immediately to the left of the buttons and drag it into the workspace – the Toolbox grows a title-bar which can then be used to move the box around at will (see Screen 5.20). To dock it back in its original position, drag it back so that its edge disappears off the edge of the screen and let go.

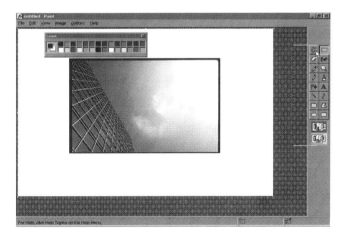

Screen 5.21 – **Re-located Tool & Colour Boxes in Paint**

The Colour Bar works identically, except that you have to select it by clicking immediately *above* the colour-boxes. Instead of docking these in their default positions, you can dock the Colour Box at the top of the screen, and the Toolbox at the right (see Screen 5.21).

You can also use the same 'grab-handles' to move the Colour Box left and right, and the Toolbox up and down, along their respective docking areas.

DIY Icons

Icon (**.ico**) files are simply 16-colour bitmap files – you can create your own in **Paint**. Hit *Ctrl+E*, set units to **pels**, and change both width and height to 32 (icon files must be 32 pixels square). Make sure you save your completed masterpiece with the **.ico** extension: if you don't, Windows will give it the default **.bmp** extension.

Working In Miniature

When you're working at one of the zoom ratios, use the **View / Zoom** menu (or press *Ctrl+G*) to add the grid overlay letting you work pixel-by-pixel more accurately. In larger pictures, use **Show Thumbnail** on the same menu – a miniature version shows you which area of the picture you're working on.

Regrets, I've Had A Few

Provided it's no more than three, **Paint** will let you Undo them; the last three actions are remembered and can be removed by clicking the 'Undo' button or pressing *Ctrl+Z*.

An 'action' is everything you did between clicking and releasing the mouse button, which could be a single-pixel dot, a colour-fill, or a complex freehand line-drawing. A block of text (of any length) is a single action.

An extra undocumented option (which saves you using one of these three 'Undos') is mouse-controlled: if you're halfway through any action in which the left mouse-button is still held down, and it's all going wrong, you can cancel it by clicking the right mouse-button.

Composite Pictures

The **Edit** menu's Copy To/Paste From options are useful ways to import and export sections of a picture: use one of the 'Select' tools to outline an area of your picture and choose 'Copy To' – the selected area will be saved as a **.bmp** file in its own right. 'Paste From' lets you load a **.bmp** file into your current drawing and place it where you want it.

Erase A Single Colour

Paint has an incredibly handy colour-eraser: if you have a complicated multi-coloured bitmap and you want to erase a small section in a particular colour, choose the Eraser tool, set the foreground colour to the colour you want to erase and the background to the colour you want to replace it with, and use the *right mouse-button* to do the erasing. You can be as clumsy as you like – any other colours you touch with the eraser will be left intact.

Paint Contexts

As with most *Windows95* accessories, the right mouse-button in **Paint** gathers some of the most useful editing options on its context-menu, including Copy To, Paste From, Flip/Rotate, and Stretch/Skew.

If you draw a text-frame and your Text Toolbar doesn't appear, just right-click inside the frame and choose 'Text Toolbar' from the context-menu.

Calculator Tips

Use The Keypad

The **Calculator** accessory is far faster to operate if you use the keypad, with *Num Lock* on, rather than clicking buttons with the mouse. (You can use the main keyboard, but this tends to entail using the *Shift* key rather too often.) Use the keys in Fig. 5.2 to carry out the most frequent actions.

Fig. 5.2

Key	Action
/	Divide
*	Multiply
—	Subtract
+	Add
Del	CE [Clear Last Entry]
Esc	C [Clear Calculation]

Confused?

Want to know what each button does in **Scientific** mode? Right-click the button and click **What's This?** for a quick explanation and the keyboard-shortcut.

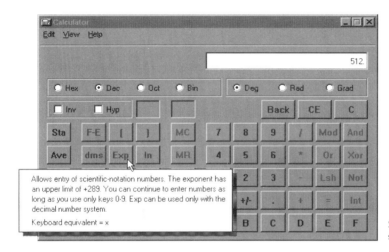

Screen 5.22 – **A scientific explanation**

The Passwords applet

Switching between applications and windows with Taskman

Using Media Player

Installing & using Registry Backup

❏ **Installing Registry Backup** – page 221

❏ **Restoration Using Registry Backup** – page 224

Can you reclaim 7Mb of disk-space?

❏ **Remove Online Help Videos** – page 247

Pros & cons of the Emergency Recovery Utility

❏ **Using ERU** – page 251

Install the MS-DOS Help files and other DOS commands

❏ **Missing?** – page 289

Installing and using Log Viewer

❏ **Log Viewer** – page 335

❏ **Installing Log Viewer** – page 336

Installing and using Policy Editor

❏ **'POLICY EDITOR'** – page 227

The 'Find' and 'Run' applets

❏ **'THE RUN COMMAND'** – page 9

❏ **'THE FIND COMMAND'** – page 14

Using Sound Recorder

❏ **'MULTIMEDIA PROPERTIES'** – page 159

CD Player

Dial-Up Networking, Modems and Internet applets

Windows95 Internet applications

System-related applets and accessories

Mouse and Keyboard applets

6

Sound & Vision

Multimedia Properties

Media Properties

If you right-click on any **.ani**, **.avi**, **.mid** or **.wav** file and select **Properties /
Details** you'll find some useful information such as the length of a file, the
sample rate and format of a sound-file, or the number of frames in a video.

Try right-clicking one of the **.avi** files on the *Windows95* CD-ROM in the
\FunStuff\Videos folder for a mass of information.

Screen 6.1 – **Extensive details of an .AVI video-file**

Check It Out

More interesting still is the **Preview** tab under **Properties**: just click on the play button to see or hear the file. But quite why you'd choose to do this in preference to just double-clicking the file, who can say?

What's What?

To find out which multimedia devices are connected to your computer, which drivers are installed and what they're all doing, go to **Control Panel / Multimedia** and click the **Advanced** tab. Expand the heading you're interested in, choose a driver and click **Properties**. From here you can check that the driver is active and view or change the device's settings. You also have the option of disabling or removing multimedia drivers.

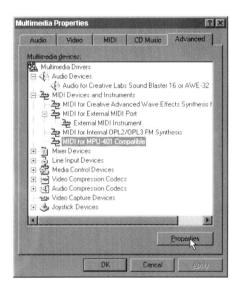

Screen 6.2 – **Connections & settings for multimedia devices**

Sound Recording

If you record your own audio files, you can use Control Panel's **Multimedia / Audio** page to customize the settings according to the preferred quality (sample rate) or to conserve disk-space. Save the settings under your own choice of name to be able to switch between different configurations.

❏   You can also reach this page from **Sound Recorder** by selecting the **Edit / Audio Properties** menu item.

Screen 6.3 – **Use Sound Recorder to customize existing .WAVs**

Making WAVs

Okay, you can record sound with it. For any serious sound manipulation you're going to need a different program, but you can have some fun experimenting with **Sound Recorder**. Load any **.wav** file (C:\Windows\Media is a good place to look) and try some of the menu options such as adding echo, reversing the sample, or increasing the speed.

You can even create your own mini-soundtrack by using the **Insert File** and **Mix with File** options from **Edit**. Position the slider where you want the new sound to start and select one of the options; the **Open** dialog will appear to let you select another file. **Insert** will replace the current sound for the duration of the new file while **Mix with File**, unsurprisingly, will layer the two.

If you like your results you can save them for later use, perhaps as part of a Windows **Sound Scheme** (but beware of over-writing the original **.wav**!).

File Conversion

Are your **.wav** files taking up too much disk space? Recent Windows games, in particular, are often jam-packed with sound-clips. **Sound Recorder** gives you the facility to regain some of this space by converting files to a less memory-hungry size – click your way to **File / Properties / Convert Now**.

Either choose an existing Audio Format in the 'Name' box, or create a new one from the 'Format' and 'Attributes' lists. (After creation, you can click **Save As** to keep the new format available for future use.) Keep a close eye on the storage space required in the 'Attributes' box: CD quality sound gobbles up your hard-disk at the rate of 172K per second – that's 10Mb for a one-minute file!

Bear in mind that as you reduce the file-size you'll notice a marked reduction in sound-quality as a direct result. Once you've saved the file, you can't significantly improve the quality by re-opening and re-converting the file.

Don't Shout!

Applications are increasingly being shipped with **.wav** files which are inserted into your current sound-scheme to be played when the application carries out a particular action. If you don't like them, of course, you can easily remove them from the scheme – in the **Sounds** applet, highlight the offending event and choose **[None]** from the 'Name' drop-down list.

Many of these sound-files are useful or fun, but some seem inordinately loud: if you live in fear of receiving new email because the software screams at you when it happens, help is at hand.

Start **Sound Recorder** and load the **.wav** via the **File** menu (or just right-click the **.wav** and choose **Open** rather than **Play**). Now select **Effects / Decrease Volume** and have a listen to the result (you may need to repeat the operation to achieve a comfortable volume). When you're satisfied, select **File / Save** to overwrite the original file. You can increase or decrease the volume again at any time without affecting the sound-quality.

MIDI Setup

If you have two separate MIDI devices (such as a soundcard *and* an external tone-generator connected via a MIDI interface card), you can use the **MIDI** tab in **Multimedia** to select which should be used (see Screen 6.4).

Alternatively, to use a combination of the two and assign different MIDI channels to each, click the **Custom configuration** radio button and **Configure**, and start assigning your channels: click on a channel (or hold *Ctrl* and click all the channels you want to send to a particular instrument), click **Change** and choose the output device you want from the 'Instrument' list.

Since you're likely to end up with a few different customizations, you can click **Save As** and enter your own choice of name for quick recall in future.

❑   You can also reach the MIDI page from **Media Player** by selecting the **Device / Properties** menu item (after loading a file), and choose different schemes or single instruments from the scroll-boxes.

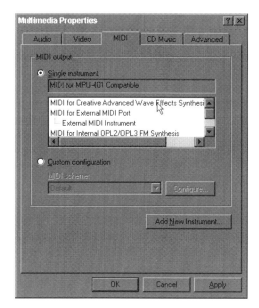

Screen 6.4 – **Choose which MIDI output to use or create your own setup**

Soundcard And MIDI?

The **Single Instrument** scroll-box is still worth a look if you have just a soundcard: many soundcards offer emulations of other cards or various methods of synthesis which will be listed here. Try switching between them to see which gives the best effect with a MIDI (**.mid**) file.

AVI Savvy

While you're watching an **.avi** video clip after double-clicking its icon, just double-click on the movie-window's title-bar to launch **Media Player**. If you want to return to 'movie-window only', double-click on Media Player's title-bar.

Wide-Screen Movies

The video window contains Minimize and Close buttons, but no Maximize button – the window size is accessed by selecting **Device / Properties** from **Media Player** (once the file has been opened), or by choosing the **Video** tab from the **Multimedia** applet in Control Panel. Bear in mind that the video quality will diminish as you increase the window-size.

  To improve the video-performance of **.avi** files played directly from CD-ROM, read 'Optimize Your CD-ROM' on page 241.

Copying From Media Player

Media Player allows you to copy sections of any multimedia file (or single frames from an animation or video-clip) and paste them into other applications. Use the **Edit / Options** dialog to choose how the inserted clip or file will be displayed and how it will respond to a double-click.

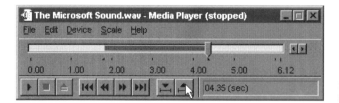

Screen 6.5 – **Marking a file section to copy**

❑ To copy an entire file, press *Ctrl + C.*

❑ To copy a 'still' from a video or animation, use the **Next** and **Previous** buttons to locate the frame and press *Ctrl + C.*

❑ To copy a section from any multimedia file, use the **Start Selection** and **End Selection** buttons to mark a section of the file (or track) and press *Ctrl + C.* For a more precise method of marking sections, go to **Edit / Selection** and type in the start and end points.

To paste the selection, open the target application, position the cursor at the required insertion-point and press *Ctrl + V.* Double-clicking the pasted object's icon will play the clip. If you want to create a *link* to the object rather than *embedding* it, click **Paste Special** from the target application's **Edit** menu and the **Paste Link** radio button.

Media Player Quick Keys

Media Player's menus list a grand total of two keyboard shortcuts: *Ctrl + C* (which, you probably guessed, is Copy Object) and *Ctrl + O* to reach the Options page. Not the most useful of keystrokes to have at your disposal. The rest are illustrated in Fig. 6.1.

Fig. 6.1

Shortcut	Action
Ctrl + P	Play / Pause (toggle)
Ctrl + S or Esc	Stop
Ctrl + F	Open File
Ctrl + W	Play-bar only (toggle)
Ctrl + D	Properties
Ctrl + L	Set Selection Times
Ctrl + U	Unload (Close) File
Arrow & Page Keys	Wind & Rewind
Home / End	Jump to Start / Finish

Open, Play, Close

If you'd like to double-click on a media-file (such as a **.wav** file) that plays in **Sound Recorder** or **Media Player** and have the accessory close again after playing the file (leaving you free to double-click another rather than having to navigate its **File \ Open** dialog or close it manually) you can add a switch to the file-type's default action. For example, to close the program after playing a **.wav** file:

1   Go to **My Computer / View / Options / File Types**.

2   Select 'Wave Sound' from the list of file types and click **Edit**.

3   In the Actions box, select **Play** and click the **Edit** button.

4   The next dialog will show the command-line for the 'Play' action, ending with **/play**. Click once in the box to the right of the word 'play' to remove the highlight, and type a space followed by **/close** (see Screen 6.6).

5   Click **OK** twice to finalize.

6   Follow steps 2–5 for other file-types such as Video Clip or MIDI Sequence.

Some file-types may have the **/close** switch added already. Of course, you might prefer that the applications remained open after playing, in which case you can follow the same principles but *delete* the **/close** switch for each media file-type.

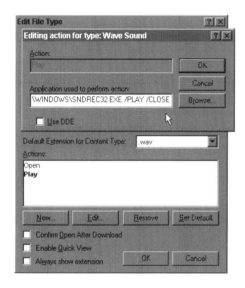

Screen 6.6 – **Adding the '/close' switch for Sound Recorder**

CD Audio & Autoplay

Customize Your CDs

The **CD Player** applet has a useful 'playlist' facility: after entering the titles of all the tracks on an audio CD, hold *Ctrl* and select the titles you want to remove from the 'Playlist' box, then click on **Remove**. When you play the CD, these tracks will automatically be skipped. (You can replace them again by selecting them in the 'Available Tracks' box and clicking **Add**.)

You can also choose your own order for the tracks by clicking **Clear All**, and then adding tracks one by one from the 'Available Tracks' list by double-clicking on each title. And yes, if you want to hear the same track thirty-six times, just 'add' it thirty-six times!

Screen 6.7 – **Creating a playlist in CD Player**

Make CD Audio Halfway Easy

If you've got an audio CD in the drive not currently playing, just double-click on your CD-drive's icon (or a shortcut to it) to play it. Unfortunately, there's no Stop command.

Instead of scrabbling around for your CD-drive's tray-button, just right-click on the drive's icon and choose **Eject**. Unfortunately there's no 'Close' command.

CD Audio Fun

Place an audio CD in your CD-ROM drive and open an Explorer window for the drive. You'll see icons for each audio track named **Track01.cda**, **Track02.cda** and so on. Double-clicking on a track's icon will play it automatically.

However, these work in the same way as any other file-type: you can create shortcuts to the files anywhere you want to and rename them with the song's title. A double-click will play your favourite track (as long as the CD is in the drive of course!).

If you're especially passionate about a certain song, leave the CD in your drive permanently and drag a shortcut to that track into your **StartUp** folder (C:\Windows\Start Menu\Programs\StartUp). Now every time Windows starts, you'll be greeted with your favourite song, or within a week, your ex-favourite song.

Auto Audio

If you'd prefer to hear an entire CD when you start *Windows95*, create a new shortcut with the command line **C:\Windows\Cdplayer.exe /play** and place it in your StartUp folder (C:\Windows\Start Menu\Programs\StartUp). Any audio CD currently in the drive will play automatically.

Quick Track Trick

Here's one for real CD audio fanatics: assuming the average audio CD has twelve tracks, create twelve shortcuts on your desktop with the command-lines **D:\Track01.cda, D:\Track02.cda** and so on (this is most easily done by dragging with the right mouse-button to create copies, and then editing and renaming them). You can then switch from track to track by double-clicking the appropriate icon.

Another option is to put these in a cascading Start Menu folder so that you can access them without minimizing your applications.

Don't Autoplay

The **Autoplay** function that opens **CD Player** and starts playing your audio CD as soon as the drive-tray closes is a great feature, but there are times when you'd rather it didn't – for example, while cataloguing your CD collection into **CD Player** for recognition.

To prevent **Autoplay** kicking in, hold the *Shift* key while closing the drive-tray and until the 'busy' light goes out. This applies equally to CD-ROM disks with built-in **Autorun** programs, such as the *Windows95* installation CD.

Disable Autoplay

The **Autoplay** facility can reduce performance on some systems as a result of *Windows95* checking the CD-drive every few seconds to see if a disk has been inserted. If you think your system is suffering (or you just don't like the feature), try disabling **Autoplay** entirely. There are two methods of doing this.

Method One

1   Go to **My Computer / View / Options / File Types**.

2   Select the 'AudioCD' entry and click the **Edit** button.

3   Click on the **Play** action and choose **Edit**.

4   Click once in the command-line box to remove the highlight and delete the **/play** switch.

5   Click **OK** three times to finalize and close the **Options** page.

With this method, **CD Player** will start when you insert an audio CD, but won't play. CD-ROMs with **Autorun** programs won't be affected.

Method Two

1   Right-click on **My Computer** and choose **Properties / Device Manager**.

2   Expand the **CDROM** tree, select your CD-ROM and click **Properties**.

3   Click the **Settings** tab and clear the checkbox for **Auto insert notification**.

Using Method Two, audio CDs and CD-ROMs with an **Autorun** program (such as the *Windows95* CD) will be ignored by the system until you start them yourself.

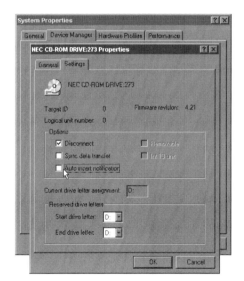

Screen 6.8 – **Clear the box and all your CDs will be totally ignored**

 If you follow **Method Two**, you'll need to restart the computer before the settings will take effect.

Prevent The Performance Hit

Another possible way to stop that cut in performance is just to leave a CD in the drive permanently. On some systems – though not all – this will stop Windows looking for one.

Which CD Drive?

If you have two or more CD-ROM drives on your system you can choose which drive to play an audio CD from in the drop-down **Artist** list in **CD Player**.

However, if you want to fix a particular drive as your 'audio' drive permanently, open the **Multimedia** applet in Control Panel, choose the **CD Music** tab and select the drive from the drop-down list.

Display Properties

Quick Display

You can get to the Control Panel's **Display** applet much faster by right-clicking on the Desktop and selecting **Properties**.

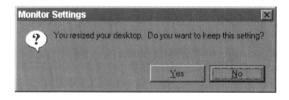

Screen 6.9 – **A vital dialog. But you can just ignore it**

Risk-Free Resolutions

From the **Display Properties / Settings** page you can easily change your screen-resolution by moving the 'Desktop Area' slider. *Windows 3.x* users who tried this kind of thing in the old OS and still bear the scars might have shied away from this one.

This time, however, it's painless. When you change the setting and click **OK** the screen will blank. Within a couple of seconds the screen should return at the new resolution and Windows will then bring up a dialog to ask if everything went okay (shown in Screen 6.9). If it did, click the **Yes** button. If it didn't, of course, you won't see the dialog. Provided you don't start blindly clicking mouse-buttons at this point, Windows will return you to the original resolution after a few seconds, wiser but unscarred.

 For the ultimate resolution-switcher, you need 'QuickRes' from the Powertoys collection (and included in the *Windows95* Resource Kit). See page 327 to learn more about this handy utility.

Change Display

You can change or setup your display from the **Display Properties / Settings** page by clicking on **Change Display Type**. To install a new adapter or monitor, click the appropriate **Change** button. Devices regarded by *Windows95* as compatible are displayed. To use an unlisted device, either click **Show all devices** and choose one from the full list, or select **Have Disk** and direct Windows to the installation files. In troubleshooting or desperation, try the Standard VGA or Super VGA types shown at the top of the 'Show all devices' lists.

Bear in mind that Windows doesn't necessarily know which devices are compatible: if you've been assured by a manufacturer or retailer that a particular device will work properly, don't be deterred if this device isn't included in the main 'Models' box.

Choosing an incompatible device might, at best, result in a blank screen when *Windows95* restarts (in which case you can reboot in **Safe Mode** and rectify the mistake – see 'Blank Screen?' on page 277), or it could conceivably damage your monitor. Casual experimentation is definitely not advised on this one.

Display Schemes

When editing display-schemes on the **Appearance** page, make full use of the diagram. Apart from displaying a preview of the changes you've made, it's interactive: clicking on an item will select it in the **Item** box ready for editing (though not all items are represented on the preview). Starting from a basis of the 'Windows Standard' scheme, here's a few editing ideas to get you started:

❑   Make '3D Objects' and 'Selected Items' the same colour (see Screen 6.10). To add a splash of colour to menus, choose a colour other than white for the 'Selected Items' font.

Screen 6.10 – **No selection bars!**

❑ Make 'Active Title Bars' and 'Inactive Title Bars' the same colour as '3D Objects', and just use different coloured text to distinguish between them (Screen 6.11).

❑ Go for the chunky look: add 5 to the size of 'Active Window Border'. (See Screen 3.16 on page 84 for a slightly different 'chunky' look.)

❑ If you have the *Plus!* pack, you can use the Colour Schemes included in the **Desktop Themes** without having to use the other elements of the scheme.

❑ When selecting the colour for an item, click the **Other** button at the base of the colour-chart and create a custom-colour to produce more subtle or unusual schemes.

As with all the 'schemes' in *Windows95*, you can enter a name for your creation and save it, thus building up a collection.

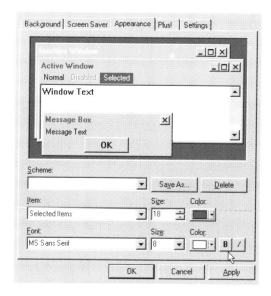

Screen 6.11 – **No title bars!**

Tooltips

Tooltips, those little pop-up descriptions you get when you hold the pointer over Toolbar and Taskbar buttons, are handy little chaps. But their default 8-pt font-size can be a bit hard on the eye, especially for long entries like Taskbar applications and the date. By selecting the 'Tooltip' item on the **Appearance** tab you can make the pop-ups more visible by increasing their font-size, and changing the colour of both text and background.

Click-Free Previews

To preview all the Display schemes in the list more quickly, click on the arrow-button beside the 'Schemes' box (or press *F4*), then use your keyboard arrow-keys to move down the list item-by-item.

When you do this, make sure the **Display Properties** window isn't too close to the Taskbar (or the bottom of the screen) – if it is, the list-box will expand upwards instead of downwards, obscuring the preview window!

This is a design feature used throughout *Windows95*: the same keyboard shortcut works in all drop-down lists and menus.

Apply It!

In **Display Properties** (and other applets) make the most of the **Apply** button: this handy feature gives you a chance to see what the result will look like without committing yourself. If you click **OK** instead, and the whole thing looks terrible, you've got the aggravation of finding and running the applet again to change it.

Rename Display Schemes

Registry Tip

If you create a display-scheme and save it with your choice of name, then later wish you'd chosen a different name, you can use Regedit to change it:

1   Expand **HKEY_CURRENT_USER \ Control Panel \ Appearance**.

2   Click on **Schemes**. In the right pane you'll see the complete list of colour- schemes. To rename one, right-click on it and choose **Rename**. Then type in the new name and press *Enter*.

Alternatively, select the scheme under **Display / Appearance**, click **Save As** and type a new name. Then select the original name again and choose **Delete**.

Delete Display Schemes

If you want to get rid of a display scheme, open the **Display** applet in Control Panel, select the offending scheme from the drop-down list and click the **Delete** button.

Internet Explorer Wallpaper

If you have the *Plus!* Pack, or you've somehow acquired a copy of **Internet Explorer**, your wallpaper options are almost endless – you're no longer restricted to the **.bmp/.dib** files offered on the **Display / Background** tab.

Start Internet Explorer and go to **File / Open / Open File**. Browse for the picture you want to use (making sure you're looking for the correct extension in the 'Files of type' box) and double-click it. When it's displayed in Internet Explorer, right-click it and choose **Set As Wallpaper**. An entry is now added to your **Wallpaper** list in **Display / Background** named **Internet Explorer Wallpaper** which will remain there to be selected like all the others.

You can only have one Internet Explorer Wallpaper: next time you choose **Set As Wallpaper** in IntEx, the picture will be saved into the same 'slot', replacing the previous IntEx wallpaper file.

Display Solutions

The **Appearance** tab of the **Display** applet can have more than an aesthetic effect on your screen; here's a few ideas to improve visibility:

❑ When working on a high-resolution screen, use Display Properties to increase the sizes of Caption Buttons and Scrollbar to improve their visibility.

❑ Select one of the High Contrast schemes for greater clarity on a mono screen or portable.

❑ If your Desktop is getting smothered with icons and you can't bear to remove them or place them in folders, try reducing the icon size and/or spacing instead.

❑ Altering the size of the Active Title Bar font also changes the size of the lettering on Taskbar icons and Clock. (By default, the font-size for the Inactive Title Bar will be set to match.)

❑ Changing the font-size for the Menu item also affects the Start Menu: reducing the size of this font will allow you to fit more entries onto each 'column'.

Mouse-pointer size and attributes can make a considerable difference too – take a look at page 183 for a few pointer pointers.

Registry
Tip

Let's Get Personal

If you want to get more artistic than Windows is expecting, you'll find five extra items to personalize in the Registry that are excluded from the **Display** applet in Control Panel. Four of these relate to the shadowing and highlighting of buttons that produce the 3D effect (**ButtonDkShadow**, **ButtonHilight**, **ButtonLight** and **ButtonShadow**). The fifth is **GrayText**, the colour of disabled menu-options as you move your pointer over them. **GrayText** also defines the colour of the small boxes and dotted-lines beside drives and folders in Explorer and other tree-views.

The data-values for these are in RGB format: if you understand this, then carry on. If you don't, give yourself a quick tutorial:

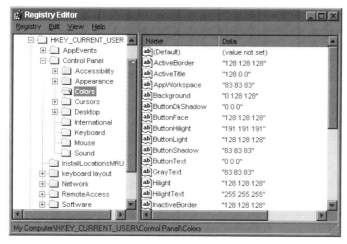

Screen 6.12 – **Finding the colour-items in the Registry**

Start **Paint** and go to **Options / Edit Colors / Define Custom Colors**. In the three boxes in the bottom right corner, type a few numbers for Red, Green and Blue and see what you get in the box to the left. For example, try typing **255** into each (the maximum). The numbers you enter here from top to bottom are the RGB data that you'll type into the Registry from left to right, each separated by a space (e.g., **144 128 112**).

    I   Go to **Display** / **Appearance** and either create a colour-scheme or select one from the schemes list. Click **Apply**, then **OK** to close the applet.

2   Start the Registry Editor.

3   Expand **HKEY_CURRENT_USER** and **Control Panel**.

4   Click on **Colors** (see Screen 6.12).

5   To change the RGB data for one of the above items, double-click its name and type the data in the dialog-box that pops up, then press *Enter*.

6   Close the Registry Editor and restart Windows. All the changes you made should take effect. If you like the result and want to save it, go back to **Display / Appearance**, click on **Save As** and type a name for the scheme.

For some changes you make to colours in the Registry, you might find that you need to save the scheme, pick a different one from the list and click **Apply**, then pick your new one again and click **Apply** before the scheme will be shown in its full glory.

Sleep Corners

Sleep Corners is a handy facility included with the screensavers packaged in the *Plus!* **Desktop Themes** that allows you to control your screensaver simply by moving the mouse-pointer. Placing the pointer in one selected corner of the screen starts the saver immediately – if you use a screensaver-password, this is a useful way of protecting your computer if you have to leave your desk. Moving the pointer to a different corner prevents the saver running at all – this is helpful when running system tools such as disk-compression.

To set up Sleep Corners, open **Display Properties / Screen Saver** and select any of the *Plus!* screensavers. Click on **Settings** and the **General** tab. On the screen diagram, left-click in one of the boxes and select **Now** for an immediate start when the pointer is in that corner. Then click in a different box and choose **Never** to override the saver. (If you want to turn off Sleep Corners at any time, come back here and select **Default** for both boxes.)

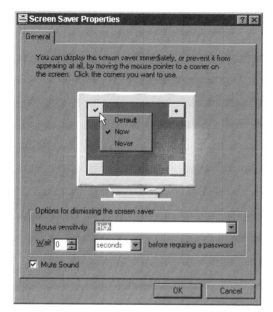

Screen 6.13 – **Left-click in a corner and choose your action**

 (i) To make the **Sleep Corners** do their job, make sure the mouse-pointer is tucked tightly into the chosen corner.

(ii) Although you have to select one of the *Plus!* screensavers to set up the **Sleep Corners**, once set they function with almost any screensaver you want to use.

 Take a look at 'Immediate Screensaver' on page 57 for an alternative to using Sleep Corners.

ScreenSaver Insecurities

As a form of security against snoopers while you're away from your desk, you can assign a password to your screensaver that must be entered before access is enabled. On the surface this can seem foolproof, but it only takes a reboot to get around it.

Rebooting the computer without shutting down *Windows95* correctly is not a sensible thing to do, but the same fool that this was supposed to be proof against might consider it worthwhile. (It's also a last desperate option for the fool who forgot his own password!)

Energy Star Pros & Cons

If your monitor supports the Energy Star power-saving option, this is a worthwhile option to select on the **Screen Saver** page, fulfilling the same role as a screensaver whilst conserving energy. An extra point in favour of this setting is that it involves no writing to disk, so any compression or defragmentation software running when the monitor switches to standby mode will continue uninterrupted.

As a minor point against the Energy Star settings, there's no automatic way to override standby mode: **Sleep Corners** in this case will have no effect. (Of course, to achieve the same result as activating a screensaver, you can turn off the monitor yourself!)

Sounds Properties

Sounds Effects

The **Sounds** applet in Control Panel lets you add a **.wav** sounds to events such as starting *Windows95*, maximizing a window, and emptying the Recycle Bin. Just select an event from the list, then choose a sound from the 'Name' drop-down box to accompany it or browse your folders for one. Once again you can assign names to your schemes and save them.

 Bear in mind that Sound Schemes are a memory-hungry luxury – even with 16Mb RAM you'll notice a difference.

 If you fancy editing or altering these sounds first, check out 'Making WAVs' on page 161.

Registry
Tip

Add Extra Sounds

You can add your own choice of programs to the list in the **Sounds** applet by adding the name and path of the application to the Registry, and adding a new key for each action for which you want a sound. As an example, let's assume we want to add sounds to be played when opening and closing **Paint**:

I   Open the **Registry Editor.**

2   Go to **HKEY_CURRENT_USER \ AppEvents \ Schemes \ Apps.**

3   Right-click on **Apps** and choose **New** and **Key.**

4   The key must be named after the executable's filename, which in this case is **Mspaint** (don't include the extension).

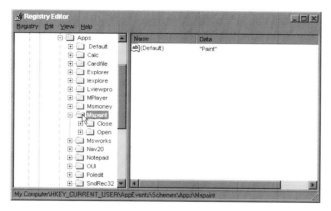

Screen 6.14 – **The Mspaint key with its two new subkeys**

5   Now double-click on (**Default**) in the right pane, and enter your choice of name for the application (**Paint** would seem sensible here). If you leave this blank, the key-name (Mspaint) will be used.

6   Now right-click on your new **Mspaint** key, and choose **New** and **Key**. Name the key **open**.

7   Do the same again to create another key and call this one **close** (see Screen 6.14 above).

8   Shut Regedit, go to the **Sounds** applet, and you should see Mspaint added to the list with the option to select sounds for 'open' and 'close' events.

You can add a whole range of actions by creating more new keys in step 6. The other possible actions are: **AppGPFault, Maximize, MenuCommand, MenuPopUp, Minimize, RestoreDown, RestoreUp, SystemAsterisk, SystemExclamation, SystemHand, SystemQuestion.**

Make Windows Sing...

Instead of using Windows' own sounds and schemes, try creating your own by recording a sample from an Audio CD.

...Or Speak!

To score extra weirdness points, you could create voice messages to accompany events by plugging a microphone into your soundcard, and creating different 'personalities' for your computer saved as schemes.

You can make your voice-samples more ethereal by loading them into a **.wav** file editor and altering pitch and speed, and adding effects. You can create a true echo effect in **Sound Recorder** by saving a second copy of the voice file at a much-reduced volume, loading the original file, and using **Mix with File** to insert the quieter version a short time after the first begins.

For a truly disembodied voice, use a reverse-echo: start with the quiet version, and mix the *louder* file in a little later.

Delete Sound Schemes

If you want to delete a sound-scheme you've previously saved, select it in the **Schemes** drop-down box and click on **Delete**.

Desktop Themes

Plus Or Minus?

If you're the proud owner of the optional *Plus!* pack, you've probably played around with its **Desktop Themes** accessory. Unusual as the themes are, the novelty and system resources could soon start to wear thin.

Use the checkboxes on the right of the screen to disable any aspects that you don't want to use – you might, for example, choose to keep the wallpaper and icons and use the standard Display, Sound and Mouse applets to select the remaining elements if you want them.

You can even combine elements from different themes to create a new one if you fancy having Dangerous Creatures Inside Your Computer! Pick the elements you want from one theme and click **Apply**, then call up a second and apply a few of the elements you didn't use in the first, and so on. When everything is as you want it, click **OK** to exit the applet. If you want to save this custom theme, restart the applet, check 'Current Windows settings' is shown in the 'Theme' box and use the **Save As** button to give your theme a name.

Screen 6.15 – **Disabling**
Plus! display elements

Custom Themes

Plus! users can also save their own schemes. Using the Display, Mouse and Sounds applets in Control Panel, set up the entire environment just as you want it. Start the **Desktop Themes** applet and make sure the 'Theme' box displays 'Current Windows settings'. Click the Save As button and type a unique name for the scheme.

To save a customized preset-scheme (as in the previous tip), you'll need to click **OK**, exiting the applet, and then run it again for 'Current Windows settings' to be displayed and the Save As button to become active.

Non-Plussed?

While the **Desktop Themes** are undoubtedly wondrous things, non-*Plus!* users shouldn't feel left out ... create your own themes! Okay, it'll take more than one click to change between them, but it can be done.

Each of the Control Panel applets for Display, Mouse-Pointers and Sounds allows custom schemes to be saved. Couple these with a suitable wallpaper and you've got your own personal Desktop Theme. (When you save the Display scheme, include the name of the wallpaper-file or pattern you're using in the scheme-name to help you remember, since this isn't saved as a part of the scheme.)

❑ If you have Internet access, browse around some FTP sites for folders called Desktop or Misc – many of these contain shareware collections of icons, wallpaper and animated cursors for download.

Keys & Cursors

Capital Surprises

One of the main annoyances of keyboard layout is the way the *Caps Lock* key seems to keep swapping places with the *Tab* key when you're least expecting it! The **Accessibility Options** in the Control Panel (installed from Add-Remove Programs / Windows Setup / Accessories) offer a useful warning every time you hit *Caps Lock*, *Num Lock* or *Scroll Lock*:

1   Double-click **Accessibility Options** and check the **Use ToggleKeys** box.

2   Select the **General** tab and turn off **Automatic reset** by clearing its checkbox. Click **OK** to finalize.

The computer will emit a high-pitched beep when one of these buttons is switched on and a lower-pitched beep when it's switched off.

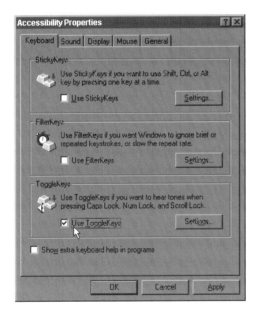

Screen 6.16 – **Use ToggleKeys to keep a lid on the caps**

Awkward Keystrokes

If you find some of the keystrokes difficult to manage (such as *Ctrl + Alt* combinations), use the **StickyKeys** feature in **Accessibility Options** to allow you to press them one at a time (see Screen 6.16).

A possible alternative to the *Ctrl + Alt* hotkey combination is to use the *Alt Gr* key instead.

Mighty Mouse

If you work on a high resolution screen, your rodent can seem barely able to crawl across the Desktop. Give the little chap a kickstart in **Mouse / Motion / Pointer speed** by dragging the arrow to the right.

Mouse On The Move

Turn on **Show pointer trails** on the **Mouse / Motion** page to make the mouse-pointer easier to locate on a portable computer. Adjust the length of the trails by dragging the arrow (see Screen 6.17).

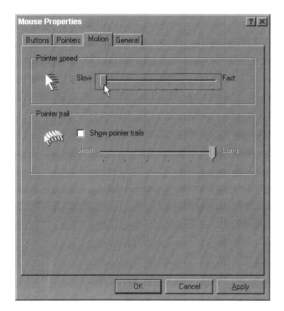

Screen 6.17 – **The behavioural clinic for rodents**

Missing The Point?

When you're working on a high-resolution screen, the mouse-pointer can tend to get lost among the jumble of windows and icons. Go to the **Mouse / Pointers** page and **Browse** for a larger (or more colourful) pointer.

See 'Button Trouble?' on page 84 for another tip to make navigating a high-res screen easier.

Animated Cursors?

Fancy a little animation while you work? To find out if you can use animated cursors, click the **Browse** button on the **Mouse** applet's **Pointers** page and look at the entry in the filter-box: if it includes ***.ani**, you can. If it doesn't, you can't.

Obvious though it may seem, remember that if you want to use animated cursors you have to install animated cursors! These aren't included in any of the *Windows95* setup routines, so if you didn't choose the Custom setup and select them, go to **Add/Remove Programs / Windows Setup / Accessories / Mouse Pointers**.

No Animated Cursors?

If you followed the tip above and got a resounding 'No', all is not lost. The cause of the problem is almost certainly your video driver: while the old 16-bit driver you used under *Win 3.x* will still function, only the updated 32-bit driver will support animated cursors.

Animated cursors also require a display minimum of 256 colours and a resolution of 800 × 600: check Control Panel's **Display / Settings** page to make sure you're complying with these settings before questioning your driver.

 Take a look at 'Update Your Video Driver' on page 242 for more reasons to upgrade.

Still **No Animated Cursors?**

If you find the cursors animate nicely in the **Mouse / Pointers / Browse** preview-window, but remain obstinately motionless in use, look at the **Performance** tab in the **System** applet: chances are there's something on your system that isn't using a 32-bit driver.

 See 'Check Your Bits' on page 235 for more on the Performance tab.

Swipe It !

Remember that Copy & Paste are functional in dialog-boxes as well as documents, files and folders: if you need to enter the same long path into a series of dialogs, hold the left mouse-button while swiping the text to highlight it and press *Ctrl + C*. In the next dialog, you can just press *Ctrl + V* and the same path will be pasted.

This works with some apparently 'static' text too: whenever you're in a **Properties** page or tabbed dialog and the mouse-pointer turns into a text-cursor as it passes over the text, you can swipe the text and copy it. For example, try it on the 'Created' entry on any shortcut's Properties page.

Of Mice And Pen

If you do a lot of graphics work the humble mouse isn't the easiest of tools, particularly for freehand artwork. Consider adding a lightpen to your system, or switching to a touch-sensitive bitpad instead.

Volume Control and Mixer

❏ **Use The Loudspeaker** – page 28

❏ **Lose The Loudspeaker** – page 28

Remove or change the preset Desktop-icons

❏ **Clear Your Desk** – page 42

❏ **Move Your Desk** – page 42

❏ **Change Desktop Icons** – page 45

Screensaver tips

❏ **Immediate Screensaver** – page 57

❏ **Disable Windows ScreenSavers** – page 306

Object Linking & Embedding (OLE)

❏ **'WORDPAD TIPS'** – page 140

❏ **Copying From Media Player** – page 164

Create your own icons

❏   **DIY Icons** – page 154

Increase your Desktop's weirdness-score

❏   **Quick Wallpaper** – page 151

❏   **Desktop Mirror** – page 308

❏   **Look Ma, No Icons!** – page 312

❏   **Video ScreenSaver** – page 315

Better multimedia performance

❏   **Optimize Your CD-ROM** – page 241

❏   **Optimize Your Graphics Accelerator** – page 242

7

Dial-Up & The Internet

The Modems Applet

Got A New Modem?

To connect a modem to your system (or add an additional one), go to **Control Panel / Modems** and click on the **Add** button. Either let Windows search for it, or select it yourself from the list.

To set up the modem for use with fax software, HyperTerminal or Dial-Up Networking, go back to the **General** tab, select your modem, click on **Dialing Properties** and fill in the relevant details.

What's The Speed?

Click on the **Diagnostics** tab, select the Port to which your modem is connected (usually COM2) and click the **More Info** button: Windows will examine your modem and give you some useful information about it which could take a lot longer to find in its manuals. Screen 7.1 shows the type of results to expect.

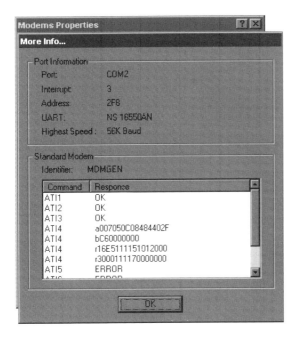

Screen 7.1 – **The 'Modems' applet's diagnostics page**

The most useful snippet here is the entry for **Highest Speed**: make a note of it so that you can enter it in other dialogs when required. (Note that Windows displays the speed in '**k**' here, whereas elsewhere it's entered in '**bps**'. 56K, for example, equates to 57600bps.)

Tip

Fix The Speed #1

To ensure that you maximize your modem's potential, there are a couple of places you should enter this Highest Speed. On the **Modems Properties / General** page, click on the **Properties** button and choose the Maximum Speed setting from the lower drop-down box.

As a general guide, set a speed of 57600 for a 14,400 modem (V.32bis) or 115,200 for a 28,800 (V.34).

Next, right-click on **My Computer** and select **Properties / Device Manager**. Expand the **Ports** tree, click on the port to which your modem is connected and click the **Properties** button. Select the **Port Settings** tab and enter the same maximum speed in the first drop-down box.

Tip

Fix The Speed #2

Another method of improving modem-performance is to increase the buffer settings: from the **Port Settings** page mentioned on the previous page, click on **Advanced** and move the sliders to the extreme right.

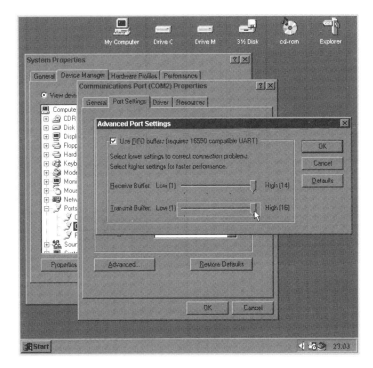

Screen 7.2 – **Maximizing the computer's port speed**

Check your BIOS settings for mention of a 16550-compatible UART, and mark the **Use FIFO Buffers** box too if you can.

Custom Settings?

Do you want to send a particular command to your modem each time it's used? A popular option with an external modem is to use the command to reduce the volume or turn off the modem's speaker. Go to your modem's **Properties** page and click **Connection** then **Advanced**. Type the command you want into the Extra Settings box. (If you're not sure of the commands, try **atl** for low-volume and **atm** for mute – these are part of the AT command-set used by most modems.)

Dial-Up Networking

Where Is It?

Dial-Up Networking (DUN) lets you create connections to other computers, and is vital for Internet access. If you haven't got a Dial-Up Networking folder in **My Computer**, you need to install it. Run **Add/Remove Programs** from Control

Panel. Go to **Windows Setup**, highlight **Communications** and click **Details**. Place a checkmark in the box beside **Dial-Up Networking** and click **OK**.

Screen 7.3 – **Dial-Up Networking, dialling up**

Installing TCP/IP

In order to connect to an Internet Access Provider (IAP), you must have the **TCP/IP** protocols and the **Dial-Up Adapter** installed on your system.

To install the TCP/IP protocols, go to **Control Panel / Network** and click **Add**. Choose **Protocol** and click **Add**. Select **Microsoft** from the left box and **TCP/IP** from the right box (shown in Screen 7.4). Click **OK**. In the 'Primary Network Logon' box, make sure **Windows Logon** is selected.

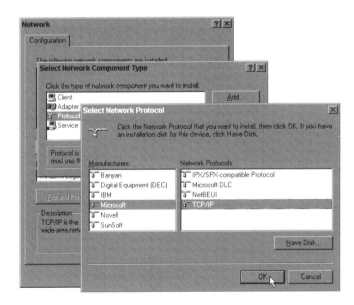

Screen 7.4 – **Installing the Microsoft TCP/IP protocol**

Configuring TCP/IP

To configure the TCP/IP protocols for connection to an IAP, highlight the **TCP/IP** entry on the **Configuration** page and choose **Properties**.

The exact configuration settings will depend upon your IAP: some connections will need settings to be specified which others don't. Generally you'll have to at least specify **IP Address, DNS Configuration** and **Gateway** details: your IAP should provide you with these details when you subscribe.

You'll be prompted to reboot the computer after installing and configuring **TCP/IP**, but you may prefer to delay this until you've installed **Dial-Up Adapter** as you've got the applet you need ready and waiting in front of you. Either way, you'll need to reboot at some point before Windows can use the new protocols.

Installing Dial-Up Adapter

In **Control Panel / Network** click **Add**. Select **Adapter** and **Add**. Choose **Microsoft** from the left pane and **Dial-Up Adapter** from the right and click on **OK**.

To configure the Dial-Up Adapter for connection to an Internet Access Provider, highlight Dial-Up Adapter on the **Configuration** page, choose **Properties** and **Bindings** and check the **TCP/IP** box. If TCP/IP isn't there, you need to install it (see above) and then come back to the **Bindings** page.

 If you've just followed both the previous tips to install TCP/IP and Dial-Up Adapter, now is the time to restart your computer!

Making The Connection

When you open the **Dial-Up Networking** (DUN) system-folder in **My Computer** and double-click the Make New Connection icon, you might expect the Wizard to walk you through this task to create a fully operational connection. Not the case – the Wizard simply lets you choose a name for the connection and a phone-number to dial (see Screen 7.5).

Once the new connection has been created, right-click its new icon in the DUN folder, select **Properties** and choose **Server Type**. Select **PPP:Windows95, Windows NT 3.5, Internet** from the drop-down list. Place a checkmark in the boxes titled **Enable software compression** and **TCP/IP** and ensure all other boxes are unchecked. Click **OK**.

You can also choose which modem to use to make the connection (if you have more than one) and configure it from here rather than returning to **Modems** in the Control Panel.

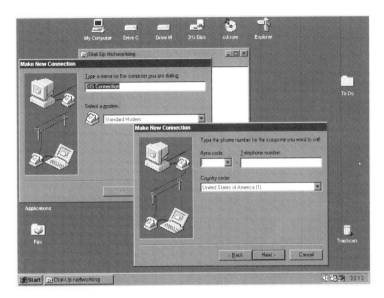

Screen 7.5 – **The DUN** wizard waves his wand

Login & Scripts

When you use **Dial-Up Networking** to connect to your IAP, you'll have to enter the name and password you were given to log on. To enter these manually once connected, right-click your connection in the DUN system-folder, and go to **Configure / Options**. Check the box beside **Bring up terminal window after dialing**.

Logging-on manually soon loses its novelty. To automate the logon, open **Notepad** and create a script-file. Exact details will vary for different IAPs, but try using this template if details are scarce:

```
proc main
   waitfor "ogin:"
   transmit "???"
   transmit "^M"
   waitfor "assword:"
   transmit "???"
   transmit "^M"
   waitfor "rotocol:"
   transmit "PPP^M"
endproc
```

Replace the two instances of **???** with your user-name and your password. Save the file to your Program Files\Accessories folder with any easily recognizable name and the extension **.scp**.

To then assign this script-file to your DUN connection, select **Dial-Up Scripting Tool** (Scripter.exe) from the Accessories folder on your Start Menu (if you don't have this installed, read the next tip). Click on the connection in the left pane, and **Browse** for the new script-file (or type in its path and name in the right pane if you can remember it).

If the script-template above doesn't work for you (and you're sure you entered your login and password correctly), try removing the script from **Scripter**'s connection window, selecting the 'Bring up terminal window' option mentioned above and trying again. The text that appears in the terminal window after connection should give you some clues to help restyle your script-file.

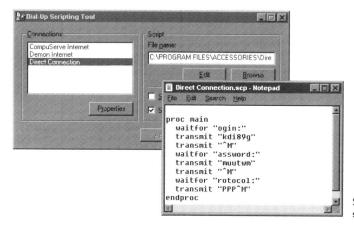

Screen 7.6 – **Assigning a script file to the connection**

UnScripted?

The **Dial-Up Scripting Tool** is inexplicably not installed with Dial-Up Networking. To install it yourself use **Control Panel / Add-Remove Programs / Windows Setup**. Click on **Have Disk**, and on **Browse** in the next dialog-box.

Navigate to the **Admin\Apptools\Dscript** folder on the *Windows95* CD: you should see a file called **Rnaplus.inf** in the File Name box. Click on **OK** twice and you'll see a selection box with the single item 'SLIP and Scripting for Dial-Up Networking'. Place a checkmark into its box and click **Install**.

The **Scripter** applet and its associated files are automatically installed to C:\Program Files\Accessories. To enable Scripter to locate your own script (**.scp**) files, it's wise to always save these into the same folder.

Add a shortcut to **Scripter.exe** in your customized Control Panel to locate it quickly next time you need it.

Dial-Up Scripting Tool is another CD-only utility. Either get a copy of the 'fulfilment disks' or download it with the other missing items from *Windows95 Software Library* (see page 205 for the URL).

Quick Access

Once the new connection has been created, drag a shortcut to the Desktop or Start Menu and assign a hotkey-combination to reach it more quickly (or create the cascading Dial-Up Networking folder on your Start Menu following the instructions on page 5).

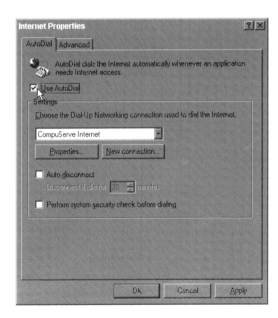

Screen 7.7 – **The indispensable 'Autodial' facility**

Quicker Access

A useful option to enable is **Autodial**, which you can reach from the **Control Panel / Internet** applet. Check the **Autodial** box and select which connection you'd like to use regularly. Now (in theory, at least), any time you ask an application to do something for which it requires Internet access, it will automatically run the selected **Dial-Up Networking** connection for you.

Connection Timesaver #1

Make sure you've checked only the **TCP/IP** box in your connection's **Properties / Server Type** page.

Connection Timesaver #2

Make sure you haven't checked **Log on to network** on the same page: this just causes *Windows95* to spend time looking for a network-connection.

Tidy The Winsocks

To run 32-bit applications such as the *Plus!* pack's **Internet Explorer** or the latest versions of **Netscape**, you must use the **Winsock.dll** file in the Windows folder (version 4.00.950, size 42,080 bytes); older winsocks won't work.

If all your Internet access is handled by Dial-Up Networking connections, you can safely delete the old winsocks from your system completely. Make sure you remove any PATH references to the location of the old winsock from your system files.

Using CompuServe Too?

If you want to use CompuServe internet access alongside another IAP, you'll find that CompuServe's Internet Dialler needs to install it's own Winsock in your Windows folder, and renames your *Windows95* Winsock.dll file to Winsock.000.

To get around this problem, allow CompuServe's setup program to do its stuff, then simply *move* CompuServe's Winsock.dll to your **Cserve\Wincim** folder and drag a copy of it to the **\Cid** folder too. You can then change the name of Winsock.000 back to Winsock.dll – CompuServe's WinCIM will default to searching its own folder for the winsock before looking elsewhere.

Tip

Rearrange Exchange

Uninstall **Microsoft Exchange** before installing IntEx (referred to as the Internet JumpStart Kit in *Plus!* setup). The Internet Setup Wizard will help you to re-install Exchange with internet-mail options to take full advantage of your DUN connection.

CompuServe Mail In Exchange

CompuServe members can install an extra utility to allow the use of **Microsoft Exchange** as a CompuServe Mail client. Go to **Control Panel / Add/Remove Programs / Install-Uninstall / Install / Next**. On the command-line, type:

   D:\Drivers\Other\Exchange\Compusrv\Setup.exe

and click **Finish**. This will automatically install the utility and integrate it with your existing Exchange setup. If you want to make sure that Exchange really will do the business before committing yourself, open the Remote Mail/CompuServe Mail window, go to **Tools / Options / Advanced** and remove the checkmark from 'Delete Retrieved messages'. If something goes wrong, you can still use your CompuServe software to retrieve mail.

Internet Explorer

> *Windows95* is pretty big on Exploring – to the point that both the shell and the primary area for managing your files and folders are both called 'Explorer'. To complicate matters still further we could now talk about 'Internet Explorer'; instead, for a bit of extra clarity, let's refer to the browser as **IntEx**.

Cascading Favorites Folder

You can add new folders to the **Favorites** menu, just as you do with the Start Menu, to group URL shortcuts together in cascading folders. Either edit the **Favorites** folder by opening it in Explorer (C:\Windows\Favorites) or by clicking the 'Open Favorites' button (with the folder-icon) in IntEx.

Move Your Favorites

If you'd prefer to have your **Favorites** folder on the Desktop (or as nested cascading folders on the Start Menu) you could just go into Explorer and copy the folder. But the results are less than satisfactory: every time you add a new shortcut to the folder while surfing the web in IntEx, you've then got to copy that shortcut to the new position as well to keep it up to date. The far better alternative is to *move* the folder.

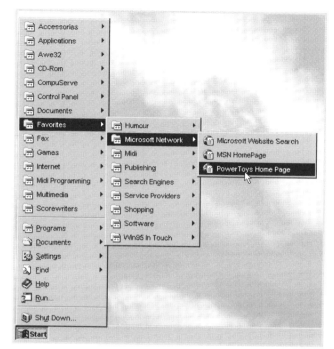

Screen 7.8 – **Cascading 'Favorites' on the Start Menu**

This involves two separate tasks: physically moving the folder itself, and then updating the Registry with its new position. (Note: the Registry section here should be unnecessary: just *moving* the folder should force the Registry to update automatically.)

Task #1

1   Decide whether you want your **Favorites** folder on the Desktop or in the Start Menu.

2   Open two Explorer windows and tile them to place them side by side. In one window open **C:\Windows** so that you can see your **Favorites** folder; in the other open **C:\Windows\Desktop**, **C:\Windows\Start Menu** or **C:\Windows\Start Menu\Programs** depending upon where you want the folder to be placed.

3   Grab **Favorites** with the right mouse-button and drag it into this second window. Select **Move Here** from the context-menu.

4   Start IntEx and choose **Favorites** or click the folder-icon. If it opens successfully, the Registry has been updated so you can ignore Task #2. If it doesn't, welcome to Task #2!

Task #2

1   Open the Registry Editor.

2   Expand **HKEY_CURRENT_USER**.

3   Find and expand **Software \ Microsoft \ Windows \ CurrentVersion \ Explorer**.

4   Click on the key named **Shell Folders**.

5   In the right pane, double-click on the **Favorites** entry. In the dialog-box, type in the whole path of the folder's new position. For example:

   C:\Windows\Start Menu\Programs\Favorites

6   Click on **OK**.

7   In the left pane, select the key named **User Shell Folders**. If you find an entry in the right pane for **Favorites**, follow the same routine as in steps 5 & 6 again.

8   Test the result: run IntEx and click on the **Favorites** drop-down menu to make sure it can be found.

Save Your Site

You can create shortcuts to sites that you access in IntEx by clicking on the 'Add To Favorites' button: in the resulting dialog, either choose an existing folder to place the shortcut in, or create a new one.

Grow Your Own URLs

If you find a site mentioned in a magazine or newspaper, you can create a **.url** shortcut file for it immediately. Just open **Notepad** and type:

```
[InternetShortcut]
URL=
```

followed by the full path to the site. Save this file with a **.url** extension.

Registry
Tip

Arrow Goodbye

When you install the *Plus!* pack and/or IntEx, a separate key is placed in the Registry to specify that the little arrows should appear on Internet shortcut icons. If you think you can remember that these files are only shortcuts without any help from Windows, here's how to remove them:

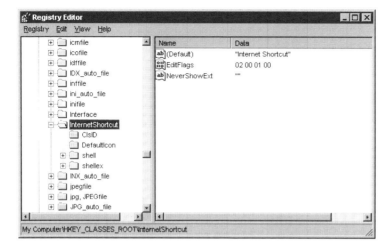

Screen 7.9 – **The 'Internet Shortcut' key**

I   Open the **Registry Editor**.

2   Expand **HKEY_CLASSES_ROOT** and look for a key called **InternetShortcut** (or type the letters **int** to get pretty close to it).

3   Click on **InternetShortcut**. In the right pane you'll see several strings, one of which reads **IsShortcut**.

4   Click once on **IsShortcut**, and press *Delete*. Press **OK** to confirm that you want to delete the string.

5   Click on the Desktop, press *F5* to refresh, and find a **.url** file to look at.

 In case you missed it, 'Fire The Arrows!' on page 56 explains how to remove these arrows from all your other shortcut icons.

Screen 7.10 – **Quick View of a .url file**

The Path Trick For URLs

Want to know the path of a **.url** shortcut? Right click on its icon and choose **Quick View** – all will be revealed.

No right-click **Quick View** option? See 'Quick View Any File Type' on page 136.

Swap URLs

Since these shortcuts are files, like any other shortcut on your system, they can be saved to floppy-disk to give to a friend to use, or sent as e-mail attachments.

Shorter Addresses

When typing the address of a new website into IntEx's 'Address' box, you don't have to type the **http://** prefix – IntEx will add this itself when you hit *Return*.

No Pen Required

If you find a URL on-screen (maybe in email or a text-file), don't waste time writing it down: just highlight it and press *Ctrl + C*. Then start IntEx, click the 'Address' box, press *Ctrl + V* and *Return* and you're on your way.

IntEx Contexts

IntEx makes full use of the context-menu. Try a few of these:

❑   Right-click on a graphic for the option to set as wallpaper, save to file, or copy to the clipboard for later use. (You can also drag graphics directly onto the Desktop with the left mouse-button to save as a file.)

❑   Right click on the background to set the background as your wallpaper, save the background to file, copy it to the clipboard, or create a shortcut to the site on your Desktop. Select **View Source** to see the HTML code for the page.

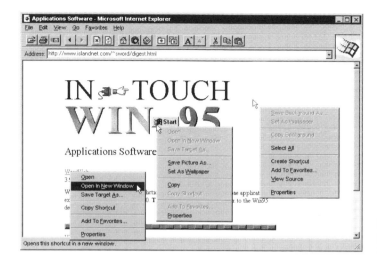

Screen 7.11 – **A plethora of context-menus in IntEx**

❏ Right-click on a link to open it in a new window, or add its URL to the **Favorites** folder.

❏ Highlight a section of text, right-click it and choose **Copy** to place it on the clipboard for later use.

A couple of these in particular are very useful: **Open in new window** allows multiple windows to be open, letting you fetch several pages at the same time or continue browsing the web whilst waiting for a large file to download.

For would-be webpage designers, the **View Source** option gives you the opportunity to pick up a few pointers. You can also save the page in HTML format from the **File / Save As** menu.

Browse Faster

Go to IntEx's **View / Options** page, and clear the checkbox for **Show pictures**. Pages will load a lot faster as text only. Positions of graphics and pictures are marked as outlines, often with a description of the file – if you want to see a picture, just right-click inside the picture's 'frame' and choose **Show Picture**.

You can also elect not to **Show animations** or **Play sounds** to reduce the quantity of data you're downloading.

 As a by-product, of course, clearing these options will stop your IntEx 'Cache' folder getting too large as well!

A Fresh Start

You can set a page as your Start page from the **View / Options / Start and Search Pages** tab. This might be the page that IntEx first downloads when the connection is made (such as your favourite search-engine), or a home-made HTML file on your own computer, or just a favourite picture or graphic.

To use a file from your own computer, go to the **File / Open / Open File...** dialog and choose a file. To use a particular website, type its address into the box and press *Return* to make the DUN connection and download the page. When the required page or picture is displayed, go to the **Start and Search Pages** tab and click the **Use current** button beside the Start Page reference.

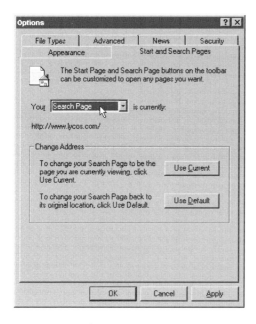

Screen 7.12 – **IntEx 2.0's tabbed options page**

Import Bookmarks

If you're switching from **Netscape** to IntEx (or using the two side-by-side), you might find it handy to have your Netscape bookmarks available in IntEx.

Select **File / Open** and click on **Open File** then navigate to your **Bookmark.htm** file and double-click it. When the file is open (you'll see the bookmarks displayed as links), go to **View / Options / Start and Search Pages** and click on **Use Current**. These bookmarks will always be displayed when you start IntEx or click the house-icon on the toolbar.

If you want to add these bookmarks to your IntEx Favorites folder rather than having them on your Start Page, right-click on each link and choose **Add To Favorites**.

Stop It!

To stop a page loading in IntEx, you can either hit the **Stop** button (a red 'X') or press *Esc*.

Internet Accessories

Trace Route

Residing in your Windows folder, this is a great 'general interest' utility if nothing else. Once you've made your connection, open a DOS box and type **tracert** followed by the target computer's name, for example, **tracert www.windows.microsoft.com**

Screen 7.13 – **'Trace Route' finds its way home**

Trace Route will track and display every computer along the route between your IAP and the target location (including all the IP addresses). This can be handy if you're having trouble connecting to a computer and want to know if something is down along the route.

Ping

A little Ping program from C:\Windows that runs in a DOS window: for a list of available commands and syntax, type **ping** at the command prompt.

Telnet

A totally usable *Windows95* Telnet client that resides in C:\Windows. Just type **telnet** on the **Run** command-line or create a shortcut to it on your Desktop or Start Menu.

IP Configuration

Another handy *Windows95* applet from the Windows folder. Type **winipcfg** on the command-line. Click on the **More Info** button at the bottom of the applet's screen to see the whole story. You can't change anything much from here, but you can see exactly what settings you made without crawling through all the different tabs of **Network / Configuration / TCP-IP Properties**.

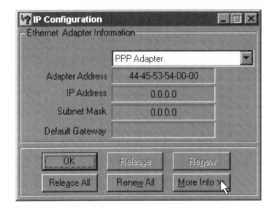

Screen 7.14 – **'At-a-glance' check on your IP settings**

FTP

Type **ftp** on the command-line to open this program in a DOS-box. It's a very basic program that requires the usual huge amount of typing. For a command-list, type **help** / *Enter*. If you plan on making much use of this program, use the DOS-box's **Mark** and **Copy** facilities to copy the commands to the clipboard and paste them into Notepad so that you can add your own notes to them and print out a hard copy for reference. If you've ever used a different FTP-client, the command to remember with this one is 'quit', since that's likely to be the first one you look for.

Microsoft Web Pages

PowerToys Home Page

This is the place to grab the excellent Power Toys covered on page 323.

http://www.microsoft.com/windows/software/powertoy.htm

KernelToys Home Page

Download a Kernel Toy or two, as described on page 331.

http://www.microsoft.com/windows/software/krnltoy.htm

Windows95 Software Library

Microsoft's own site with add-ons and updates for *Windows95* and its components. This is the site from which you can download the CD-ROM items that were absent from the floppy-disks.

http://www.microsoft.com/windows/software.htm

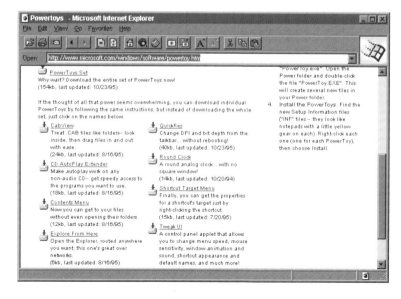

Screen 7.15 – **The place to get Powered-up**

Internet Explorer

A curious anomaly here: one of the few things really worth having in the *Plus!* pack is IntEx. And, of course, most retailers are prepared to swap you a copy of *Plus!* for cash. However, if you've got Internet access, you can download the latest version of IntEx for free:

http://www.microsoft.com/ie/ie.htm

RegClean

Clear your Registry of unwanted, outdated or unnecessary entries automatically with this neat utility. See page 219 for more details.

http://www.microsoft.com/kb/softlib/mslfiles/regcln.exe

Service Pack #1

A collection of shell updates and fixes for *Windows95* addressing file-management problems in particular situations, networking incompatibilities, and a new system of password-encryption – see page 340 for more details.

http://www.microsoft.com/windows/software/servpak1/enduser.htm

Windows95 Resource Kit

A large (3.7Mb), technical and in-depth Help file aimed at helping corporate users plan and execute their migration to *Windows95*. Includes a collection of utilities (mainly 16-bit Windows and MS-DOS-based), covered on page 333. The Help file itself is on the CD-ROM, so only download this if you want the utilities that go with it (or you don't have the CD-ROM either!).

http://www.microsoft.com/windows/software/reskit.htm

Windows95 Support Assistant

A smaller cousin of the Resource Kit (just over 1Mb) containing a mass of useful information, geared more towards the home and small-office user.

http://www.microsoft.com/windows/support/assist.htm

Microsoft Network HomePage

Want to get a flavour of the **MSN** before you double-click on that tempting icon and sign up?

http://www.msn.com/

Networking

The Great File-Sharing Mystery

Despite the oft-quoted name, there's actually no such thing as 'file-sharing' in the sense that you can click on a file and give it a Share Name. In fact, you can do that with almost anything *except* files. You can, however, mark a file in a shared folder as Read-Only or Hidden on its properties page to ensure it remains safe.

When you set up a folder's share details, make the most of the options available. Adding a 'Comment' in the appropriate box to explain what the folder contains can save users' time when browsing in Details view in Explorer.

Secret Sharing

If you want to share a particular folder or other resource in a workgroup without making it visible, you can add a $ (dollar-sign) to the end of its Share Name, such as "Reports$". To be able to access the resource, a user must know its full name.

Avoid Oversharing

If your workstation has no particularly sensitive files on it, you may have opted just to share the entire contents of its drives. But do all users need access to all folders? Assigning access rights only where they're needed could reduce traffic and help users find what they need more quickly.

Traffic Control

On a peer-to-peer network, try to divide the most frequently used files and applications between different workstations to spread the load evenly across the network. For especially heavily used applications you might find it more efficient to install the software onto each user's own computer.

Whose Bin?

Assigning a user full access to a drive or folder means that that user can delete your files as if they were on the user's own hard-disk. The good news is that you should be able to retrieve them from the Recycle Bin. The bad news is that you've got to find out *whose* Bin they're in – files deleted in this way are placed in the user's own Bin!

Network Folder Mapping

The easiest and most flexible way to connect to a shared folder is to map it as a drive, causing *Windows95* to treat it as if it were a drive on your own computer. Just right-click the remote folder and choose **Map Network Drive**, then select the drive-letter you want to assign it from the drop-down list. If you check the box marked 'Reconnect at Logon' you can opt to reconnect to the same folder using the same configuration next time you logon to Windows. If you need the connection only for this session or only occasionally, don't check the box. The primary benefit of drive-mapping is that this drive appears in applications' Open and Save As dialogs just as any physical drive.

Network Folder Shortcuts

A similarly easy way to deal with remote folders and other resources is to create shortcuts to them. Right-click on the resource and choose **Create Shortcut**. A dialog will explain that you can't create a shortcut in the Network Neighborhood window and offer to place it on the Desktop; click **Yes**.

Just like any other shortcut, you can double-click it to open it, drag items onto it to be copied (or printed, if the resource was a printer), or drag items into your applications to be opened.

Multiple Network Shortcuts

Along similar lines to the previous tip, you might find that there are several folders on one or more workstations that need to be accessed pretty frequently by most users. Create shortcuts to each of these folders and place them in a single folder on one computer. You can then create shortcuts to *this* folder on everyone's Desktop, providing fast access to all the most-used resources and, again, easing traffic by reducing browsing-time.

Unnecessary Log-On?

If you're on a LAN you probably see the log-on screen every time you start *Windows95* and have to enter a password. If you don't need immediate or constant use of the network's resources, open the Control Panel's **Network** applet, choose **Windows Logon** from the 'Primary Network Logon' drop-down list, and click **OK**. Next time you start *Windows95*, just hit the *Enter* key without entering a password.

WinPopup

WinPopup is a tiny, but magical, accessory hidden in your Windows folder, built especially for workgroups. Ideally this should be in your StartUp group.

Messages can be sent and received over the network – either to individuals or to the entire group – and the WinPopup window can be configured to 'pop up' and display a message as soon as it's received. If you prefer not to be interrupted by the up-popping of this window, you can just keep an eye on its Taskbar icon which changes to indicate a message has arrived.

If you use a remote printer, one of the major benefits of **WinPopup** is that it automatically notifies you when a print job you requested has been completed.

Share Your Desktop

The Desktop is the ideal place for sharing files if you work on documents jointly: newly arrived files can be spotted immediately. Open Explorer and navigate to your Windows folder. Right-click on the Desktop folder (C:\Windows\Desktop), select **Sharing** and assign a Share Name (and password if required).

If you have **Microsoft Office95** and use its Shortcut Bar, try setting it to display the Desktop toolbar. In this way, when something new lands on your desk, the arrival of a new icon on the toolbar will let you know (in a similar way to **WinPopup**'s changing icon).

Easy Desktop Sharing

If you and others in your workgroup follow the tip above, put shortcuts to their Desktop folders in your Send To folder to make the passing to and fro of documents a quick and easy process.

Put your Dial-Up Networking folder on the Start Menu

❏ **Cascading System Folders** – page 5

Open a Web-page from the command-line

❏ **Run A Website** – page 12

The modem icon in the Tray

❏ **Use The Modem** – page 29

❏ **Ins & Outs Of The Modem** – page 29

❏ **Lose The Modem** – page 30

Using HyperTerminal

Keep .url files handy

Use a picture in any graphics format as your wallpaper

Find out more about Microsoft's 'PowerToys' *et al.*

8

The Registry & Policies

The Registry

What Is It?

The **Registry** is home to a vast majority of the system settings needed by your computer and by *Windows95*. All the settings relating to hardware and software configurations are stored here, as well as most user-selectable preferences, largely replacing the **.ini** files used in *Windows 3.x*.

Forming such an important part of the operating system, if the Registry files become corrupted they may prevent Windows from starting or the entire system from booting.

Where Is It?

The **Registry** consists of two files: **System.dat** and **User.dat,** both of which are kept in your Windows folder:

❏ **System.dat** contains the system data, including details of installed hardware components and the resources they use. This is by far the more important of the two files since *Windows95* can't start without it.

❏ **User.dat** contains the user-preferences such as colour-schemes, software preference-settings and so on.

Both files are hidden – unless you've selected **Show all files** from Explorer's **View / Options** menu, they'll be invisible to prevent accidental alteration or deletion.

If you opted to set up multiple Desktops (as in 'Desktop Duality' on page 36), each user-name will have its own personal copy of **User.dat**. As soon as you specify multiple users, Windows creates a folder called **Profiles** under C:\Windows, and creates one folder per user-name within **Profiles**. When you log on to Windows with a particular user-name, you're effectively telling Windows which Profiles subfolder to look in to find a copy of **User.dat**.

Because of the vital nature of the Registry files, Windows makes backups of **System.dat** and the current **User.dat** files (with the extension **.da0**) whenever you start or restart your computer making it theoretically possible to restore the Registry to how it was the last time you started *Windows95* successfully. (See 'Restoring The Registry' on page 223 for details.)

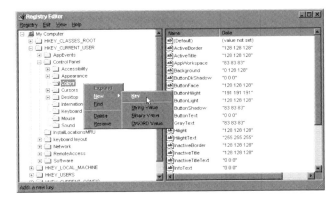

Screen 8.1 – **Right-click on a key to create a new sub-key**

The .INI Files

Although the two **.dat** files have superseded the use of **.ini** files, you'll still find **Win.ini** and **System.ini** in your Windows folder. These are needed for backward-compatibility with older Windows applications. On booting up, *Windows95* reads these two files and transfers any changes into the Registry.

This is a one-way street however: changes you make to the Registry won't update the two **.ini** files. That's worth remembering – if you make some change to the Registry and find it keeps returning to its original setting, it usually means the setting is included in either **Win.ini** or **System.ini** and needs changing there as well. In addition, many applications create their own **.ini** files which shouldn't be deleted unless you know what you're doing!

 The easiest way to view or edit these two .ini files is to use the System Editor – see page 258.

System.1st

You might have also noticed a file called **System.1st** in your root folder (hidden by default). This is a copy of the first **System.dat** file created when you first installed *Windows95*. This is kept for troubleshooting purposes – as a backup, it's probably hopelessly out of date!

If you did decide to use this file to restore the Registry, the reinstallation and reconfiguration of more recently added software and hardware could be a long and tortuous affair. Nevertheless, as long as you're prepared for that, it *is* still an option.

Registry Layout

When you first start the Registry Editor (**Regedit.exe** in your Windows folder), you'll see an Explorer-like view containing six keys in the left pane. Expanding one of these keys (by double-clicking it or clicking on its ' + ' box) reveals the level of keys beneath it, many of these also expandable in the same way.

Right-clicking on a key will display a context-menu with options to create a new key beneath the one you clicked on, or to create a new value in the right pane. You can also rename or delete a key from this context-menu.

Clicking on (almost) any key will display its list of values in the right pane: these may be string, binary or DWORD values: a string value uses a red '**ab**' icon, the other two a blue '**011110**' icon.

Information in the right pane is split into two: the *value-name* (beside the icon) and the *value-data* (to the far right). Double-clicking on a value-name will allow you to modify its data. A right-click on the name will produce a context-menu with the same option, plus the choice of renaming or deleting the value.

Almost all registry-editing involves locating the correct key in the left pane, choosing the correct name in the right pane and either deleting it or modifying its data.

Where Am I?

The view from anywhere in the Registry looks pretty much the same, so it's easy to get lost. Instead of scrolling up and down the left pane searching for clues, look in the status bar (providing you've selected that option in the **View** menu) – your full current path is listed there.

Stay Away From Reg

Browsing through Explorer, you might happen upon the occasional file with the extension **.reg** (carrying the same icon as **Regedit.exe**). These are sometimes installed with software to enter the Registry settings needed by an application.

If you double-click on one of these files, the data it contains will automatically be inserted into the Registry, with no warning, overwriting the data of any keys with the same name – this could potentially damage your Registry.

If you ever feel a compelling desire to double-click one of these files, first right-click it and choose **Edit** to view and compare its contents with the data already in the Registry, noting anything that will be changed by it.

Reg Needs Protection

With so much of *Windows95* hidden from view to make it more difficult for the inexperienced to mangle it, it's an odd quirk of design that double-clicking a Registry (**.reg**) file should automatically merge it into your Registry, no questions asked. To protect your Registry from accidental merges, go to **My Computer / View / Options / File Types** and make the following change:

I   Find **Registration Entries** in the list, select it, and click the **Edit** button.

2   In the 'Actions' window, click once on 'Edit' and click the Set Default button. You should see 'Edit' now turn to boldface type to indicate that it's become the default action for a double-click.

From now on, double-clicking any **.reg** file will open it in **Notepad**. To copy the file's contents to the Registry, you have to right-click it choose **Merge** – not so easy to do by accident!

The Deeper Meaning Of Keys

Data in the Registry is organized into particular areas, with each of the six main keys acting as a kind of 'subject divider' from the user's point of view. In fact, from the *computer's* point of view, there are just two: **HKEY_LOCAL_ MACHINE** (containing all the data from **System.dat**) and **HKEY_USERS** (containing the user-preferences from **User.dat** for each of the computer's users). The remaining four keys act as 'shortcuts' to particular areas of these two.

If you've followed any of the tips in this book involving Policy Editor, you've probably noticed this yourself: when you choose **File / Open Registry**, instead of the full six keys being represented you see just two – Local User and Local Computer.

Here's a run-down of how Regedit's six keys are organized:

❏   **HKEY_CLASSES_ROOT:** A quick route to **HKEY_LOCAL_MACHINE**'s list of file-extensions, file-types, and the applications associated with them.

❏   **HKEY_CURRENT_USER:** The current user's preferences (Desktop, colour schemes, wallpaper, sounds, software-settings etc.), a shortcut into the appropriate key of **HKEY_USERS**.

❏ **HKEY_LOCAL_MACHINE:** All hardware configuration data and system-software settings.

❏ **HKEY_USERS:** Preference settings for each user (in a multi-user setup) and/or the default-user (for a single-user setup).

❏ **HKEY_CURRENT_CONFIG:** Settings for more hardware and system-software; a shortcut into **HKEY_LOCAL_MACHINE \ CONFIG**.

❏ **HKEY_DYN_DATA:** System performance data and statistics for the current session – this data is constantly changing, and never saved.

Editing The Registry

Which User Am I?

You'll notice there are two keys with a certain similarity: the **Current_User** key and the **Users** key. The layout of the **Users** key – and the way you edit the Registry – will depend upon whether your system is set up for multiple users or not (see 'Protect Your Desktop Settings #1' on page 40).

Single User

If you have *Windows95* set up for a single user (the default setting, with which you don't have to logon to Windows at startup), below the **Users** key you'll find a single key called **.Default**. Expanding this will present the same key-names and hierarchy as beneath the **Current_User** key.

This is because the only *Users* of the system are the *Current User* (ungrammatical, but true). Under this setup, an alteration made under either the **Current_User** key *or* the **Users \ .Default** key will automatically update its twin.

Multiple Users

If you've opted to have multiple user names (ie. you have to enter a user-name to log on to Windows), the **Current_User** key will contain the settings specific to *you*. This is what enables you to have several vastly differing Desktop layouts, Start Menu structures and colour/sound schemes and switch between them – when you enter a logon name, Windows finds and implements the preferences associated with that name.

Under this scenario, therefore, when you make an alteration under the **Hkey_Current_User** key, this will have no effect on the settings of other registered users. If you expand the **Hkey_Users** key, you'll see the **.Default** key and the keys relating to each of the other users of your computer. The **.Default** key contains the settings that would be implemented if you returned to single-user mode. The profile-keys for the other user-names contain the same set of subkeys as both **.Default** and **Hkey_Current_User**, though the actual data they contain may obviously differ for each.

If you want to make changes that will affect *all* the users of your computer, you'll need to add or edit the same data in each profile-key individually. So when Registry tips in this book specify **Hkey_Current_User**, substitute this with **Hkey_Users** and carry out the tip in each of the profile-keys (and, if you choose, the **.Default** key too).

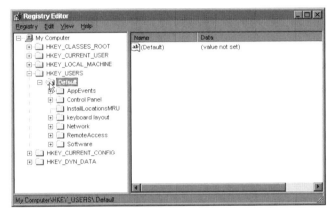

Screen 8.2 – **Finding the .Default key in HKEY_USERS**

 Edits made to other keys, such as **Hkey_Classes_Root** or **Hkey_Local_ Machine**, will automatically apply system-wide irrespective of whether your computer is configured for single or multiple users.

Editing Registry Data

To run the Registry Editor, select **Run** and type **regedit** on the command line. The Registry Editor uses the same tree-structure as the left pane of a dual-pane Explorer-window.

- ❑ To expand a key, double-click it (or click on the small cross beside it).

- ❑ To search for a specific string, or to repeat the previous search, press *F3*.

- ❑ Right-clicking on a key in the left pane allows you to rename or delete it, add a new key beneath it, or to add a new name to its entry in the right pane.

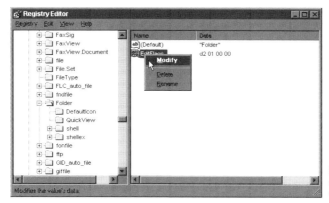

Screen 8.3 – **The context-menu for value-entries**

❑ Right-clicking or double-clicking a value-name in the right pane allows you to modify its name or data in a dialog-box (see Screen 8.3).

❑ Keys and strings can be deleted by highlighting them and pressing *Delete* (followed by **OK** in the obligatory confirmation-dialog).

❑ When you first open the Registry you can use *F3* to start a search even though this keystroke is actually a shortcut to 'Find Next'. If you've already made one search and you want to enter a new search-string, use *Ctrl* + *F* to bring up a fresh search-box.

Regedit In DOS

You can also use a version of **Regedit.exe** under MS-DOS (though not in a DOS-window under *Windows95*) to import and export Registry files. A copy of Regedit is also added to your Emergency Startup Disk (see page 249) to make sure this option is always available. Type **regedit/?** at the command-prompt for details and syntax.

 Take a look at 'Registry Creation In DOS' on page 224 for details of using the MS-DOS version of Regedit to recover from a corrupted Registry.

Registry
Tip

Working With Reg

Registry files can be a handy way to make your *Windows95* life easier, and perhaps cut down the time you spend editing the Registry or changing settings in Control Panel. Let's take an example...

Let's assume you use **Policy Editor** to prevent your settings being saved on shutdown (following the 'Protect Your Desktop Settings' tips in Chapter 2). Once in a while, you'll want to change your desktop settings and resave them. Instead of using Policy Editor to switch the option on & off, just export the appropriate Registry branch twice, the first time with NoSaveSettings set to **1**, the second with it set to 0. You can then just right-click on either file and choose **Merge** whenever you want to change the setting. Much quicker!

To use this example, open Regedit and use the Find command (*Ctrl+F*) to locate **NoSaveSettings**. When this string is highlighted, go to **Registry / Export Registry File**. If **NoSaveSettings** is set to **(1)** type **C:\Windows\Desktop\Keep** in the 'File name' box and click **Save**. Now go back to **NoSaveSettings** and set it to **(0)**. Export this is the same way, entering **C:\Windows\Desktop\Change** in the 'File name' box.

Merge the 'Change' file when you want to change your Desktop settings, then merge the 'Keep' file after you've restarted Windows.

You can probably find other settings logged in the Registry that take a lot of mouse-clicks in Windows, and export them in the same way. If you decide to try some others, backup your Registry first and test the exported files immediately (while the backup is still fresh!) to make sure they function as they're meant to when you merge them.

Here's one they don't tell you: when you're in Regedit you can import any **.reg** file from the **Registry** menu, regardless of name. But if you want to just right-click on a file and choose **Merge**, the filename must be no longer than eight letters!

Hedge Your Bets

When carrying out a Registry edit, avoid closing the Registry until you're satisfied with the result and know you want to keep it (unless, of course, you have to restart Windows). To check the effect of your edit, click once on the Desktop (minimizing Regedit if it's in the way) and press *F5* to refresh, and then run a test of the setting you edited. If you don't like the result, you still have the edited key in front of you ready to restore.

Safety First

Unlike most other applications, Registry Editor has neither **save** nor **undo** commands, so if you muck something up you can't just close the application to prevent it taking effect. If you change an entry and immediately regret it, you have to change it back to its previous setting yourself, so either make a careful note of the original setting or don't change it!

The other option, worthy of serious consideration, is to export the Registry-branch you're about to edit as a **.reg** file. This acts as a backup that can be merged into the Registry to reverse any modifications you made or replace any data you deleted. See 'Working With Reg' earlier in this chapter for details.

 Exporting a single Registry-branch should absolutely *not* be regarded as an alternative to full Registry backups! They didn't replace seat-belts with airbags did they?

Still **At It?**

Pushing buttons, double-clicking icons, checking boxes – it's what experimentation is all about. And here's one to avoid: when you're in Registry Editor, pressing the * (asterisk) key on your numeric-keypad expands every sub-key below the current position. And it's not a quick operation at all. You can try it for yourself if you've got the time...

Clean Your Registry

If you have Internet access, grab a copy of Microsoft's **RegClean**. This utility scans your Registry files and removes any entries that shouldn't be there, resulting in smaller System.dat and User.dat files and, potentially, solving a few problems along the way too. To anyone who upgraded from *Win3x*, the benefits will be obvious: remember the vast number of orphaned **.ini** files and file-type associations you ended up with after installing and removing various software? Since the Registry has all but replaced these, the same entries are collected here instead but are just as superfluous.

Once the RegClean Wizard has done his business, you can take a look at the entries that were removed (highlighted in red). The removed entries are saved to a **.reg** file which can be merged back into your Registry if you encounter problems. You can download RegClean from:

> **http://www.microsoft.com/kb/softlib/mslfiles/regcln.exe**

Backing-Up The Registry

Backup Methods

Backups of the Registry's **.dat** files are vital things, whether you intend editing Registry-data yourself or not: badly behaved software installations, viruses and good ol'-fashioned mistakes can cause as much damage as clumsy editing if the gods aren't smiling on you.

Windows95 creates its own backups of the **.dat** files on bootup which are a handy safety-net, but shouldn't be relied upon. There are three additional types of backup, usually requiring one floppy-disk and less than 10 minutes' work:

I   Export the Registry's contents to a **.reg** file in your Windows folder.

2   Use **Registry Backup**. This is included on the *Windows95* CD-ROM, but not automatically installed. If you want to have the option of using this recovery method, you must install the program yourself and create at least one backup of the registry *in advance* of trouble occurring (i.e., now!).

3   Make backups to floppy-disk of **system.dat** and **user.dat**.

The following tips explain how to create these backups in more detail.

An important part of the recovery/restoration procedure is being able to boot to MS-DOS. For this reason, make sure you've made an Emergency Startup disk (see page 249), and check it works before filing it away in a disk-box!

The Import/Export Business

The first method of backup (also useful for copying Registry data from one computer to another) is the Import/Export option within the Registry Editor itself. This allows you to save ('export') the entire database as a **.reg** file, or to load ('import') a previously saved file. The **.reg** file can be edited within a text editor such as **Notepad**.

You can also opt to save the contents of a single key (and its subkeys, if any) by selecting that key before choosing the **Export** option and clicking **Selected branch**, or by typing the key's name into the **Export** dialog box.

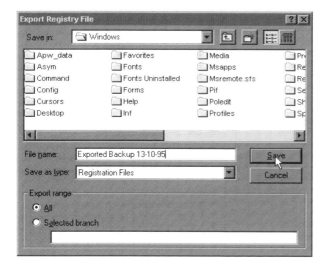

Screen 8.4 – **Regedit's Export File dialog**

To use this method as a backup, of course, you must *export* a copy of the registry to file before trouble strikes! Start **Regedit.exe**, click on **Registry** and **Export Registry File**. Type a name (such as 'Backup 1'), select a target folder to save the file to and click **Save**.

Installing Registry Backup

For extra peace of mind with your Registry, install the **Registry Backup** program from the *Windows95* CD-ROM. This lets you save backups of your Registry to the Windows folder, and will allow up to nine before you're forced to replace the older ones.

Installation is simple: open Explorer and double-click your CD-drive's icon. Navigate to **D:\Other\Misc\Cfgback** and copy the two files you find there into your Windows folder. Create a shortcut to **Cfgback.exe** in your customized Control Panel.

Registry Backup is extremely easy to use, simply requiring you to enter a name for the file and click the **Backup** button. Nevertheless, it's a good idea not to check the box that removes the instruction-pages – they're always a comforting sight in a crisis!

In the same way as **Regedit**'s Import/Export option, the main benefit of **Registry Backup** is not so much in recovering from disaster as in protection against mistakes: clearly, if you can boot to Windows and run the program, you haven't really *had* a disaster, but accidents such as hitting *Del* instead of *Return* can happen to anyone on a bad day. The backups also give you defence against badly behaved software-installation programs.

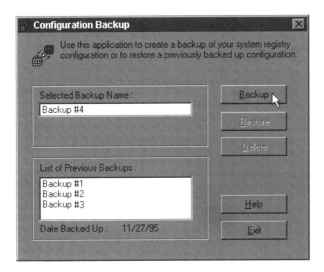

Screen 8.5 – **The registry-backup program in all its simple glory**

By default, **Registry Backup** saves its backup-files to your Windows folder. You can, of course, move these to a different folder or to floppy disk if you want to, but they must be returned to the Windows folder if you need to restore the Registry from one of them.

Cfgback won't backup **User.dat** files if you have *Windows95* configured for multiple users. While this isn't too serious (the System data is the more vulnerable by far), it *is* an extra reason to heed the next tip...

 Cfgback is also included in the ***Windows95 Resource Kit*** – see page 333 for details on this pack.

If You Want It Done Well ...

Having two extra methods of backing up the Registry may at first make you think you're secure if you use them both. Certainly you're *more* secure having the addition of **Registry Backup** than you would be without it, and the Export/Import options in Regedit are a comforting extra. But you haven't got it licked yet ...

The **Import** option and **Registry Backup**, as mentioned above, are only of use to you provided you can boot into Windows to run the necessary utilities. And depending upon what caused the problem, and when, and what you've done since, it would be unwise to rely on the backups (**.da0** files) that Windows creates each session.

The only sure way to have safe working copies of **System.dat** and **User.dat** is to make them yourself. The two files will fit easily onto a high-density floppy-disk. (These are hidden files, so make sure you've selected the **Show all files** option from Explorer's **View / Options** page.)

Go to your Windows folder, hold *Ctrl* and click on the two files. Then right click one of them and choose **Send To / Floppy Disk**.

There's no need to backup the Registry files for every little change you make (in fact it's better not to). If you install or remove hardware or software, wait until you've booted and shutdown the computer two or three times and you're sure that everything's okay, then overwrite your old backups with new ones.

Remember that the files will still be 'hidden' when copied to floppy-disk: depending on your settings, the disk may apparently be empty. You might prefer to remove the checkmark from the **Properties / Hidden** box for these backups.

Restoring The Registry

Restoration Methods

In most cases, *Windows95* should detect a corrupt Registry when booting up and automatically restart in Safe Mode to let you fix it – this unexpected switch to Safe Mode would usually be the first you knew of a problem.

If the computer won't load Windows in any form, this suggests the damage is more severe and can probably only be fixed from MS-DOS (booting either from hard-disk or your emergency startup floppy-disk), though it may still be possible to force a Safe Mode start from the DOS-prompt.

You should have at least two, and possibly four, available methods of restoring the Registry:

❑ If you can still boot to *Windows95* (in Safe Mode or otherwise), the easiest is to use the Registry Backup program **Cfgback.exe**.

❑ A possible second option is to use the **Export / Import** facility within Regedit itself. This can be done either from Windows or MS-DOS.

❑ If you can't start Windows, you'll need to restore the Registry from MS-DOS by replacing the corrupt **.dat** files 'manually'. You should have two subtly different methods of doing this: *Windows95*'s own **.da0** backups and the copies you saved to floppy-disk.

The following tips cover the various restoration methods one-by-one.

Restoration Using Registry Backup

This is the quickest, easiest, and most painless restoration method there is: start **Cfgback.exe** and click the **Continue** button until you see the list of backup files you saved. Choose the most recent backup that you know to be safe, according to the date noted below, and click **Restore**.

When you click Restore, you get a dialog box that says 'You are about to backup over a previous backup. Do you want to proceed?' This rather confused message should read 'You are about to replace the current configuration...'

Restoration Using An Exported File

The simplest method of restoring the Registry from an exported **.reg** file is to open an Explorer window, locate the file (or the most recent 'safe' file), right-click it and choose **Merge**: its data will be automatically incorporated into the Registry by replacement of (or addition to) existing data.

The other method of producing the same result is to start **Regedit**, click **Registry / Import Registry File** and select the file from the standard dialog.

Registry Creation In DOS

You can also use the DOS version of Regedit, which is included on the floppy when Windows creates your Emergency Startup Disk. Obviously, if you can boot to Windows, you don't want to be dealing with cumbersome command-line applications like this to handle something as delicate as the Registry, but if you have no choice DOS Regedit can *create* a new Registry for you from a previously exported **.reg** file.

The command uses three switches: **/L:** to specify the location of the current **System.dat**, followed by **/R:** to specify the location of **User.dat**, and **/c** to specify the location and name of the **.reg** file to create a new Registry from. The following example assumes that your corrupt **.dat** files are in C:\Windows (their default location), and you want to replace them with the data in a file called **Mydata.reg** on a floppy disk:

```
regedit /L:c:\windows\system.dat /R:c:\windows\user.dat /c a:\mydata.reg
```

Remember the **/c** switch stands for 'Create' – when you use it, your new Registry files will consist only of the data in the file you specified. If you mistakenly specify a file that contains only one branch for example, you'll end up with a Registry consisting of one branch!

This has a positive side though: as previously explained, when you use Regedit in Windows to import a file, it's *merged* with existing data so any branches that were *added* since you exported the file won't be removed. Since added branches shouldn't harm Windows to any great extent this doesn't matter too much, but it isn't the tidiest result. The **/c** switch in DOS *replaces* all the existing data.

Tip

Restoration Using The Automatic Backups

If the damage to Registry data is more serious, you may not be able to boot to Windows at all. If this is the case, you'll need to boot to MS-DOS instead and replace the **.dat** files with the **.da0** backups that *Windows95* creates each session.

This involves removing the **System, Hidden** and **Read-only** attributes from the **.dat** files and renaming them, and then renaming the backup files to take their place.

Restart your computer with your emergency startup floppy disk in the drive. When you reach the command-prompt, type the following (pressing *Enter* at the end of each line):

```
c:
cd windows
attrib -r -h -s system.dat
attrib -r -h -s system.da0
ren system.dat system.bad
ren system.da0 system.dat
attrib -r -h -s user.dat
attrib -r -h -s user.da0
ren user.dat user.bad
ren user.da0 user.dat
```

Remove the emergency disk from the floppy-drive and restart the computer.

If you can successfully boot to *Windows95* after this operation, and everything seems to be okay, find System.dat and User.dat, highlight them both (using *Ctrl + click*) then right-click on one and choose **Properties**. Check the boxes for **Hidden**, **System** and **Read-only**. Finally, either delete the files renamed with a **.bad** extension or move them to a floppy disk for analysis.

Restoration Using The Manual Backups

Windows' own **.da0** files are almost certainly going to be more recent than the backups you created manually but, depending on the circumstances, may be flawed themselves. If this turns out to be the case, you're having a pretty bad day – good thing you've got the 'manual' backups!

Use your Emergency Startup Disk (see page 249) to boot the computer. At the command prompt, replace this disk with your write-protected registry-backup disk and type:

```
c:
cd windows
attrib -r -h -s system.dat
attrib -r -h -s user.dat
ren system.dat system.bad
ren user.dat user.bad
copy a:\system.dat c:\windows\system.dat
copy a:\user.dat c:\windows\user.dat
```

Remove the floppy-disk from the drive and restart the computer. When Windows has finished loading, reassign the **Hidden**, **System** and **Read-only** attributes to the **.dat** files in your Windows folder.

Next, if you have a more recent backup file created with **Cfgback** or by export from Regedit, follow one of the earlier tips to restore this file and restart the computer before carrying out any further fine-tuning.

Forcing Safe Mode

If *Windows95* didn't reboot in **Safe Mode** of its own accord upon detecting a corrupt Registry, you may still be able to do it by restarting the computer and pressing *F5* when you see the **Starting Windows95...** message appear.

If the Registry files have been badly damaged or deleted, a Safe Mode start may still not be possible in the normal way. If this happens, boot to the DOS-prompt (using your emergency startup floppy-disk if necessary) and copy the files **Ifshlp.sys** and **Himem.sys** from the Windows folder to the root folder:

```
copy c:\windows\ifshlp.sys c:\ifshlp.sys
```

```
copy c:\windows\himem.sys c:\himem.sys
```

To then run Windows in Safe Mode from the command-prompt, type:

```
cd c:\windows
win /d:m
```

If Windows loads and the Safe Mode desktop appears, either rename and replace the **.dat** and **.da0** files or use a **Registry Backup** file to restore the data. If you can't load *Windows95* in Safe Mode, your only option is to work from MS-DOS using the automatic or manual backups.

Summary

Due to the nature of the Registry's contents, here's a quick summary of the precautions you should take before editing any Registry data by hand:

1   Copy the hidden files **System.dat** and **User.dat** from your Windows folder to a blank high-density floppy disk.

2   Install the **Registry Backup** program and use it to make one backup of your registration data.

3   Run **Regedit.exe** and select **Registry / Export Registry File** from the menu. Choose a location for the file and a name.

Make sure you have a *working* Emergency Startup Disk (see page 249) – there's no point in having the Registry data so well protected if you've got no backup method of starting your computer!

Policy Editor

What Are Policies?

The central reasoning behind Policies is to restrict access to certain parts of a computer or network. This is made possible by 'switching off' access to particular settings, options and software for different users, and then removing access to the policy-setting software itself to prevent the user simply switching it back on again.

Clearly the main benefits of Policies lie in network-management, but there are certain settings that may be handy for users of standalone computers, perhaps to prevent the kids trashing your hardware or virtual-memory settings, or to remove options you find unnecessary such as the Find command on the Start Menu. The settings you make are logged in the Registry, but the easiest method of making and changing the settings themselves is to use **Policy Editor**.

Installing Policy Editor

Some of the more practical (and safe) uses of **Policy Editor** have been covered in earlier chapters, but this handy utility isn't included in the *Windows95* installation procedure – if you want it, you have to install it yourself. Here's how:

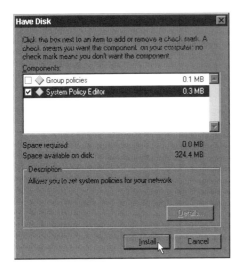

Screen 8.6 – **The 'Have Disk' selection screen**

1   Place the *Windows95* CD-ROM in your CD drive: the CD's **autorun** program should start. If it doesn't, double-click on your CD drive's icon to start it.

2   Click on the **Add/Remove Software** icon at the bottom of the screen.

3   Choose the **Windows Setup** tab and click on **Have Disk...**

4   In the 'Copy manufacturer's files from' box, type

   d:\admin\apptools\poledit

   and click **OK**.

5   A new dialog called 'Have Disk' will pop up; place a checkmark in the box beside **System Policy Editor** and click on **Install**.

Create a shortcut to **Poledit.exe** somewhere accessible (your customized Control Panel if you have one) – you're sure to need it regularly.

The first time you run Poledit.exe, you'll be prompted for a template file. If Windows doesn't suggest one, close Policy Editor, navigate back to the **Poledit** folder on the CD and copy the file **Admin.adm** to your Windows folder. Now run Policy Editor again and double-click this file when the prompt appears. Policy Editor will remember the location of this file in future.

Policy Editor is now ready to use: just follow the step-by-step instructions in the earlier chapters and the following tips.

Lock Out

This seems to be the chapter for warnings and exhortations of care, and here's another one: **Policy Editor** makes it all too easy to lock yourself out of areas of your computer. Not just 'lock out' in the 'That's going to waste ten minutes' sense, but 'lock out' in the 'I've got to reinstall *Windows95*' sense.

It's pretty easy to do as well. Policy Editor lets you create a list of allowed software, remove access to the Registry Editor and some of the Control Panel applets, and so on. Take a handful of restrictions, forget to add Policy Editor to the list of allowed applications, and you've done it!

If your computer is set up for multiple users (see 'Desktop Duality' on page 36) and you've locked one user out of the system settings, there's no problem. That's what Policy Editor is for. You can log on as a different user, use the **Passwords** applet to switch back to single-user mode and put things right. But if you make these changes in single-user (*default-user*) mode, you can transform your computer from hi-tech tool to expensive ornament with just a few mouse-clicks.

The bottom line is that it's vital to consider the implication of every restriction you impose – if you don't understand a setting or you're unsure of its potential effect when coupled with other restrictions, leave it alone!

Tip

Keeping The Kids Out

One of the main uses for Policy Editor on a standalone computer is to prevent your offspring doing unwholesome things to your system while still allowing them access to their games and educational software.

First make sure the kids have their *own* user-profile; as mentioned above, restricting any form of access to the default user is not advisable. After logging on to the kids' desktop, make sure you check 'Hide files of these types' in **My Computer / View / Options / View**. Now assign the 'Hidden' attribute to your Windows folder and any others containing system-tools and private files, but make sure you keep a shortcut to Explorer or My Computer so that you can still find and run these hidden files if you need to.

Run **Policy Editor** and open **File / Open Registry / Local User**. Here are a few options you may wish to make use of:

❑ **Control Panel**   Each of the five subkeys lets you choose to disable particular pages and tabs from Control Panel applets: check the applet's box and then choose the pages to disable in the lower window.

Screen 8.7 – **Removing access to vulnerable system-settings**

❑ **Desktop**   Specify a fixed wallpaper or colour-scheme that can't be changed.

❑ **Shell \ Custom Folders**   Choose to create a custom Programs folder on the Start Menu. Check **Hide Start Menu subfolders, Custom Programs Folder** and **Custom Start Menu**. When you check the last two of these, the default folders listed in the window below will be contained in the kids' user-profile folder in C:\Windows\Profiles. You can edit the contents of these folders to add shortcuts to their own programs and games and delete the rest.

❑ **Shell \ Restrictions**   These are largely self-explanatory. Many of these restrictions are covered in earlier chapters, and they tend to be a good place to start: for example, by checking **Remove folders from 'Settings' on Start Menu**, the entire Control Panel becomes unavailable to all but the more inquisitive user (see 'Too Helpful' and 'CPL Removal' below), saving the need to decide which applets and tabs are 'safe' in the Control Panel key above. Removing **Run** and **Find** ensures that there are fewer temptingly 'clickable' items around.

❑ **System \ Restrictions**   It's worth checking **Disable Registry editing tools** (you can still access the Policies area of the Registry from Policy Editor). If you check **Only run allowed Windows applications** you can type in a list of apps that can be run, but make sure you allow yourself access to Policy Editor. The act of applying the 'Hidden' attribute to your Windows folder will prevent access to its contents unless the kids know the filenames and have access to Run, Find, or the MS-DOS prompt.

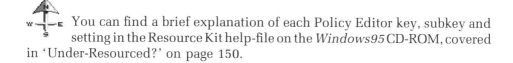 You can find a brief explanation of each Policy Editor key, subkey and setting in the Resource Kit help-file on the *Windows95* CD-ROM, covered in 'Under-Resourced?' on page 150.

Too Helpful

If you've removed the folders from 'Settings' on the Start Menu, removed Run & Find, hidden most folders in Explorer and created a small Start Menu of shortcuts to nothing but games, you may think you've set a pretty stringent Policy. If so, you've reckoned without **Help**.

There's no option to remove **Help** from the Start Menu, and *Windows95* Help files are packed with handy 'click-me' buttons for almost every Control Panel applet (including Device Manager, Add New Hardware and Add/Remove Programs), plus applications such as DriveSpace and Internet Explorer. The only way around this is to create a list of allowed applications, as above, making sure that C:\Windows\Control.exe is not among them. Make sure that you can still run Explorer.exe and Poledit.exe and either keep shortcuts to them, or don't remove the **Run** command from the Start Menu.

CPL Removal

Removing the entire Control Panel (by removing system folders from 'Settings' on the Start Menu as above) is rather a radical step if all you want to do is prevent another user accessing the Passwords or System applets for example. The easy answer is just to remove the appropriate **.cpl** file from C:\Windows\ System and either put it in another folder (perhaps a hidden one, but not C:\, C:\Windows, C:\Windows\Command, or any folder specified in your PATH= statement) or move it to a floppy-disk.

Bear in mind that not all the applets are **.cpl** files, so your choices are slightly limited. An extra limitation is that Main.cpl covers both Mouse and Keyboard, so to remove one means removing both.

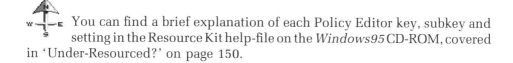 For more on the PATH= statement, take a look at 'Stating A Path' on page 265.

Working with Policy Editor

❏ **Remove The System Folders** – page 6

Make a Startup Disk from the Add/Remove Programs utility

Make a Startup Disk from the Format command

Making security backups of other vital files

Pros & cons of the Emergency Recovery Utility

Creating, saving & editing a **.set** file in Microsoft Backup

System & Performance

System Overview

The Big Picture

Almost all the nitty-gritty of your system that affects (or is controlled by) *Windows95* can be found in **System Properties**. To get here quickly, right click on **My Computer**, and choose **Properties**. Alternatively, double-click the **System** applet's icon in Control Panel.

Many of the settings that can be viewed or edited in **System Properties** can also be accessed from other, more specific, Control Panel applets such as **Display** or **Multimedia**; however, some settings found in one will be missing from the other.

Device Manager

The first tab you come to is **Device Manager**. This follows the familiar 'tree-structure' used in Policy Editor and Registry Editor. From this page, you can:

- ❏ view all the devices connected to your computer
- ❏ add/remove or disable/enable devices
- ❏ see which drivers are used for particular devices and change them
- ❏ check and change settings, addresses and IRQs
- ❏ check and alter port settings (mouse, modem, printer etc)
- ❏ make sure that each device is working properly

It's well worth taking a browse through **Device Manager** even as an inexperienced user: expand trees, select devices and choose the **Properties** button for each. Provided you don't actually change anything, this is risk-free. For the nervous, the simple way to change nothing is: Never click **OK** – always use **Cancel**.

Screen 9.1 – **The connection tree, with a warning sign**

Tip

Warning Sign

Keep a lookout for any items whose icons are obliterated by a yellow exclamation-mark (as in Screen 9.1 above). This means that the device has a problem: select it and choose **Properties** to find out what the problem is. It could be one of several things:

❑   It may be that the device has been disabled in favour of an alternative.

❑   There may be a conflict of system resources. Click on the **Resources** tab to see if this is the case.

❑   The device might be using an out-dated 16-bit driver – see 'Drivers In Bits' on page 239 to try a 32-bit replacement.

❑   It may be that the Device Manager settings don't match the settings made in the hardware. This could involve either changing the Device Manager settings (provided you can find non-conflicting settings that are compatible with your hardware) or some intimate tweaking of DIP switches or jumpers on the device itself.

After making any changes, use the **Refresh** button to update the view: this is a handy way to find out if new devices or drivers are working, or whether you've managed to solve a device conflict.

Tell Me About It

By selecting **Print** from the **Device Manager**, you have the option to print out a detailed report of your various devices, connections and resources, or a smaller summary. By first selecting a class or a single device you can print a report just on that, to help troubleshoot a particular connection.

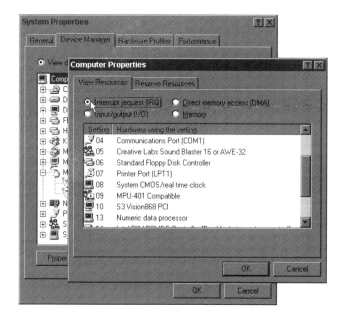

Screen 9.2 – **Ready-sorted views of allocated resources**

Locate & Compare

By selecting the **Computer** entry at the top of the **Device Manager** list and clicking **Properties**, you can view devices by resource: for example, click the **Interrupt Request** radio-button to see which IRQs are in use, and by which devices (see Screen 9.2).

Check Your Bits

Check out the **Performance** tag in **System Properties**. Ideally, every subsystem listed should show either **32-bit** or **Not installed**. If the **Performance** page shows the message 'Your system is configured for optimal performance', all is well. If the message reads 'Device xxx is using MS-DOS Compatibility', the specified device is using an out-dated real mode driver and probably reducing your system's performance.

If it's a hardware problem, you can usually get updated 32-bit drivers from the retailer, or locate them on the Internet or a BBS. (Check first that you're not loading the real mode driver in your Config.sys. If you are, remove the entry – see 'Drivers In Bits' on page 239 – Windows may be able to replace it with the protected mode driver.) Software problems are often related to older system-software such as disk-compression utilities.

Shooting Your Troubles

Windows95 provides a friendly Help-based Hardware Conflict Troubleshooter which aims to solve conflicts in question-and-answer style. Run **Help** from the Start Menu, click the **Contents** tab, then double-click 'Troubleshooting' and 'If you have a hardware conflict'.

Adding Hardware

Plug & Play

The idea of Plug & Play is that the first time you start your computer after installing new hardware (by slotting the board inside your computer's case, or plugging it into a port), *Windows95* will notice this new device, decide what it is, and add the necessary drivers for it automatically. If all goes smoothly, you should just see a brief on-screen message as your Desktop appears announcing that a new device has been detected and is being configured. As well as installing driver files, the Plug & Play system covers the allocation of resources for the device, such as assigning correct and non-conflicting DMA channels and IRQs if necessary.

Microsoft supplies its own drivers for a huge range of hardware: you might be prompted to insert your *Windows95* installation disk(s) for Windows to copy the required files to your disk. If Windows detects a Plug & Play device but can't provide a driver for it, you'll be prompted to insert the disk containing the driver-files packaged with the hardware.

The *Windows95* drivers are usually at least as good as those created by the manufacturer, so if Windows installs its own driver automatically and every-thing seems to function correctly, you might as well stick with it even if you have the manufacturer's own driver. If you want to swap drivers, you can use the **Add New Hardware** wizard to do it (see 'Change Hardware Drivers' below).

Plug & Play Compatibility

Full Plug & Play support relies on having a Plug & Play BIOS as well as Plug & Play hardware. Nevertheless, if one or both of these items are non-Plug &

Play compatible, *Windows95* will still have a brave stab at identifying the new device.

If neither are Plug & Play compatible, however, you'll probably find you need to get your hands dirty in Device Manager to assign non-conflicting resources. This will always depend upon the type of hardware you're installing, and what's installed already (see 'Resource Settings' on page 239).

Change Hardware Drivers

Tip

Despite its name, the **Add New Hardware** wizard lets you *change* hardware-drivers as well as install new hardware. If Windows didn't manage to detect your device, or you want to install an updated driver, go to Control Panel and run the wizard.

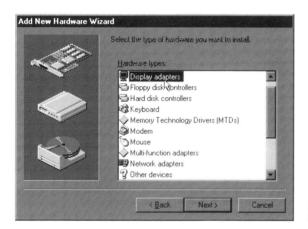

Screen 9.3 – **Pick your hardware-type from the list**

1   Click the **No** radio-button to prevent Windows searching for the device.

2   On the next page, double-click the type of hardware for which you want to change drivers.

3   If Windows failed to detect your hardware, look at the 'Manufacturers' and 'Models' lists to see if the device is listed. If it is, select it and click **Next** to install it. (If it isn't, read the next tip.) If you want to install an updated driver, or the driver that came with the software, click **Have Disk...** and direct Windows to the location of the files.

4   Installing new drivers will always require that you restart the computer for the change to take effect.

You can also change the driver in **Device Manager**. Find and double-click the device, click the **Driver** tab and click the **Change Driver...** button. You'll see a similar dialog to that shown in Screen 9.4.

Neither the **Add New Hardware** wizard nor **Device Manager** will let you change your monitor – you have to use the Control Panel's **Display** applet instead. See 'Change Display' on page 171. You can change the display adapter from here though, and install a new printer – the **Add Printer** wizard is no more than a shortcut to **Add New Hardware**'s Printers page.

You Bought A *What?*

Sometimes Windows just hasn't got a clue what your device is: it can't detect it, and doesn't list a driver for it. If the manufacturer didn't package a driver with the hardware, all is not lost ! Many drivers will work with different devices, so use the **Add New Hardware** wizard to try a few. It's a trial and error process, so it could involve a lot of booting and rebooting, but you'll usually get there in the end.

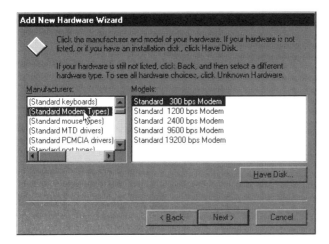

Screen 9.4 – **The 'Other Devices' page**

The first thing to try is the range of generic drivers supplied for most device types: after clicking the **No** radio-button as in step 1 above, double-click **Other Devices** in the 'Hardware types' list.

You'll see a list of bracketed entries in the left pane such as **(Standard display types)** and **(Standard mouse types)**. Click the correct type and choose what you think is the closest match in the right pane, then click **Next** to continue the installation.

Time And No Motion

When you agree to let Windows search for the latest addition to your hardware arsenal, the **Add New Hardware** wizard builds a device-list, churns the hard-disk, pauses for a while to take in a movie and have a bite to eat, and just when you'd given up hope, returns with a result and asks if it found the right device. By the time it's done all this, 'new' hardly seems like a fitting description. To save yourself some time, click **No** to the search offer and take a look to see if your device is listed, following the steps in 'Change Hardware Drivers' earlier in this section to install it.

Drivers In Bits

In a perfect world, you're using only 32-bit ('protected mode') drivers for your hardware. The quick way to find out is to run **System Editor** (Sysedit.exe in C:\Windows\System) and take a look at **Config.sys**. Calls to any device-drivers included in this file are 16-bit ('real mode') drivers (see the 'Tweaking' section on page 278). In addition to their limited functionality, using 16-bit drivers makes you more likely to get 'Out of Memory' messages, even when your computer is stuffed to the gills with RAM and swapfile disk-space.

Remark out the references to these drivers and restart your computer. If Windows can't detect the device(s) to which these real mode drivers refer (and you'll know because they won't work!), try following the previous tip to install one of the generic drivers – you should notice a great improvement in performance and functionality as a result (as well as more available conventional or upper memory when you run MS-DOS games and programs in a DOS-session under Windows).

Resource Settings

Assuming your computer has a Plug & Play BIOS, when you install a Plug & Play device, *Windows95* allocates the resources for it automatically. On the **Resources** tab of a device's **Properties** page in **Device Manager** you should see that the 'Use automatic settings' box is checked. This lets Windows juggle resources between different devices if you install more Plug & Play hardware, so this box is always best left checked.

With a Plug & Play BIOS, Windows will still try to allocate correct resources for a non-Plug & Play device, but these may not always suit the hardware itself. If they don't, you'll need to clear the 'Use automatic settings' checkbox and specify your own settings instead.

If neither hardware nor BIOS are Plug & Play compatible, the 'Use automatic settings' box will be greyed out and you'll have to identify and set the resources yourself.

Different hardware will require different resources, such as **IRQ** (Interrupt Request), **DMA** (Direct Memory Access) channel, **I/O** (Input/Output) range, and **Memory address**. The following tip explains how to carry out the common operation of changing the interrupt (IRQ) setting. The procedure is the same to change the setting for one of the other resources – just select the resource you want to change in the 'Resource Settings' window.

Changing IRQs

Tip

To change the IRQ, highlight the offending device in **Device Manager** and click **Properties** followed by the **Resources** tab, and highlight the 'Interrupt Request' entry in the 'Resource Settings' window. If 'Use automatic settings' is checked, uncheck it and click the **Change Setting...** button. Change the interrupt setting in the 'Value' box, keeping an eye on the lower box for an indication that you've picked a non-conflicting setting.

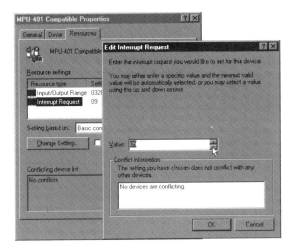

Screen 9.5 – **Specifying & conflict-checking a device's IRQ setting**

Of course, not only do you have to choose an IRQ that doesn't conflict with other installed devices, it must be one that your device can respond to, and some devices respond to a very limited number. You might be able to juggle IRQs for other devices to free-up a compatible one, but it's possible you'll have to replace the device itself with one with greater IRQ support.

If you can find an available IRQ that is compatible with your device, you may have to alter jumper or DIP switch settings on the hardware accordingly.

Some devices offer different preset configurations: before modifying any resource settings, take a look in the drop-down list titled 'Setting based on'. A different configuration may give you the settings you need, or may let you change settings that were fixed in a different configuration.

Avoid Overplugging!

When you install new hardware on the system using the **Add New Hardware** applet, install only one new device at a time. Plugging in two or three at one go could make any subsequent troubleshooting a real headache.

To Plug Or Not To Plug?

When you install a **Plug & Play** device, *Windows95* immediately dashes off to set it up for you. Usually this is what you want so there's no problem; however, if you're in the middle of a task and absently pop a PC Card device in the slot, you're suddenly on an enforced break. The moral is: If you don't want to play, don't plug!

Refreshing SCSI Hardware

SCSI devices are a different kettle of fish: if they were switched off while *Windows95* booted up, just switching them on afterwards won't make Windows recognize them.

To make these devices available without restarting Windows, open the **System** applet in Control Panel; on the Device Manager page click on **SCSI Controllers** and click the **Refresh** button. Windows will take another look at the connections and update itself.

Memory & Optimization

Optimize Your CD-ROM

If you click on the **Performance / File System** button and choose the **CD-ROM** tag, you can set your CD-ROM drive to work to its fullest potential: choose **Quad speed or higher** from the drop-down box and pull the slider to the right to maximize the cache-size (see Screen 9.6). This can make a dual-speed drive perform like a quad-speed – particularly noticeable when playing videos or graphics-intensive games from CD-ROM.

 If you're running *Windows95* with less than 12Mb RAM, you might find that these settings reduce the general performance of your system. If this seems to be the case, reduce the supplemental cache-size to minimum and set the access pattern to **Single-speed drives** to make the most of your RAM.

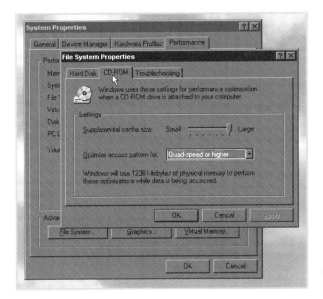

Screen 9.6 – **Turbo-charge your dual-speed drive**

Optimize Your Graphics Accelerator

If you have a graphics-accelerator card, click the **Graphics** button on the **Performance** page and drag the slider to **Full** to make the most of it.

Tip

Update Your Video Driver

Most of the video drivers that worked under *Windows 3.x* will work under *Windows95*, but there are a whole host of reasons not to use them (including the need to reboot if you want to change video resolution, and the lack of Energy Star compliance and support for animated cursors). The updated 32-bit drivers should be faster and less resource-hungry than their 16-bit counterparts into the bargain.

Memories Are Made Of This

RAM – there's no escaping it. You can't possibly have too much, but *Windows95* makes it rather easier than it was to have too little. The basic operating system will run in 4Mb, but many of the applications built for it (such as Microsoft Exchange) require a minimum of 8Mb. Running several applications at once (*multitasking*), as *Windows95*'s new interface encourages you to do, needs more memory to keep up a good level of performance.

It has been said that *Windows95* crawls in 4Mb, walks in 8Mb and runs in 16Mb. For most uses, the optimum RAM is 16Mb – beyond this, the performance increase you get for your money declines noticeably.

Silent Running

An easy way to reduce performance is to have unnecessary applications and utilities running – they may not make much difference to processor-use, but they're using valuable memory.

Take a look in your StartUp folder (Start Menu \ Programs \ StartUp), at the icons in the Tray, and at the **Close Program** dialog (by pressing *Ctrl + Alt + Del*): chances are you'll have several utilities running permanently behind the scenes that spend most of their time doing nothing, but using resources while they do it.

Over-Coloured

If your display-adapter and monitor support High Colour or True Colour displays, it's tempting to use them. For most uses, however, 256 colours are quite adequate. Keep in mind that memory requirements increase vastly as you increase the colour-depth, and you might notice a decline in the speed of screen-refreshes.

Similarly, using a 1280 × 1024 screen is a resource-hungry luxury: if you can work in 800 × 600, your system will thank you for it.

Plus! Negatives

If you installed Microsoft *Plus!*, the **Plus!** tab in the **Display** applet gives you a few Visual Enhancements in the form of font-smoothing, large icons, wallpaper stretching and maximizing icons' colours. Once again, these are aesthetically pleasing luxuries – if system performance means more to you than the precise shade of a few pixels in your icons, make sure you disable these options.

If you have neither a graphics accelerator nor a fast processor, font-smoothing and full window drag are both to be avoided.

 See page 337 for more details of these and other *Plus!* inclusions.

Optimize Hard Disk Performance

If you're running *Windows95* on a low-memory system, Windows will fill the available RAM quickly and be forced to swap to disk more than is desirable, resulting in a significant performance hit. To optimize the disk read/write times on a desktop-computer with *less* than 8Mb RAM, click the **Performance** tab in **System Properties**, click the **File System** button and set the 'Typical role of this machine' to **Mobile or docking system**.

Optimize Your Virtual Memory

Virtual memory involves using an area of your hard-disk to emulate RAM and is vital to the performance of your system. Go to the **Performance** tab in System Properties and choose the **Virtual Memory** button at the bottom of the page to check the settings.

In *Windows 3.x* it was quite usual to make your own Virtual Memory ('swapfile') settings, and you were encouraged to create a permanent swapfile: if you upgraded from *3.x* to *Windows95* you might find that these settings have been 'imported'. *Windows95* handles Virtual Memory a great deal better than *3.x*, so unless you know what you're doing it's best to check the box for **Let Windows manage my virtual memory settings**.

 See 'Optimize Your Swapfile' on page 248 to get the best performance from your virtual memory.

Change Virtual Memory Settings

If Windows has control over virtual memory, its swapfile is *dynamic* – in other words, it shrinks and grows whenever necessary to produce the best performance. At these moments, when the disk-drive suddenly starts working, you might find yourself unable to get any response to keyboard or mouse input for several seconds: setting a fixed-size permanent swapfile should put an end to these sudden bursts of activity.

In addition, some applications (particularly graphics-intensive apps) need large amounts of virtual memory. If you record audio or video in real-time to hard disk, Windows can't resize its dynamic swapfile fast enough to cope with the incoming data. In situations like this the application may fail or the system may crash, making a permanent swapfile imperative.

Click your way to the **Performance / Virtual Memory** page of the **System** applet, and click the radio-button for **Let me specify my own virtual memory settings**. In the newly active dialogs below, choose the drive on which you want the swapfile created, and set **Minimum** and **Maximum** to the same size. Click on **OK** twice to confirm and restart the computer.

To get an idea of the size of swapfile needed, try running **System Monitor** for a while during normal computer-use, keep an eye on the swapfile's largest size, and add a couple of megabytes for safety.

 To maximize the effectiveness of your permanent swapfile, make sure you defragment the drive on which you want the file located before you create it: a fragmented swapfile will not perform as well as a contiguous one. You can keep your swapfile on a compressed drive without reducing its performance.

For more details on System Monitor, see 'Monitor Your System' on page 257.

Drive Management

Drive Info

To check the free space and total capacity of a drive, open **My Computer** and click on the drive's icon: the information is displayed on the status-bar (as long as you've got **Status Bar** checked in the **View** menu).

To see the same information graphically portrayed in pink and blue, as in Screen 9.7, right-click the drive and choose **Properties**.

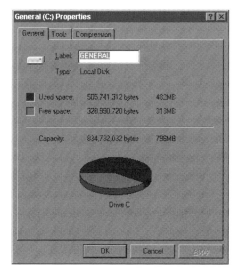

Screen 9.7 – **Glorious technicolour to soften the blow**

Drive Labels

To assign a new label to a disk (including a floppy-disk), just type it into the **Label** box on the drive's **Properties / General** page, shown in Screen 9.7.

Optimize Your Disk Space

Running on an almost full hard-disk can hit system performance hard, but there are several methods of grabbing some of this space back again...

Recycle Bin and Internet Explorer (for *Plus!* users) can each grow to take up 10% of your disk for deleted and cached files respectively if you let them. In total, on the average hard disk, that's a potential 100Mb of (mostly) garbage! Since the Recycle Bin sits on your Desktop, you probably remember to check it and empty it pretty regularly. Both Recycle Bin and IntEx give you the option to modify their maximum disk-space allowance (in **Properties** and **View / Options / Advanced** respectively), so make good use of it.

IntEx also has an option to empty its Cache folder. This is a pretty radical move: you might prefer to look at its contents in Explorer and delete files manually instead. Hang onto graphics files from sites you visit regularly since these take longest to download. Equally, deleting graphics files from sites you never intend to visit again could give you several megabytes more free disk-space.

Unchecking the 'Show Pictures' / 'Play Sounds' / 'Show Animations' boxes on **IntEx's View / Options / Appearance** page will keep your cache folder at a more manageable size as well as reducing your on-line time.

Here's a few other space-saving suggestions:

❑ Remove applications you don't need. Either uninstall them (see 'Install/Uninstall' on page 122) or move them to floppy disk in zipped form and delete their folders. (Make sure you note the folder structure in case you ever need to replace them.)

❑ Remove any Help files you no longer need to floppy disk, both from applications' own folders and from C:\Windows\Help.

❑ Clear out small files (such as icons) to floppy disk, or create a single **.zip** file for them – depending on your disk's cluster-size, a single icon may use 32K of disk-space which is almost exactly the same as a **.zip** file containing 50 of the little rascals!

❑ Consider compressing your hard-disk – see 'Drive Optimization' below.

❑ Keep an eye on your 'Temp' folder, and use **Find** to search for old **.tmp** files from time to time (some applications create temporary files in their own folders). On occasions, temp files don't get deleted; for example, when an application crashes.

Remove Online Help Videos

If you selected the **Online User's Guide** when custom-installing *Windows95*, you have a small collection of **.avi** video files in C:\Windows\Help demonstrating basic tasks such as resizing windows, using scrollbars, and opening folders. If you can live without these files, you can recover a pretty incredible 7.1Mb of disk-space!

Run the **Add/Remove Programs** applet from Control Panel and choose the **Windows Setup** tab. Select **Accessories**, click on **Details** and remove the checkmark next to **Online User's Guide**. Click **OK** twice to confirm.

Drive Optimization

By right-clicking a drive's icon in **My Computer** and selecting **Properties / Tools** you can see when the drive was last scanned, defragmented and backed-up: just click on one of the three buttons to do the job right away.

Screen 9.8 – **Power-up your disk access from here**

A third tab, **Compression**, allows you to check or adjust the **DriveSpace** settings. (*Plus!* pack users can also run **Compression Agent** from here.)

See the 'System Tools' subheading on page 251 for more information about these disk-utilities.

The Wonders Of Compression

There's a hidden advantage to compressing your hard-disk: obviously if the files themselves are compressed you'll gain disk-space, but a compressed disk also uses smaller clusters. A single icon (**.ico**) file, for example, must use at least one cluster, and clusters can't be shared between files. On an uncompressed disk, your 766 byte icon will be using a whole 32K cluster. On a compressed disk, it will use two 512 byte clusters – a total of 1K! For the best of both worlds, you can compress the disk and opt to have no compression on the files themselves, thus gaining space without sacrificing disk-performance (but make sure you backup your files first for safety).

Optimize Your Swapfile

A common cause of a performance hit in terms of disk-access is Windows' handling of Virtual Memory: since the swapfile size may change often, limited space on its drive (coupled, perhaps, with a fragmented disk) could slow it down badly. If you have another drive with more free-space, try creating the swapfile there instead. Otherwise, consider creating a permanent swapfile (see 'Change Virtual Memory Settings' on page 244).

Nippy Floppy Copy

To format or make a copy of a floppy-disk, right-click on a floppy-drive's icon or shortcut and select **Copy** or **Format**. If you've got a bundle of disks to format, you can speed up the process slightly by removing the checkmark from the box labelled **Display summary when finished**.

 See 'Alternative Format' and 'Alternative Disk Copy' on pages 289 & 290 for a method of copying and formatting floppies from a shortcut.

Quick Format

To erase and initialize a previously formatted floppy-disk, select the **Quick** radio-button in the Format dialog.

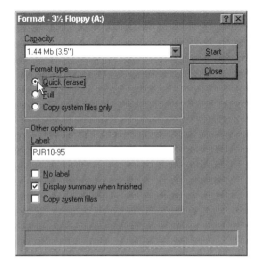

Screen 9.9 – **Fast formatting for previously used disks**

Save & Format

If you've just created a file you want to save to floppy-disk and you realize your only available floppy is unformatted, you can format it without leaving the application you're working in. Choose **File / Save As**, press *F4* to open the drive-box and click on **My Computer**. Then right-click on the floppy-drive's icon and choose **Format**.

Emergency Startup Disk

When you installed *Windows95* you were given the option of creating a startup floppy-disk to boot the system in the event of a serious crash. If you didn't (or if your computer arrived with *Windows95* pre-installed thus denying you the prompt), grab a high-density disk and your *Windows95* installation disk(s) and do it now:

I   Start the **Add/Remove Programs** applet in Control Panel.

2   Click the **Startup Disk** tab and then click on **Create Disk**.

3   Once the disk has been created, shutdown and restart the computer (not Windows) with this emergency disk in the drive to make sure it works. You should arrive at the DOS command-prompt (**A:\>**). If you do, it works. Remove the disk and restart your computer. Write-protect the emergency floppy and keep it somewhere safe.

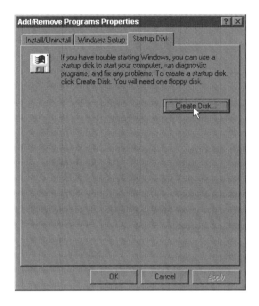

Screen 9.10 – **The all-important startup disk: 30 seconds well spent**

This disk will only boot you to DOS. For maximum safety, create a second disk in the same way and manually copy Msdos.sys to it from your root-folder (or the root-folder of your host-drive on a compressed disk). This disk will enable you to boot to *Windows95*.

No Installation Disks?

If you've ended up in the situation of having *Windows95* installed, but no installation disks, you can still create a startup disk. Put a floppy-disk in the drive, and choose **Format** from the floppy's context-menu. After selecting the correct capacity for the disk, check the box under 'Other options' marked **Copy system files**. This will add the files needed to restart the computer and take you to the command-prompt.

To these you should also add **Autoexec.bat** and **Config.sys** from your root folder, **Attrib, Chkdsk, Edit,** and **Scandisk** from C:\Windows\Command and **Regedit** from C:\Windows. Don't forget to test the disk as in step 3 above!

Keep System Backups

Keep backups of important system files such as **Autoexec.bat, Config.sys, Msdos.sys**, and all **.ini** files on a floppy-disk or other removable media, and keep them updated.

One method of doing this is to use **Backup.exe** (see 'Using Backup' on page 255) but this gives you the fiddly task of adding new **.ini** files to the backup-list every time you install new software. A quicker method is to use **Find** to search your boot-drive for ***.ini** and use the context-menu's Send To option to copy these to the floppy drive.

 It's more important still to keep backups of the Registry files. Read the section titled 'Backing Up The Registry' on page 219.

Using ERU

The *Windows95* CD-ROM hides a backup utility called **ERU** (Emergency Recovery Utility) which creates backups of Autoexec.bat, Config.sys, Msdos.sys, Io.sys, Win.ini, System.ini, Protocol.ini, Command.com and the Registry files System.dat and User.dat. There's no installation routine for this program – just navigate to **D:\Other\Misc**, copy the whole **Eru** folder to your hard disk, and create a shortcut to **Eru.exe** in your customized Control Panel. Alternatively, you can run the utility straight from the CD itself.

In fact, ERU is really only included here for completeness: its method of working is somewhat self-defeating. If you opt to create the backups on a floppy, which is preferable, ERU asks for a system-disk (created from the 'Format' command) to add the backups to. Unfortunately, the presence of the system files on the floppy means that ERU usually has to remove System.dat from its list of files to be copied due to lack of space!

You can of course backup to a folder on your hard-disk, but you're not secure without at least one set of backups on floppy-disk: once you've gathered these files onto a floppy disk yourself, you can copy them anywhere else you want them without ERU's help (or hindrance).

If you *do* decide to use ERU, you can restore all or some of the backed-up files by booting to the command-prompt and running **Erd.exe**, which is automatically created in the hard-disk folder (or on the floppy-disk) containing the backups.

System Tools

Keep 'Em Together

If you opted to create a 'Fake Control Panel' folder (see page 54), use it to keep all your system-related applets and accessories together. You're sure to need them all once in a while, and some you'll probably use pretty often. Here's a list of the programs to which you might want to create shortcuts in this folder (and you've probably picked up a few other utilities along the way too):

❑ **ScanDisk (C:\Windows\Scandskw.exe)**   Checks the integrity of files, folders and disk surfaces and reports/repairs errors. Should be run weekly with a standard test, plus a monthly thorough test.

❑ **Disk Defragmenter (C:\Windows\Defrag.exe)**   Gathers the pieces of file scattered over your hard-disk and brings them together to make the files contiguous and thus speed up disk-access. Should be run weekly.

❑ **System Info (C:\Windows\Msapps\Msinfo\Msinfo.exe)**   Diagnostic utility that lists (among others) system configuration, connected printers, currently running applications, and a full list of the **.dlls** on your system. (The 'Applications Running' section is rather selective; for a more comprehensive list, look at the **Close Program** dialog by pressing *Ctrl + Alt + Del*).

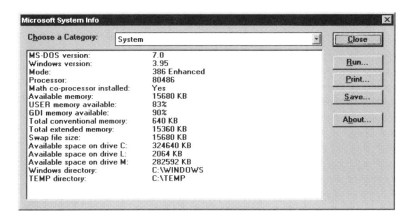

Screen 9.11 – **System Info tells it like it is**

❑ **Backup (C:\Program Files\Accessories\Backup.exe)**   Allows you to backup the entire system to a tape-drive or (more economically) to create your own list of files or whole folders to backup to floppy-disk. You can edit this list to remove or add items.

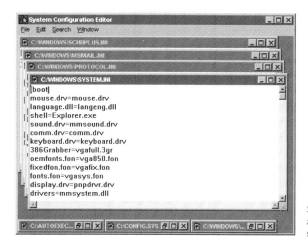

Screen 9.12 – **Sysedit autoloads the essential system files**

❑ **System Editor (C:\Windows\System\Sysedit.exe)**   To save you opening Notepad and hunting through folders for **Autoexec.bat**, **Config.sys** and the main **.ini** files, this little utility opens them all ready for you, and creates automatic backups (see Screen 9.12).

❑ **System Monitor (C:\Windows\Sysmon.exe)**   Colourful view of the ongoing state of your system's resources. (Included on the CD-ROM only.)

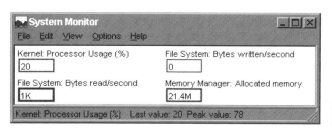

Screen 9.13 – **Not just a pretty face**

❑ **DriveSpace (C:\Windows\Drvspace.exe)**   Compress your files to gain more disk-space. (*Plus!* users have the updated version *DriveSpace3*.)

❑ **Compression Agent (C:\Program Files\Plus!\Cmpagent.exe)** 'Caretaker' software for *DriveSpace3*-compressed drives.

❑ **Registry Editor (C:\Windows\Regedit.exe)**   See 'The Registry & Policies' chapter beginning on page 211.

❑ **Registry Backup**   Outrageously easy-to-use utility for backing up Registry data. See 'Installing Registry Backup' on page 221.

❑ **Resource Meter (C:\Windows\Rsrcmtr.exe)**   Simplified Tray-icon display of system resources – if it goes into the red you're overdoing it! Double-click the icon for more details. This is a popular candidate for putting in the **StartUp** folder, but bear in mind that it uses some of those valuable resources itself!

Screen 9.14 – **Either watch the icon or click for graphic details**

❑ **Policy Editor**   Protect a variety of system-settings from other users (and from Windows itself!). See page 227 for details on installing and using **Poledit.exe**.

❑ *Plus!* **Setup (C:\Program Files\Plus!\Setup\Setup.exe)**   Add and remove Microsoft *Plus!* components, such as individual Desktop Themes.

ScanDisk Safety

If you allow **ScanDisk** to automatically fix errors by checking the corresponding box, make sure you click on the Options button before running the program and also check **Do not repair bad sectors in hidden and system files**. Right-click the box to get a 'Help' pop-up explaining why.

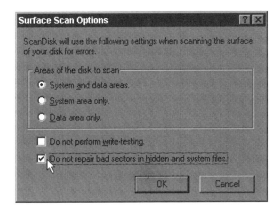

Screen 9.15 – **Generally a pretty good box to check – read the pop-up!**

Tip

DriveSpace Info

You can run **DriveSpace** to check the details of your compressed drives such as compression ratio and total capacity, and 'move' free space from one compressed drive to another (via the host drive). By clicking on the **Advanced** menu you can change the letter associated with a compressed drive, or create a new empty drive.

Compression Depression?

If you're halfway through a **DriveSpace** operation such as creating a compressed drive and your computer goes down for some reason, don't panic. Windows can remember what was going on and will resume when you restart the computer.

If it doesn't, just run DriveSpace again – it'll remember it had been busy and will give you the opportunity to cancel, defer, or continue the task.

Compression Agent

If you have the *Plus !* pack and a compressed hard-disk, run **Compression Agent** once a week to maximize its effect by recompressing the files you used in the intervening time. The easiest way to do this is to schedule a weekly 'appointment' for it in **System Agent**.

Selective Compression

Compression Agent users have an extra handy option at their disposal. While the default settings (balancing compression with fast disk-access) will suit most users, you can select individual files, folders or file-types for special attention. For example, you could choose to have no compression for **.exe** files, or select rarely-accessed folders to be Ultrapacked.

Run **Compression Agent** and click **OK** to clear the drive-prompt. Then go to **Settings / Exceptions / Add** and click the appropriate radio-button for file/folder/extension. Either click **Browse** to select a file or folder, or type a file-extension in the dialog-box. Choose the type of compression required and click the **Add** button. To select further items, repeat the same process for each.

When you're done, click **Close** and you'll see a list of the items you selected and their corresponding compression setting – these can be changed or removed from the list by selecting one and clicking the appropriate button.

If you don't want to actually recompress the drive(s) right away, click the **Exit** button – the new settings will still be saved.

 See page 339 for more details on **Compression Agent**.

Using Backup

Unless you have a tape- or zip-drive (or a second hard drive), the default Full System Backup file is out of the question ! Nevertheless, **Backup** is the ideal way to keep copies of regularly updated files such as spreadsheets and databases.

The easiest method is to create a Backup (**.set**) file containing all the important documents on your system.

Using the Explorer-type tree structure, check the boxes for single files or the contents of folders to be backed up. Click Next Step and select the drive (such as A:) or folder to which the backed-up files should be saved.

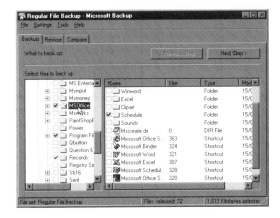

Screen 9.16 – **The familiar tree-view & checkboxes combine in Backup**

Click your way to **Settings / Options / Backup** and choose the settings you require. (The **Quit Backup...** option is worth selecting as an aid to automating the process; choosing the appropriate **Always erase...** option ensures that your drive doesn't become full of out-of-date backups.)

Now choose **File / Save As** and type a name for the selection-file (this enables you to backup the same files whenever you want to without going through the file-selection process over again). When you've saved the file, click **Start Backup** and type a name for the backup-file (for convenience, give this the same name as the selection-file).

You can run the same backup in future by double-clicking the file (or a shortcut to it). *Plus!* users can schedule **System Agent** to update it regularly. Note that **System Agent**'s command-line must include reference to an **.exe** file – to schedule **Backup** to run a particular file, the command line should be in the following form (with no quotes around the **.set** filename):

> "C:\Program Files\Accessories\Backup.exe" My Files.set

Editing A Backup File

To add new items or remove unnecessary ones from a previously created **.set** file, run **Backup**, use **File / Open** to load the selection-file, and check or clear the required boxes. Select the target drive or folder as before and **File / Save**. When you click **Start Backup**, you'll have to re-enter the name for the backup-file too – this is why it's easiest to use the same name for both!

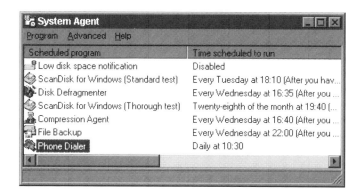

Screen 9.17 – **Add any program you like to Sage**

Secret Agent?

Despite its system connotations, and the fact that it loads and controls system applications by default, *Plus!* owners can use **System Agent** to run any type of application from its **Program / Schedule a new program** dialog.

For example, if you created the batch file that empties your Recycle Bin and clears your Documents Menu, you could schedule it to run at 9:05a.m. on Mondays in preparation for a new working week or keep your Documents Menu 'permanently' empty by scheduling the batch-file to run every 30 minutes.

If you stay organized to the point that you always like to make your calls or answer your mail at 10:30a.m., schedule your email client or **Phone Dialer** to open at that time to give you a reminder.

Bear in mind that **System Agent** requires its command-line entries to point to an application, with the filename added as an argument – see 'Using Backup' above for an example.

 Read 'Clear The Lot' on page 9 for the low-down on the batch-file mentioned above.

Monitor Your System

From the **Edit / Add Item** dialog in **System Monitor**, you can choose between a far wider range of settings than the default view would have you believe – 24 in fact. Click on a 'group' in the **Category** column and then select an item to monitor from the right pane. To see a (rather minimal) explanation of the selected item, click the **Explain** button.

Much of the information displayed can be misleading and even worrying: for example, the almost constant processor usage figure of 100% or the apparently low amount of free memory could have you dialling Tech Support in a panic, but are actually normal figures brought about by *Windows95*'s handling of resources.

The most helpful settings to monitor are those relating to Swapfile Size, Swapfile In Use, and Disk Reads/Writes per second.

Use System Editor

Whenever you want to make changes to **Autoexec.bat, Config.sys**, or one of the primary **.ini** files, use **System Editor** (in your Windows\System folder) to do the job. Not only does it load these files for you itself, it creates automatic backups of any files you change with a **.syd** extension: if something goes wrong, you can just replace the file you edited with this backup.

It's Obvious, But... (part 1)

Before you run **Defrag** or compression software, make sure you empty the **Recycle Bin**!

It's Obvious, But... (part 2)

When running **ScanDisk** or **DriveSpace/Compression Agent**, either disable your screensaver or make use of the *Plus!* 'Sleep Corners' facility (see page 176) to prevent the operation being restarted, aborted or botched.

Printing

Right-Click & Print

Many word-processors use the command-line argument /**p** for direct printing of a document. This switch can be used to add the 'print' option to your context-menu for word-processor documents.

1   Go to **My Computer / View / Options / File Types**.

2   Select the file-type corresponding to your chosen application and click **Edit**.

3   Click on **New** to create a new action.

4   In the 'Action' box, type **print**. In the box below it, type the full path to your chosen application followed by a space and /**p** (see Screen 9.18).

5   Click **OK** to close each page in turn.

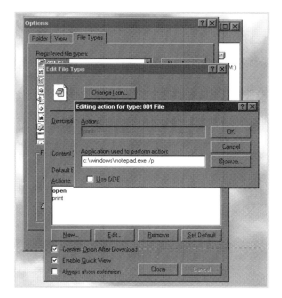

Screen 9.18 – **Add the '/p' switch to print from the context-menu**

When you right-click on one of these files, you can now select **Print** from the context-menu without needing to run the application. (Some applications will open anyway when you select the print option and then shut down again immediately after you click a confirmatory **OK** – it doesn't look as cool, but it's still a lot quicker!)

Send It!

Use your right mouse-button to drag your printer's icon from **My Computer / Printers** into your **Send To** folder (C:\Windows\Sendto). To print a file, you can just right-click on its icon, choose **Send To** and click on your printer.

 Take a look at 'Desktop Printing' on page 59 for another quick-print option.

Fast Printing

To speed up printing, right-click on your printer icon, and select **Properties / Details / Spool Settings / Print directly to the printer**. Instead of printing in the background this can have the effect of taking over your computer, so schedule your print jobs for a time when you'll be away from your desk.

Printer Contexts

To pause your printer in the middle of a print-job, just right-click on its icon and choose **Pause Printing**. When you want to restart, choose **Pause** again to remove the checkmark. If you want to stop printing this document and any others in the queue, choose **Purge Print Jobs** instead.

Print Troubleshooting

Lurking in the depths of the *Windows95* CD-ROM is the **Enhanced Print Troubleshooter**, a small question-and-answer utility that helps you sort out printing problems such as slow printing, mangled graphics, and missing fonts.

To 'install' the troubleshooter, open **D:\Other\Misc**, copy the whole **Epts** folder to your hard-disk, and add a shortcut to **Epts.exe** in your customized Control Panel. (If you prefer, you can just run the utility direct from the CD when you need it by double-clicking the **Epts** icon.)

Printer Setup

Right-click on your printer icon and choose **Properties / Details / Setup**. From here you can access a variety of print-variables including paper size and orientation, print quality and resolution (the exact details and the options available will vary according to your printer and printer-driver).

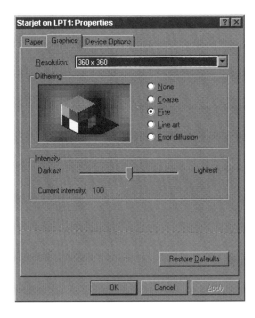

Screen 9.19 – **Fine-tune your printer's output from here**

Print To File

WordPad, Paint, and compatible applications like **Office95**, give you the option to print a document to file instead of your printer. This can be a useful way of passing a document to someone who doesn't have the required application to open it, and it can also help you stay organized if you're working on a portable computer and can't print the files until you get back to your desk.

Choose **File / Print**, check the box marked 'Print To File' and click **OK**. You'll be prompted for a location and filename – make sure you include the **.prn** extension to identify the file-type as a printer-file.

 No 'Print To File' option? Create a dedicated printer for the job – see 'Binary File Printer' on page 262.

 Once you've got a **.prn** file you need to be able to print it. Read 'Printing .PRN Files' on page 262.

Text File Printer

A similar option to the tip above is to print the document to a text-file: this creates a **.prn** file containing only the ASCII-text portions of the file and ignoring everything else. Apart from its use in troubleshooting font-related printing problems, the Text Printer can be handy for printing a 'quick'n'dirty' reference copy of a heavily formatted spreadsheet or word-processor file.

1   Open the Printers folder and double-click the **Add Printer** wizard.

2   From the 'Manufacturers' list choose **Generic**. The 'Printers' list should show **Generic / Text Only**.

3   In the next dialog, choose **FILE:** as the output port.

4   Next, type your choice of name for the new printer, and make sure 'No' is selected at the offer to make this the default printer.

5   Finally, right-click on your newly created printer's icon and click the **Paper** tab. For 'Paper Source' select **Continuous – No Page Break** and click **OK**.

You can now choose this printer in any application's **Print Setup** or **Print...** dialog; as in the previous tip, you'll be prompted for a location and name for the **.prn** file.

Binary File Printer

If applications you regularly print from don't have a 'Print To File' option and you don't want to make do with a text-only printout, create a printer especially for the job. Run the **Add Printer** wizard and choose your regular printer from the Manufacturer/Printer lists. In the next dialog, choose **FILE:** as the output port, then type a name for the printer on the next page.

When you finish, the wizard may prompt you for your *Windows95* installation disks to copy printer files, and will therefore probably find it impossible to copy the printer-driver because it's in use – click on **Skip File** if this occurs (since you've just created a copy of your printer, all the files are already in place anyway). Printing to this printer will create a **.prn** file with the correct formatting for your printer.

Printing .PRN Files

If you've followed any of the tips above and saved a **.prn** file you'll have noticed that one of the many things it doesn't do when you double-click it is print! Instead you get the **Open With** dialog. You can print one of these files from the command-line (either in a DOS-window or the **Run** command) but the easiest way is to create a batch-file containing the command and associate **.prn** files with it to print them with a double-click. Open **Notepad** and type:

> **@echo off copy /b %1 lpt1:**

Save this file as C:\Windows\Printer.bat (making sure you include the **.bat** extension). Find and right-click this batch-file's icon to open its **Properties** page, go to the **Program** tab, select **Minimized** in the 'Run' box and check **Close on exit** then click **OK**.

Now double-click your **.prn** file to display the **Open With** dialog. Use the **Other** button to browse your way to your new **Printer.bat** and double-click it. Check the box marked 'Always use this program to open this type of file' and click **OK**.

If you'd like your **.prn** files to have their own icon to make them more easily identifiable, go to **My Computer / View / Options / File Types**, find the **PRN File** entry and click **Edit / Change Icon**. (Instead of scrolling down the list, just type *prn* with no pauses to find the entry quickly.)

 You can edit a batch-file easily by just right-clicking it and choosing *Edit*. The Edit command is associated with **Notepad**.

The printer Tray-icon

❏ **Print Control** – page 30

Check the size of a folder's contents

❏ **Exact Folder Size** – page 94

Deleted a vital file? Use Extract to replace it

❏ **Opening Cabinets** – page 131

Find hidden details about .dlls and .exes

❏ **Quick View Tricks #1** – page 138

Checking and changing multimedia drivers

❏ **What's What?** – page 160

Methods of defeating CD Autoplay

❏ **Don't Autoplay** – page 168
❏ **Disable Autoplay** – page 168

Changing screen-resolution

❏ **Risk Free Resolutions** – page 170

Changing monitor or display adapter types

❏ **Change Display** – page 171

CD-ROM driver hazards in Config.sys

❏   **Changing CD-ROM Drivers** – page 280

Configuring multimedia devices

❏   **'MULTIMEDIA PROPERTIES'** – page 159

Optimize your modem- and port-speed

❏   **'THE MODEMS APPLET'** – page 187

10

Bootup & Shutdown

Booting Up

Stop The StartUp Folder

If you want *Windows95* to ignore your **StartUp** folder and not load the programs it contains, hold *Ctrl* as Windows starts and the cursor first appears.

Tip

Stating A Path

When you use command-line applets such as **Run** or **Go To**, or enter a filename into a new shortcut, you need to specify the **path** to tell Windows (or MS-DOS) where to find the file – i.e., the drive to look in, the folder(s) to open, the file to choose. Doing this all this typing too often becomes a chore.

The 'path statement' in your **Autoexec.bat** file (located in your root folder, usually C:\) takes care of this by giving the system a list of places to look in advance. The Registry defines the path to C:\, to C:\Windows and to C:\Windows\Command (or equivalent, depending upon the name and location of your Windows folder). Therefore, if you type the name of an item contained in one of these folders on the command-line, it can be found. Type the name of an item in C:\Program Files, however, and Windows will display an error message.

To make finding and opening files and folders quicker, start **System Editor** and maximize the **Autoexec.bat** window. Find the line beginning SET PATH= (or add it yourself) and add any well-used paths to the line. Separate each new path with a semi-colon (;) and remember to enclose paths using long folder-names in quotes ("). Part of your path statement could look like this:

   SET PATH=C:\Windows\Media;C:\DOS;"C:\Program Files";E:\;E:\Reports;

When you've added what you need, select **File / Save** and exit System Editor. The paths will become active the next time you boot-up.

Change Your Boots

When you switch on your computer and the BIOS has done its business, you see a message that reads **Starting Windows95...** If you press *F8* as soon as this message appears you'll be presented with a menu of options. Exactly which options you'll have will depend on your hardware and connections, but the basics are:

❑ **Normal** – boots straight to *Windows95* in the usual way.

❑ **Logged** – boots to *Windows95* as usual and creates a log-file called **Bootlog.txt** in your root folder (**C:**) as a troubleshooting reference.

❑ **Safe Mode** – loads *Windows95* in a default configuration as a temporary fix to let you troubleshoot and correct any problems that prevented your own configuration running.

❑ **Step-By-Step Confirmation** – steps through each entry in your system files and asks whether to process it or not; use the *Enter* and *Esc* keys to select Yes and No respectively. This enables you to temporarily 'remove' any entries you think may be causing a problem without physically editing your system files.

❑ **Command-prompt only** – processes your system files and leaves you at the DOS-prompt to either run an MS-DOS session or continue booting to Windows.

❑ **Safe-mode Command-prompt** – takes you straight to the command-prompt without processing your system files.

You can use the arrow-keys and *Enter* to select an option, or type its number.

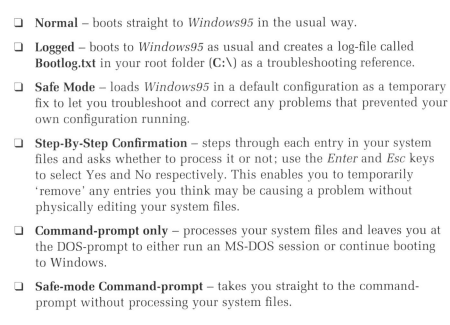 You can customize the way the Boot Menu operates by editing **Msdos.sys**. See 'Automatic Boot Menu' on page 269 and 'Maximize Your Boot Options' on page 270.

Bypass The Boot Menu

If you know exactly where you want to go today, you can bypass the Boot Menu and get there faster. Instead of hitting *F8* at the **Starting Windows95...** message, type one of these:

Safe Mode – *F5*

Command-prompt only – *Alt* + *F5*

Safe-mode Command-prompt – *Shift* + *F5*

Step-By-Step Confirmation – *Shift + F8*

Move On Up

If you booted to MS-DOS (command-prompt only) and now want to load *Windows95*, just type **win** at the command-prompt.

Hello . . . Goodbye

If you select the **command-prompt only** option, only to see your command-prompt flit by and your Windows Desktop appear, check your **Autoexec.bat** (in the root folder of your boot-drive, usually **C:**). The last entry of the file is probably **win** (the command to load Windows).

In Command-Prompt Only mode, *Windows95* processes your system files but doesn't execute its in-built command to start Windows. However, if the command is contained in your **Autoexec.bat** then of course it'll be processed along with the others.

To check it out, run **System Editor** (C:\Windows\System\Sysedit.exe) and select the **Autoexec.bat** file. If you find a line beginning WIN, type REM before it, followed by a space (this converts it to a remark rather than a command), select **File / Save** and try rebooting to the command-prompt again.

Msdos.sys Boot Options

Msdos.sys Precautions

Msdos.sys is one of the vital system files that resides in the root folder of your boot-drive, usually **C:**. (If you compressed your hard-disk with DriveSpace or another disk-compression utility, the active **Msdos.sys** file will be on the *host* drive of your computer rather than the *compressed* drive.)

Msdos.sys has *hidden* and *read-only* attributes to prevent accidental alteration or deletion – if the file is deleted, the computer won't start. Before making any changes at all, use Explorer's **View / Options / View / Show all files** option to make the file visible, then copy the file to floppy-disk and, for extra safety, to a different folder on your hard-disk.

When you open the file in **Notepad**, you'll see it contains several lines of **xs**; these are to ensure that **Msdos.sys** is greater than 1024 bytes in size and should not be removed under any circumstances.

And one final point: don't make any changes to the [PATHS] section of the file – you may prevent your computer from starting.

 Msdos.sys is a vital file that enables your computer to boot to *Windows95*. For this reason, it's useful to have a second Emergency Startup Disk (see page 249) that contains this file as well as the files *Windows95* places on a system-disk which will only get you as far as DOS.

Editing Msdos.sys

Tip

Once the file is visible, right-click it and open its **Properties** page. Remove the checkmarks from the **Hidden** and **Read-only** boxes.

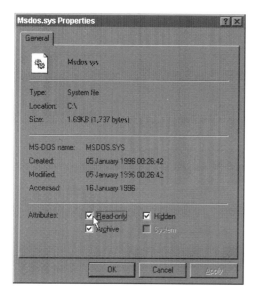

Screen 10.1 – **Changing the attributes of Msdos.sys**

To open the file, click on it once to highlight it, press *Shift* and right-click on it. Choose the **Open With...** option and select **Notepad** from the application list.

When you've finished editing the file, make sure you return to its **Properties** page, and reassign the same attributes.

Instead of mucking about with the **Open With...** dialog to open this file (or any other) in Notepad, follow the tip titled 'View Any File Type' on page 103 to put the option on the context-menu.

Boot To The Command-Prompt

If you want to boot to the command-prompt every time you power-up your computer, rather than directly into Windows, you can do so:

Find the line in the [OPTIONS] section that reads BOOTGUI = 1 and change it to BOOTGUI = 0.

At the command-prompt, you can type **win** and *Enter* to start *Windows95*.

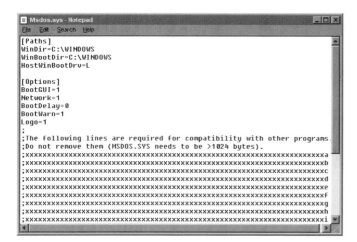

Screen 10.2 – **Msdos.sys waits expectantly**

Faster System Restart

Open **Msdos.sys** as above, and add the line BOOTDELAY = 0 to the [OPTIONS] section. This prevents Windows displaying the **Starting Windows95...** message and pausing for user-input, thus starting the boot-sequence sooner.

To access the boot-menu by pressing *F8* (see 'Change Your Boots' on page 266), you'll need to be able to recognize when the BIOS has done its business and act quickly as soon as the boot-sequence starts. After editing **Msdos.sys**, restart the computer and try it for yourself to make sure.

The BootDelay is set in seconds, with a default of 2. If you want a longer pause instead, add the desired delay time to the line after the = sign.

Automatic Boot Menu

If you find yourself frequently pressing *F8* when the **Starting Windows95...** message appears and selecting different boot-options, you can edit **Msdos.sys** to display the menu automatically every time you boot the computer:

In the [OPTIONS] section, add the line BOOTMENU = 1. The Boot Menu will remain on screen until you select one of its options.

Maximize Your Boot Options

To have the best of all possible worlds, you can force the Boot Menu to appear, wait for input from you, and continue loading Windows should none be forthcoming. Add the following lines to the [OPTIONS] section:

    BootMenu = 1
    BootMenuDefault = 1
    BootMenuDelay = 10

The first line forces the automatic display of the Boot Menu; the second specifies which boot-option should be taken if you don't specify something different (in this case, Option 1 – a normal boot to *Windows95*); the third line is the time in seconds for which the menu should be displayed before following the option in the second line.

On start-up, the Boot Menu will be displayed with an on-screen countdown from 10 to 0. If you don't choose a different option during the countdown, *Windows95* will be loaded automatically.

Lose The Startup Logo

If you're tired of seeing the animated startup logo, add the line LOGO = 0 to the [OPTIONS] section of your **Msdos.sys** file. If you ever want your logo back, re-edit the line replacing the 0 with a 1.

 You can edit the startup logo (and the two displayed during shutdown) for an extra bit of personalization. See pages 281 & 283.

Shutting Down

Always Shut Down!

Always, but always, shut down the computer correctly at the end of a Windows session by selecting **Shut Down** from the Start Menu and choosing the required option. If you just switch off, data may be lost or damaged as a result.

Screen 10.3 – **What we've all been waiting for?**

Always wait until you see the on-screen logo announcing **It's now safe to turn off your computer** before hitting the Off-switch.

Don't Restart The Computer

Selecting **Restart the computer** from the Shut Down dialog does just that, almost as if you'd turned it off and back on again. After clicking the **Restart the computer** button, hold *Shift* as you click on **OK** – this restarts *Windows95* rather than the whole system and takes about half the time!

Do I Have To?

Some of the changes you make to the system send up a dialog prompting you to restart the computer for the changes to take effect. Pressing *Shift* while clicking on the **OK** button works in most of these dialogs too – you'll then see Windows pause to update the system before restarting. Some changes to system or hardware settings do need a system-restart, but in these cases Windows will do that anyway even if you're holding *Shift*.

Quick Shutdown/Restart

Shutting down the computer or restarting Windows seems like a lot of mouse-action for what should be a simple job; using the keyboard speeds the process along...

❑ **Shutdown** – press *Alt+F4* then *Return*.

❑ **Restart Computer** – press *Alt+F4* then *R* then *Return*.

❑ **Restart Windows** – press *Alt+F4* then *R* then *Shift+Return*.

❏   **Restart in MS-DOS Mode** – press *Alt* + *F4* then *M* then *Return*.

❏   **Logon as a different user** – press *Alt* + *F4* then *C* then *Return*.

Auto Restart

Okay, so you can restart *Windows95* instead of rebooting the computer – that saves some time. You can use keystrokes to do it which speeds it up even more. Wouldn't the world seem a little cosier if you could just double-click something? You can, and once again it's the DOS batch-file to the rescue...

I   Start **Notepad**, and type **@exit**. Save this file to your Windows folder with a sensible name like **Restart.bat** (make sure you include the **.bat** extension).

2   Open your Windows folder in Explorer, find your new **Restart.bat**, and use the right-mouse button to drag a shortcut onto the Desktop.

3   Right-click this shortcut and choose **Properties / Program**. Check the box marked **Close on exit**.

4   Click the **Advanced** button, and check the **MS-DOS mode** checkbox. Remove the checkmark from the box labelled **Warn before entering MS-DOS mode**. Click **OK** twice to confirm and close the **Properties** pages. (If you want to choose a new icon, click **Change Icon** before the second **OK!**)

Double-clicking this tiny program, after closing any running applications, will move you into MS-DOS mode, at which point the program's only command ('exit') will close MS-DOS mode and restart Windows.

If your computer reboots instead, this means you have TSR programs being run as you enter MS-DOS mode which require a reboot. These are in a file named **Dosstart.bat** in your Windows folder which was automatically created when you installed *Windws95* to give you mouse and CD-ROM drivers for MS-DOS mode sessions.

If you don't use MS-DOS mode (or don't need these drivers when you do use it), right-click **Dosstart.bat** and choose **Edit**. Type REM followed by a space at the beginning of each line in the file then choose **File / Save** and quit Notepad. You should now find that your Restart shortcut works perfectly.

If you do use these drivers in MS-DOS mode, make a copy of **Dosstart.bat** and call it something like **Drivers.bat**, then edit **Dosstart.bat** as above. When you run an MS-DOS mode session, just type **drivers** at the command prompt to run this file.

(i) If you're concerned that you might double-click this icon accidentally, leave the **Warn before entering MS-DOS mode** box checked – this is especially worthwhile if you put the shortcut on the Start Menu where only a single click is needed !

(ii) Because it's a shortcut, you can create a hotkey combination for it too. This makes accidental restarts even easier though, so heed point (i) above if you do it.

Quick MS-DOS Mode

If you want to restart the computer in MS-DOS mode, there's an option on the **Shut Down** menu for just that purpose. And it works. But here's a tip for all the shortcut fanatics out there: use **Find** to locate **Exit To Dos.pif** and use the right mouse-button to drag it to the Desktop and create a copy (or put it on the Start Menu). This acts as a shortcut to MS-DOS mode.

By default you'll get a warning dialog before Windows closes. If you can trust yourself not to click the shortcut accidentally, go to its **Properties / Program / Advanced** page and clear the checkbox for 'Warn before entering MS-DOS mode'.

Alternative Shutdown

Rather than using the **Shutdown** command from the Start Menu, you can use the **Close Program** dialog to do it just as safely: press *Ctrl + Alt + Del* and either click the **Shut Down** button or press *Alt + S*.

In this case, however, using the *Shift* key to try to restart *Windows95* only will have no effect.

And Another Thing...

Windows95 suffers from the lack of a direct-cable connection to your brain: it allows you to shut down the computer and watch the graphics-screens appear before you remember the *other* thing you wanted to do before quitting.

The obvious option is to restart the computer, but you may have a quicker method. If you booted to Windows from the command-prompt (i.e., pressed

F8 at the **Starting Windows95** message, chose the **Command-Prompt Only** option and then typed **win**), *Windows95* returns to the command-prompt when you shut down – it's hidden behind the 'It's now safe to turn off your computer' logo, but it's there. To return to Windows, type **co80** (still invisibly) and hit *Enter* then **win** and *Enter*.

Quit To DOS #1

The above method is okay as long as you *want* to restart Windows – perhaps you'd like to hang onto your options a while longer. If you rename the two logo-files that are displayed on shutdown (or remove them from your Windows folder), Windows will exit to the command-prompt. You can then type **win** to restart Windows, or (as is displayed on the screen) switch off, press *Ctrl + Alt + Del* to restart the computer or continue working in **MS-DOS**.

The easiest and safest method is to rename the logo-files: open your Windows folder, find the files **Logos.sys** and **Logow.sys** and rename them **Old Logos.sys** and **Old Logow.sys**. This will, of course, mean that you'll no longer see the logos when you shut down, but if you can live with that sad thought, your options are greatly increased.

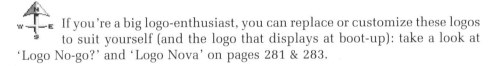 Again, you need to have started *Windows95* from the command-prompt in order to be returned to it. If you didn't, you'll see the same on-screen text but no command-prompt.

If you're a big logo-enthusiast, you can replace or customize these logos to suit yourself (and the logo that displays at boot-up): take a look at 'Logo No-go?' and 'Logo Nova' on pages 281 & 283.

Quit To DOS #2

If the idea of quitting to DOS is attractive, but you don't fancy having to boot to the command-prompt first, here's a trick to get around it: add the line BOOTGUI = 0 to the [OPTIONS] section of **Msdos.sys**, and add WIN as the last line of your **Autoexec.bat**.

The result is that you'll automatically boot to the command-prompt, but *Windows95* will immediately load due to the Autoexec.bat line – you won't notice any difference from the normal boot. Just rename the logo files as in the previous tip, and you'll be returned to DOS on shutdown without having to make any sacrifices!

If you take this option, make sure you know how to use the Boot Menu's 'Step-by-step confirmation' option to override the 'win' line in case you ever need to boot to the command-prompt and stay there!

Troubleshooting

Help!

To get help from *Windows95*, select **Help** from the Start Menu, click on the **Find** tab and type **trouble** in the first box. In the box at the bottom you'll find topics regarding memory, hardware conflicts, disk-errors and more.

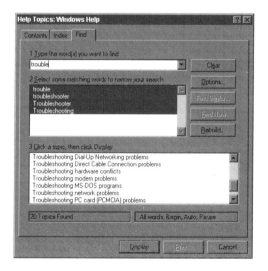

Screen 10.4 – **Type 'trouble' to see what Windows95 can offer in the way of support**

Tip

The Three-Finger Trick

If an application hangs, press *Ctrl* + *Alt* + *Del* and you'll see the **Close Program** dialog, containing a list of the currently running applications. Select the offending application from the task-list and click on **End Task** to get rid of it without having to restart the whole system. (Be patient at this point: *Windows95* sometimes has to grapple with the app for a while before it can show you a confirmation dialog.)

The task-list itself can be a useful tool at any time to find out what accessories and utilities are running in the background that don't appear on the Taskbar. If you're only accessing it for information, however, make sure you close the dialog by pressing **Cancel**.

Pressing *Ctrl+Alt+Del* a second time while the **Close Program** dialog is on the screen will restart the computer. This should be regarded as a last resort in the unlikely event that you lose all control over *Windows95* and can't access **Shut Down** on the Start Menu to quit safely.

Safe Shutdown

Using the *Ctrl+Alt+Del* combination a second time to restart the computer (i.e., while the **Close Program** dialog is on the screen) should always be regarded as a desperation-option. Try one of the following first to avoid taking unnecessary risks:

❑ Click on the **Shut Down** button in the **Close Program** dialog: this shuts down the computer in the same orderly manner as the Start Menu's **Shut Down** command.

❑ If you still have mouse-control, try to access **Shut Down** from the Start Menu.

❑ If you don't, try *Ctrl+Esc, U, Return* or *Alt+F4, Return.*

Safe Mode

If you make some ill-advised change to the system that results in *Windows95* not starting or not running correctly, reboot the computer in **Safe Mode** by pressing *F5* as soon as you see the **Starting Windows95...** message on the screen. This will present a slightly unusual-looking *Windows95* Desktop in 16-colour low-resolution, and will disable a few features, but it does allow you to put right your mistake and then reboot normally.

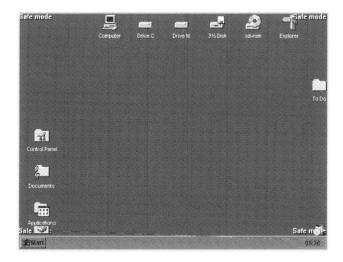

Screen 10.5 – **The reassuring sight of Safe Mode**

You can also select **Safe Mode** from a menu of other options by instead pressing *F8* when you see the **Starting Windows95...** message.

See 'Forcing Safe Mode' on page 226 for more details and possible problems with launching Windows in Safe Mode.

Boot Menu Troubleshooting

The boot-menu that appears when you press *F8* at the **Starting Windows95...** message offers a couple of extra troubleshooting options. Use the **Logged** option to create a file called **Bootlog.txt** in your root-folder detailing all the actions taking place during bootup. Using **step-by-step confirmation** mode, you can choose to have Windows ignore some or all entries in your system files if you believe one of these to be causing a problem.

Blank Screen?

If you make the common experimental mistake of installing a non-compatible display-type that leaves you with a blank screen after rebooting, don't panic! When the screen goes blank instead of displaying the *Windows95* Desktop, don't just turn off the computer – this could cause you many more problems.

When the hard-disk stops working and *Windows95* has finished loading, just press *Alt + F4* to (invisibly) bring up the **Shut Down** dialog and then hit *Return*. Give Windows about 30 seconds to go through its usual shut-down procedure (still invisibly) and *then* press your computer's 'warm restart' button and boot to **Safe Mode** following the instructions on the previous page.

A Missing Explorer?

It shouldn't be possible for *Windows95* to run without its shell application (which, unless you've changed it, is Explorer.exe) but, as they say, stuff happens. In some unfortunate circumstances, Explorer can apparently shut down leaving you with an empty, but still wallpaper-covered screen.

If this happens to you, don't reach for the computer's warm-restart button. Just press *Ctrl + Esc*. If Explorer's still lurking in the background, you'll get the Start Menu and the chance to restart safely. If Explorer really is in a deep sulk, you'll get **Taskman** instead – this is better still! Go to **File / Run Application** on Taskman's menu, type **explorer** and hit *Return*. Explorer will reappear, giving you the chance to save open files, close applications, and perhaps do a bit of troubleshooting before you go to the Shutdown dialog.

Tip

'Broken' System Files

Windows95 can be very sensitive about the treatment of its system files: changing or removing the file-extension can sometimes cause Windows to lose track of it entirely. You can see it, highlight it, and select its **Properties** page but you can't alter, delete or rename it – *Windows95* suddenly believes it doesn't exist.

If you find yourself in this situation, MS-DOS is the answer. Open a DOS-prompt window, switch to the correct folder and type **dir /w** to view the folder's contents. You should now be able to see the file displayed with its current name and use the **ren** command to rename it.

For example, if **Msdos.sys** had accidentally been renamed to just **Msdos.s**, and Windows wouldn't let you do anything about it, go to the command-prompt and type:

    ren msdos.s msdos.sys

Tweaking

Driver Error

If you're using a Windows-only system, *Windows95* will have replaced all (or most) of your drivers with the new 32-bit drivers. Any old 16-bit drivers in your system files are the slow link in the chain; if you remove all references to them, when Windows starts and carries out its usual search for any device without a driver, it should find these devices and try to load the correct 32-bit drivers for them.

All driver data is now kept in the Registry so drivers and TSRs loaded via Config.sys or Autoexec.bat will be either the old 16-bit ones or unnecessary references to the new ones, unless you have unusual hardware that *Windows95* doesn't provide drivers for. Take a look at the 'Adding Hardware' section beginning on page 236 for details of installing and replacing drivers, and configuring resource settings.

For more on the question of 16-bit vs. 32-bit drivers, see 'Check Your Bits' on page 235.

Tidy Your System Files

If you upgraded from *Windows 3.x*, your system files (**Autoexec.bat** and **Config.sys** in the root folder of your boot-drive) probably contain plenty of unnecessary entries, and may even be reducing your system's performance. Ideally, you should be able to delete **Config.sys** and have nothing in **Autoexec.bat** except environment variables (PATH= lines).

Before doing anything to them, create backups of the files to a floppy-disk. (Make sure you read the 'Changing CD-ROM Drivers' tip on page 280 too!)

Next, run **System Editor** and select **Config.sys**. Type **rem** followed by a space at the beginning of each line, select **File / Save**, and close System Editor. ('Unnecessaries' (see below) lists the entries you can remove in complete safety, but don't limit yourself to these.)

Now select **Start / Shut Down** and press *R* followed by *Return* (don't just restart *Windows95* – the computer must reboot). If you've remarked-out any device drivers, *Windows95* should detect the devices and try to load updated 32-bit drivers for them, in which case you may be prompted to insert your *Windows95* installation disks.

If any of your older devices fail to function after doing this, (perhaps because Windows couldn't identify the hardware, or due to a resource conflict) read 'You Bought A What?' on page 238 to try installing one of the generic drivers. If this doesn't work, remove the REM from the device's Config.sys line and restart your computer to get the hardware working again, and contact the device's manufacturer for a 32-bit driver.

System Configuration Editor

File   Edit   Search   Window

C:\AUTOEXEC.BAT

@ECHO OFF
SET PATH=C:\QTW\BIN;C:\WINDOWS;C:\WINDOWS\COMMAND;C:\DOS
SET SO
SET BLA
SET MID
C:\SB16
C:\SB16
C:\SB16

C:\CONFIG.SYS

rem DEVICE=C:\WINDOWS\HIMEM.SYS
rem DEVICE=C:\WINDOWS\EMM386.EXE RAM HIGHSCAN AUTO
REM BUFFERS=30,0
REM FILES=40
REM DOS=UMB
REM LASTDRIVE=Z
REM FCBS=4,0
REM DEVICE=C:\WINDOWS\SETVER.EXE
DEVICEHIGH /L:1,24336 =C:\CDROM\CD12J27.SYS /N:1 /D:NEC_CD
REM DOS=HIGH
rem DEVICE=C:\WINDOWS\COMMAND\DRVSPACE.SYS /MOVE
rem DEVICEHIGH /L:1,17184 =C:\WINDOWS\COMMAND\DISPLAY.SY
rem Country=044,850,C:\WINDOWS\COMMAND\country.sys

C:\WINDOW...   C:\WINDOW...   C:\WINDOW...   C:\WINDOW...

Screen 10.6 – **A Config.sys angling for deletion**

Edit your **Autoexec.bat** file in a similar way, but you don't want to delete it – just REM out everything but the PATH= statements. These are still needed since *Windows95* doesn't include its own support for PATH=.

Changing CD-ROM Drivers

If you remove your old CD-ROM driver's entry from **Config.sys**, Windows will find the hardware next time you boot up and will try to install its own driver. To do this, it needs the original installation disk, so if you installed *Windows95* from CD-ROM you're in a catch-22 situation.

To pre-empt the problem, use the **Add New Hardware** wizard in Control Panel to install the *Windows95* driver for your CD-ROM *before* removing its line from **Config.sys**. (See the 'Adding Hardware' section starting on page 236 for details on installing or replacing drivers, and configuring hardware.)

Unnecessaries

Apart from the question of drivers, a collection of other entries included in *Windows 3.x* system files are now handled by *Windows95* without assistance. The following lines and references should be removed (or remarked-out) unless you need to set different values than these defaults for any of them:

  FILES = 60
  BUFFERS = 30
  FCBS = 4
  STACKS = 9,256
  LASTDRIVE = Z
  DOS = HIGH,UMB

```
SETVER
HIMEM.SYS
SMARTDRV
DRVSPACE
SHARE
IFSHELP.SYS
PROMPT = $P$G
SET TEMP = C:\WINDOWS\TEMP
WIN
```

For example, if you prefer your Temporary folder to be C:\Temp you'll need to leave a line in Autoexec.bat that reads SET TEMP = C:\TEMP.

Customizing

Turn Off NumLock

By default, Windows loads with the *NumLock* key on. If you'd prefer it were turned off, just add the line NUMLOCK = OFF to your **Config.sys** file. (If you've deleted your Config.sys file but would like to use this option, create a new one: start a text-editor such as **Notepad**, type the line, and save the file as C:\Config.sys.)

Override The Startup Logo

If you'd like a break from seeing the *Windows95* logo during startup, press *Esc* once when you see the **Starting Windows95...** message appear.

For a permanent farewell to the logo, see 'Lose The Startup Logo' on page 270.

Logo No-go?

Had enough of the dry logo-screens *Windows95* displays on startup and shutdown? Why not liven them up a bit?

Windows95 uses three separate screens: the startup logo (clouds), the shutdown logo ('Please wait while your computer shuts down'), and the ever-popular 'It's now safe to turn off your computer'.

These logos are saved in the files **Logo.sys, Logow.sys** and **Logos.sys** respectively, the first in your root folder (C:\) and the others in your Windows folder. (Don't be put off by the **.sys** extension – these are just ordinary 256-colour bitmap files.)

First, make backups of any of the files you want to edit and place them in a separate folder together in case you want to revert to them. Now choose a file to change, hold *Shift* and right-click it. Select **Open With**, choose **Mspaint** from the list and click **OK**.

When **Paint** starts with the file open for you to edit, press *Ctrl + W* to reach the Stretch/Skew dialog and stretch horizontally by 167%: this is a temporary manoeuvre to make the image's aspect ratio easier to work with. Click **OK** and start editing!

When you've finished, go back to Stretch/Skew and stretch horizontally by 60% (actually reducing the width of the image). Next, press *Ctrl + E* to open the Image Attributes page, set the **Units** of measurement to **pels** and change the **Width** setting to 320 (the image must be exactly 320 × 400). Select **File/Save**.

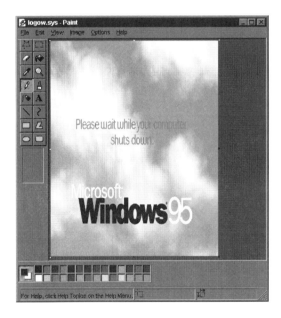

Screen 10.7 – **Logow.sys in Paint before ratio-adjustment**

(i) Logo.sys is an animated bitmap file: if you edit it in an ordinary graphics-editor like **Paint** (or use a different graphic in its place), the animation effect will be lost. This is purely an aesthetic addition -you may feel it's a sacrifice worth making.

(ii) If your hard-disk is compressed, the active Logo.sys file will be located on your computer's *host* drive.

Logo Nova

Because the three logo screens are simply 256-colour bitmap files, you can create your own from scratch. (Once again, be sure to make backups of the originals in a different folder before overwriting them.)

The only constraint upon you is that the images must be exactly 320 × 400: this is an unusual aspect ratio to be working in for a rectangular screen and makes it hard to be sure what your finished result will look like, so use the better working size of 534 × 400 until the design is ready to save. Run **Paint** and press *Ctrl + E* to reach Image Attributes. Set the Units to **pels**, set the Width to **534** and the height to **400** and click **OK**. Now get creative!

When you've finished, press *Ctrl + W* to bring up the Stretch/Skew dialog and stretch the image horizontally by 60% (reducing its width). Then, to fine tune the size exactly, hit *Ctrl + E* again and in the width box type **320**.

Now save the file to the path and filename you want to replace, such as C:\Windows\Logow.sys. (Make sure you type the **.sys** extension: without it, **Paint** will save with the default **.bmp** extension.)

New Light Through Old Windows

If you're missing those old *3.x* days, remind yourself what it was really like – use **Program Manager** as your shell again! Use **System Editor** to find **System.ini** and locate the line in the [BOOT] section that reads SHELL = EXPLORER.EXE. Change this to read SHELL = PROGMAN.EXE, save the file and restart Windows.

A popular hack with *Win3.x* was to use **File Manager** as the shell; this one still works as well – type SHELL = WINFILE.EXE instead.

Want the best of both worlds? Create a 'Fake Program Manager' (see page 314).

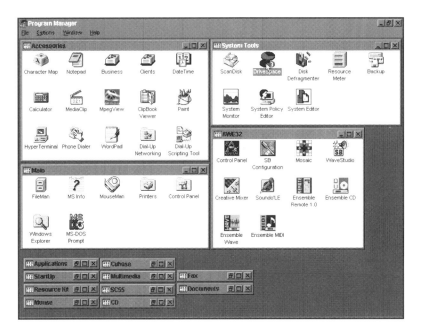

Screen 10.2 – **'It's program Jim, but not as we know it'**

Forgotten your screensaver password at the wrong moment?

❏ **ScreenSaver Insecurities** – page 177

Making a system disk

❏ **Emergency Startup Disk** – page 249

Making backups of vital system files

❏ **Keep System Backups** – page 250

Suggestions and troubleshooting for the StartUp folder

❏ 'THE STARTUP FOLDER' – page 21

11

MS-DOS & Games

Commands

Useful DOS Commands

If you're new to MS-DOS, it can be hard to locate the basic commands. Here's a few to get you started:

❑ Type **/?** after a command to get specific help on it (e.g., **dir /?**). For lengthy instructions type **/? |more** to view the details in window-sized chunks.

❑ Type **edit** to open the text-editor, or **edit myfile.txt** to edit a particular file

❑ To move up to the parent folder, type **cd..**

❑ To move up two levels, type **cd...** or three levels **cd....**

❑ To move down one level, type **cd myfolder**

❑ To view the contents of the current folder type **dir**

❑ To view the contents a screen at a time (for large folders) type **dir /p**

❑ To view titles only (wide-screen), type **dir /w**

❑ To view all files (including hidden files), type **dir /a**. These switches are additive – you can type **dir /w /p /a**.

❑ To view only files with a **.txt** extension in the folder specified by the command-prompt, type **dir *.txt**.

❑ To change to a particular folder, type **cd** followed by a space and the full path to the folder. If the folder in question uses *Windows95* long filenames (such as C:\Program Files), enclose the full path in quotes.

❑ To run a DOS program (**.exe** or **.bat**), type the program's name (preceded by the full path if necessary).

❑ To close a DOS-prompt window and return to *Windows95*, type **exit**.

❏ To run *Windows95* from MS-DOS, type **win**.

❏ To open an Explorer window for the current folder, type **start .**

❏ To open an Explorer window for the parent folder, type **start ..**

❏ To open an Explorer window for the root folder of the drive shown by the prompt, type **start **

❏ To open an Explorer window for another drive (such as your floppy-disk drive), type **start A:**

❏ Remember the distinction: **C:** is a drive; **C:** is a folder.

The following tips cover some of the other useful DOS commands, with examples of the types of operation you'll probably want to use most often. Almost all of these commands have further parameters and switches not included here – to find out what's available, type the command name (or its abbreviation) followed by **/?**.

Attrib

The 'attrib' command is used to set the assignment of attributes to files; **r** for read-only, **h** for hidden, and **s** for system, with + and – signs to set or remove them.

❏ To show a file's attributes, type **attrib myfile.txt**.

❏ To remove read-only & hidden attributes, type **attrib -r -h myfile.txt**.

❏ To make a file read-only, type **attrib +r myfile.txt**.

Mkdir

The command for 'Make Directory' (or 'create a new folder' in *Windows95* language). If you want to create a folder with a long name, remember to use the infamous quotes (").

md c:\windows\myfolder or **md "c:\windows\My New Folder"**

Rmdir

The 'Remove Directory' command, to delete an empty folder. (To delete a folder and its contents, use the **deltree** command below.)

rd c:\windows\myfolder or **rd "c:\windows\My New Folder"**

Deltree

To delete a folder and all its contents, including subfolders and their contents. The 'deltree' command will also delete read-only, hidden, and system files – in other words, it ignores attributes and just gets on with the job.

deltree c:\windows\myfolder or **deltree** "**c:\windows\My New Folder**"

Delete

The file-delete command. Remember that files deleted in MS-DOS are gone for good – they're not whisked away to the Recycle Bin!

del c:\myfolder\myfile.txt

Move

As you'd expect, this command moves a file or folder from one location to another. A handy extra is in its ability to rename it at the same time, or even to leave it where it is and rename it (the same result as using **ren**).

❑ To move c:\myfolder to c:\windows\myfolder, type **move c:\myfolder c:\windows\myfolder**

❑ To rename myfolder to His Folder, type **move c:\myfolder** "**c:\His Folder**"

❑ To do both in one operation, type **move c:\myfolder** "**c:\windows\His Folder**"

Copy

Another obvious one, although this command is used only to copy files. In a similar way to 'Move', you can specify a different name for the copy.

❑ To copy c:\myfile.txt to c:\windows\myfile.txt, type **copy c:\myfile.txt c:\windows\myfile.txt**

❑ To copy the file to C:\Windows but with a different name, type **copy c:\myfile.txt c:\windows\hisfile.txt**

Xcopy

The 'xcopy' command is the copy command for folders. The **/e** switch forces folders to be copied even if they're empty; the **/k** ensures that a file's attributes are copied too. To copy a folder, its contents and subfolders to a floppy-disk using these switches, type

> xcopy c:\windows\myfolder a:\myfolder /e /k

You can also use **xcopy** to copy floppy disks. If you have one floppy drive (**A:**), type **xcopy a: a: /e /k**. If you have two floppy drives (**A:** and **B:**) and you want to copy the disk in **A:**, type **xcopy a: b: /e /k**.

The **xcopy** command using the **/k** switch doesn't correctly assign folder-attributes such as Hidden or Read-only to the copied folder, only to the files it contains. You'll need to use Explorer to assign these attributes yourself.

Rename

The simple command for renaming files. (To rename a folder, use the 'move' command.) Assuming you're already in the folder containing the file to be renamed (indicated by the command-prompt), just type

> ren myfile.txt hisfile.txt

One massively useful benefit of **ren** is in the use of wildcards: changing a file's extension in Windows is a painful process, and changing a collection of files with **.txt** extensions to **.doc** is only slightly more fun than being electrocuted. But in DOS it's easy. Assuming once again you're in the folder containing all the **.txt** files, just type the following to change all the extensions:

> ren *.txt *.doc

Tree

Displays a graphic depiction of folder tree-structure, rooted to the folder you specify (long filenames and quotes not supported). For example, to show the tree structure of your Program Files folder, type

> tree c:\progra ~ 1

To view longer tree-structures, such as your Windows folder, add a space and the |**more** switch to the command. To view files as well, add **/f** |**more**.

Expand

A lot of the major software you install (apart from recent Microsoft applications) is distributed in a particular compression format characterized by the files on the disks having two-letter extensions followed by a _ sign, such as **progman.ex_**. Provided you know what this missing letter should be, **Expand** lets you grab single files from these disks and decompress them ready for use.

And it's easy – type **expand** at the prompt, and you'll be asked which file you want to decompress. Type its full path, such as **a:\progman.ex_** and press *Enter*. You'll then be prompted for a destination path and name: type something like **c:\temp\progman.exe** and it's all over.

Quickies

A few short, useful or amusing commands to have at the ready:

❑ **cls**   clears the screen, leaving just the command prompt.

❑ **time**   displays the current time, together with a prompt to change it. Press *Enter* if no change is needed.

❑ **prompt**   changes the command-prompt. Typing **prompt** by itself reverts to the default **c >**. Type **prompt td** to show current time and date. The usual prompt (displaying current folder) is **prompt pg**.

❑ **|more**   with any command that results in output that won't fit on the screen, add a space and **|more** to the end of the command to force the information to be displayed one screen at a time.

Missing?

If you didn't upgrade to *Windows95* from *Windows3.x* and its requisite DOS you'll be missing some of the commands mentioned above, but you can find the required files on the *Windows95* CD-ROM in the **Other\Oldmsdos** folder. Just copy what you want into C:\Windows\Command.

If you ever do anything in DOS at all, make sure you copy the two files named **Help**. These are DOS 6.22 versions and so a little out of date, but still extremely useful. To access the help file in DOS, just type **help** and *Enter*. Either click on a command to see its entry, or reach it by typing the command's initial letters or using the arrow-keys and pressing *Enter*.

Alternative Format

If right-clicking on your floppy-drive's icon and choosing Format isn't to your taste, create a shortcut on the Desktop to do the job in a DOS-window.

❙ Right-click on the Desktop and choose **New** and **Shortcut**. On the command-line type:

   format a: /f:720 or **format a: /f:1.44**

where **a:** is your floppy-drive and **720** or **1.44** refer to a double-density and high-density disk respectively. (To specify a Quick Format, for previously used disks, add a space and **/q** to the end of either command.)

2   In the next dialog, type a name for the shortcut and choose an icon.

3   Finally, right-click on the new shortcut, choose **Properties** and the **Program** tab, check the **Close on exit** box, and select **Minimized** from the 'Run' box. If you want a different icon, click **Change Icon**.

For details of the other switches available, open a DOS window and type **format** **/?** and press *Enter*. You can of course just type the command given in step 1 at the command-prompt if you're in the middle of a DOS-session and don't want to go back to Windows just to format a disk.

Alternative Disk Copy

In the same way as Format, you can create a Copy Disk shortcut: on the shortcut command-line, type:

  diskcopy a: a:

where the first **a:** is the source-drive and the second the destination-drive, and follow the same steps 2 & 3 above.

Type **diskcopy /?** at the command-prompt for details of the additional switches.

MS-DOS Prompt Tips

Run DOS In Windows

Lurking beneath *Windows95* is MS-DOS 7.0. It comes in various shapes and forms, but if nothing else, it's younger and prettier than its ancestors. As in previous incarnations of Windows, you can still boot to the MS-DOS prompt to run a 'real' DOS-session by means of the Boot Menu (covered in the previous chapter), but a huge leap forward in DOS/Windows integration is the addition of MS-DOS mode and the DOS-prompt window.

MS-DOS is still, however, a 16-bit operating system – running a MS-DOS mode session in which you need to use your mouse or CD-ROM drive requires that you load the old real-mode drivers into conventional or upper memory, leaving less breathing space for the program. Running DOS under Windows (whether in a window or full-screen) retains full 32-bit functionality, using the same protected-mode *Windows95* drivers already loaded into your several megabytes of extended memory, thus releasing a good deal more conventional memory for the DOS-programs you want to run.

MS-DOS Mode Options

MS-DOS mode provides a halfway-point between 'real DOS' and 'Windows DOS' – it's still the old real-mode operating system, but has the two additional features of being able to be switched into from Windows almost instantaneously (either from a shortcut to a DOS program or from the Shut Down menu), and to specify different configurations for individual programs. Sadly, these two features are mutually exclusive.

❏ The default method processes a batch file in your Windows folder called **Dosstart.bat** containing calls to 16-bit drivers originally in your Autoexec.bat and replaced by updated versions when *Windows95* was installed. This file should include a mouse driver and a reference to **Mscdex.exe** for CD-ROM functionality; your CD-ROM will only function in MS-DOS mode if you've left the reference to its real-mode driver in your Config.sys (or you add it to a custom Config.sys, using the second method). When you're ready to leave MS-DOS mode and return to Windows, type **exit**.

❏ The second method lets you add your own choice of commands to Autoexec.bat and Config.sys files specific to the program you want to run. Since this replaces the default configuration, the computer needs to reboot into this form of MS-DOS mode. (See 'Customize Your DOS Sessions' on page 298.)

Where's The PIF Editor?

Ex-*Windows3.x* users will probably remember PIF Editor. In fact, they'll probably *always* remember PIF Editor. Another advance in Windows/DOS integration has seen the automatic creation of PIFs (Program Information Files) coupled with far easier configuration of DOS programs, making a dedicated PIF editor pleasantly unnecessary.

When you first run a DOS program a PIF is created in the same folder; this takes the name of the program with a **.pif** extension and the colourful MS-DOS icon. Right-clicking this file and choosing **Properties** allows you to make all the settings you need for the program on a straightforward set of tabbed pages (see the 'Fun & Games' section on page 298). Clicking **Properties** on the executable's context-menu will similarly create a **.pif** (or edit the existing one) if you make any changes and click **OK** to close. (You can even edit the configuration while the program is running in a window – just click the **Properties** button on the toolbar.)

The **.pif** file is now the DOS equivalent of a *Windows95* shortcut: you can make copies of these files anywhere you want to, and launch the corresponding program with a double-click. Alternatively, you can create a shortcut to a DOS program using any of the methods you'd use for a Windows program.

Long Filenames In DOS

Even when working in DOS you can usually use the standard *Windows95* long filenames, such as C:\Program Files instead of C:\Progra ~ 1, but they (and the whole path if specified) must be enclosed in quotes (*"***C:\Program Files***"*).

Don't Quote Me

Annoying things, those quotes. Particularly since, if you forget them, you have to retype the whole path again. There's no real escape from the leading-quote, but for almost everything you do at the DOS command-prompt, you *can* leave out the closing quote-mark. (That goes for the *Windows95* **Run** command too !)

Missing Quotes?

If your *Shift + 2* quote-mark turns into something else when you open a DOS-box, leaving you unable to use long filenames, try typing **keyb uk** and *Enter* and trying it again. If that doesn't work, type

   keyb uk,, c:\windows\command\keyboard.sys

(note the double comma). Whichever of these does the trick, type the same thing into Notepad, save it as C:\Quotes.bat and go to your MS-DOS Prompt shortcut's **Properties / Program** page. In the box labelled 'Batch file', type **C:\Quotes.bat** to have this run automatically every time you open a DOS-box.

Copy & Paste In DOS

You can copy and paste text and graphics in a DOS window or application, and even paste the selections into a Windows program. Click the **Mark** button and select an area of the screen with the pointer, then click the **Copy** button to copy it to the clipboard.

To paste the selection in Windows, run the target application and press *Ctrl + V* or select **Paste** from the **Edit** menu.

You can use the same method to copy to the DOS-window itself: selecting paste in the DOS-box will place the copied selection at the cursor position. This can be a real typing-saver if you want to re-run an earlier command.

Hasty Pasting

Although pasting selections into DOS that you copied in Windows is a perfectly normal and civilized thing to do, DOS sometimes doesn't think so. In particular, the combination of older DOS apps and large amounts of data can cause selections to be pasted incorrectly. To solve the problem, click the **Properties** button on the toolbar, go to the **Misc** tab, and clear the checkbox beside **Fast Pasting**.

QuickEdit

While the method above makes it possible to copy from DOS, it's not as fast or intuitive as the Windows 'button-free' method of simply swiping the pointer across the object to be selected. But, once again, there's a solution...

Click the **Properties** button on the Toolbar (or right-click your MS-DOS Prompt shortcut and choose **Properties**) and select the **Misc** tab. Check the **QuickEdit** box and click **OK**. You can now select any object at any time without first clicking the **Mark** button.

In **QuickEdit** mode, the mouse will constantly act as a selection-tool. To use the mouse as a 'point-and-click' device in DOS (for example, when clicking the hot-links in MS-DOS Help), you'll first need to disable **QuickEdit**.

Run Windows Apps From DOS

You can start a Windows application from within a DOS-box by just typing the path (if required) and filename. For example, try typing **notepad** at the command-prompt.

Screen 11.1 – **Program launching the DOS way**

You can even add switches to the command to specify that the application runs maximized or minimized by prefixing the command with **start**, and select a file to be opened with the application. For on-screen details, just type **start** at the command-prompt. (See Screen 11.1 for these details and a few example commands.)

StartUp Control

When you place shortcuts in your StartUp folder they're run automatically as *Windows95* finishes loading, but there's no way to specify the order in which this happens. If you need your StartUp entries run in a particular sequence, the solution lies in the MS-DOS batch-program: use **Notepad** to create a file named something like Startup.bat containing the command-line for each entry on a separate line in the order you want them run. Here's an example:

```
@echo off
start /m explorer /n, /e, /select, c:\
c:\windows\dialer.exe
echo y | del c:\windows\recent\*.*
"c:\program files\accessories\wordpad.exe" "e:\things to do.txt"
cls
```

(The final **cls** entry in a batch-file closes the prompt-window when the program has finished.) Create a shortcut to Startup.bat in your StartUp folder to replace its current contents, and set it to run minimized in its **Properties / Run** box.

Custom StartUp

From the basis of the previous tip, you can use a batch-file to let you pick and choose which programs and documents you want to run at startup. Create the Startup.bat file as above, but remove the **@echo off** line, and replace **cls** with **exit**. Save the file to your Windows folder.

Now open **Notepad** and type:

```
@echo on
command /y /k c:\windows\startup.bat
cls
```

Save this file somewhere convenient with a **.bat** extension and create a shortcut to it in your StartUp folder. On startup, the prompt window will open and offer to run Startup.bat. Press *Y* for Yes, and choose which programs to run as they're presented. When you reach the **exit** command, type *Y* to close the prompt-window or *N* to keep it open.

Pathed Out?

If you've had enough of typing long paths at the DOS-prompt, do it the easy way: drag a file or folder into a DOS-window and its full path will be entered at the current cursor position.

DOS App Variables

If your DOS application needs different settings each time you run it, you can still create a shortcut to it and force it to prompt you for the required parameters when it runs.

Right-click on the program's icon (or its shortcut icon) and choose **Properties / Program**. In the **Cmd line** box, click once to the right of the entry to clear the highlight and add a space and a question-mark (**?**) to the end of the path.

Open In A DOS Window

If you want to open a particular folder in an MS-DOS window, the quickest way to do it is to add the option to your context-menu:

I	Go to **My Computer / View / Options / File Types**.
2	Select the **Folder** entry in the list and click **Edit**.
3	Click on **New** to add a new Action.
4	In the resulting dialog, type **O&pen DOS Window** in the 'Action' box, and **C:\Windows\Dosprmpt.pif** in the 'Application used to perform action' box. (The ampersand allows the hotkey 'p' to be used for this action instead of a mouse-click.)
5	Click on **OK**, and on **Close** twice to finalize.

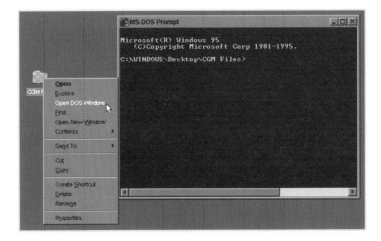

Screen 11.2 – **Ready for work in DOS at a single click**

Now when you right-click a folder or drive-icon on the Desktop or in either pane of a dual-pane window, you can choose the **Open DOS Window** option to start a DOS session in this folder rather than the default C:\Windows. (If you select this option from a single-pane window, however, the *parent* of the folder you clicked will open.)

Double Dose Of DOS

If you're running an application in a DOS window and need to access a different DOS app, click on the **Background** button on the DOS box's toolbar. With this button depressed, you can now open a second (or third, or fourth...) DOS box and use it independently while the first application continues running.

Window Dressing

By clicking the **Font** button on the Toolbar, you can customize the size, shape and font-size for your DOS-window: the preview screens show what the result will look like, with the font shown at actual size and the window-preview reflecting the actual position of the DOS-box on your screen.

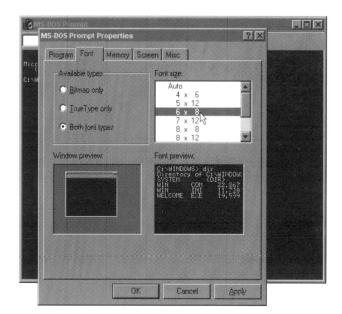

Screen 11.3 – **Setting DOS-window preferences**

Each window is treated independently, so if you have two or more DOS-prompt windows open you can use different settings for each.

Where's My Toolbar?

If your DOS-box's Toolbar seems to have taken a hike, just right-click on the title-bar to access all the options (including the Toolbar) from the control-menu.

Where's Windows?

Switching DOS from a window to full-screen is easy: there's a tempting little box full of arrows begging to be clicked. Once you've clicked it, and Windows has vanished behind a black screen taking the toolbar with it, it isn't obvious how to get back again.

The secret is *Alt + Return* – this key-combination toggles back and forth between the two.

DOS Is A Task

In many ways, Windows DOS is a task like any other application that might be running. And in the same way, you can use the *Alt + Tab* key combination to switch between even full-screen DOS and your other apps and windows.

Using MS-DOS Mode

Sometimes a DOS application isn't happy running in a window, usually for reasons of compatibility or an avaricious attitude to system resources. The next best solution is **MS-DOS Mode**: find the application's executable file in Explorer (it should have a **.bat** or **.exe** extension), right-click it and select **Properties / Program / Advanced**. Check the box beside **MS-DOS mode** and click on **OK** twice to finalize.

When you run the DOS program, *Windows95* will close any open windows and running applications and launch the DOS program in real-mode DOS. When you've finished using the program, type **exit** at the command prompt and you'll be automatically returned to Windows.

Customize Your DOS Sessions

You can set your own preferences for DOS sessions by adding your own commands to the **.pif** file that kicks in when you choose 'Restart the computer in MS-DOS mode' from the Shut Down dialog.

Look in your Windows folder for **Exit To DOS.pif**, right-click on it and choose **Properties / Program**. Click the **Advanced** button and check the box marked 'Specify a new MS-DOS configuration'. In the boxes below, you can now enter your own choice of Autoexec.bat and Config.sys settings and commands.

 Whether you create a custom configuration or use the current one, add a copy of **Exit To DOS.pif** to your Desktop or Start Menu: you can then move into MS-DOS mode with a quick click instead of using the **Shut Down** menu.

For more on the custom-configuration settings, turn to page 301.

Fun & Games

A New Game

GUI-based operating systems are memory-hungry beasts, and *Windows95* has a particularly voracious appetite. For this reason, game producers still create games that run in MS-DOS in order to have maximum resources at their disposal. Of course, there are many non-game DOS programs out there still being used (and the tips in this section apply equally to them) but for the most part these will run in a DOS-window with consummate ease. Games, on the other hand, often come with a frightening looking list of memory-demands in their manuals, all couched in acronyms, which often take varying degrees of experimentation, inspiration, and pure luck to set up correctly.

Getting a game to work might, on occasion, be a struggle, but the good news from *Windows95* is that once you've managed to fix the settings you need they can be retained for the next time you play, and you shouldn't have the worry of whether your other games will still run after all that tweaking!

Since a collection of variables is involved, there can be no concrete solutions given here: the appropriate settings will depend on the game, your installed hardware and drivers, and your available memory. For this reason, it's best to approach this section with a particular game in mind and a list of its requirements in front of you; so let's assume you've just become the proud owner of a shiny new game...

Will It, Won't It?

After carrying out any installation of the game-software that may be necessary, look in Explorer for the file used to start the game (with a **.exe** or perhaps a **.bat** extension) and create a shortcut to it somewhere accessible. Right-click the shortcut's icon and choose **Properties**. On the **Program** tab check the 'Close on exit' box to ensure you'll be returned to Windows when you've finished playing; on the **Screen** tab click the 'Full Screen' radio button (most games won't run in a window). Provided you're not intending to run other applications in the background, clear the checkbox for 'Dynamic Memory Allocation' to help channel available resources to the game.

Now, the moment of truth – double-click the shortcut, and see what happens! If the game runs, you're done (though you may want to consider a few of the tips later in this chapter to see if you can make any useful modifications). If it doesn't run, it's probably time to read the instructions...

Hide Windows

The usual reason a game won't run is through lack of memory: if you had any Windows programs running when you tried the game, shut them down and try again – some Windows applications use a small amount of conventional memory which might make the difference.

Before tweaking memory-settings, let's try something else. Since most DOS games expect to have exclusive rights to system resources, just a sniff of *Windows95* can send them into a sulk. Go back to the **Properties / Program** tab and click the **Advanced** button. Check the box marked 'Prevent MS-DOS-based programs from detecting Windows', and make sure 'Suggest MS-DOS mode as necessary' is also checked. Click **OK**, and try running the game again.

Fixing Memory

If the previous tip didn't do the trick, it's time to look at the settings shown in the game's manual. Go back to **Properties** and click the **Memory** tab. There are three types of memory you're concerned with here: Conventional, Extended (XMS), and Expanded (EMS). By default these are all set to Auto allowing dynamic allocation of resources, but the great advantage of *Windows95* over its predecessors is that you can set the amount of each type of memory required for an individual program in these boxes.

Maximum conventional memory is 640k and specifying, for example, that you want 600k in the 'Conventional memory' box would have little effect if you don't have this much available. The primary method of gaining more free conventional memory is to remove unnecessary drivers from **Autoexec.bat** and **Config.sys** (see the 'Tweaking' section on page 278).

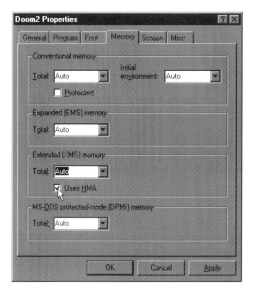

Screen 11.4 – **So many memories...**

Following the memory-requirements given in the game's manual, type the figures into the appropriate boxes for EMS and XMS as well. Clear the **Protected** checkbox under Conventional Memory to gain a little extra performance from the game. Click **OK** and run the program again – if it's going to run under *Windows95*, it's going to do it now!

 If you find your game crashes, taking *Windows95* down with it, go back to the **Memory** tab and check the **Protected** box again.

Memory Check

To find out how much Conventional and Extended (XMS) memory you have free, open a DOS-window and type **mem /c** and hit *Enter*. If you manage to find and remove some unnecessary TSRs and drivers from your system files, take a look at these results again after rebooting your computer, paying particular attention to 'Largest executable program size' – this is the amount of conventional memory you have available, and it's probably increased.

MS-DOS Mode

If you've run through the previous tips and your game is still resolutely refusing to run, it's time to try MS-DOS mode. Head back to the **Properties / Program** tab and click the **Advanced** button. Check the box marked **MS-DOS mode**, and ensure the **Warn before entering MS-DOS mode** box is checked too: the warning is usually worth having since this is a single-application mode so all currently running applications are shut down when you use it.

Now, by all means, click **OK** and try running the program – you might just avoid some more intimate dealings with memory-settings.

> Still no luck? You don't have to go back to Minesweeper just yet – *Windows95* has another trick up its sleeve that should do the job. Go back to **Properties / Program / Advanced** and click the radio-button marked **Specify a new MS-DOS configuration**. This lets you create custom Autoexec.bat and Config.sys settings for the program by typing them directly into the boxes below. The following four tips cover entries to include to maximize the three types of memory...

Conventional Memory

As previously mentioned, to gain the most free conventional memory you need to be sure you're not loading unnecessary drivers. For example, if your game doesn't run from CD-ROM, don't bother loading your CD-ROM driver. Similarly, if you can bear to run the game without sound, that's another chunk of memory kept available for the game itself.

Those items you do have to use should be loaded into upper memory (making sure you've included the EMM386.EXE statement covered in the next two tips).

❑ Programs should be loaded in Autoexec.bat, using the LOADHIGH (LH) command, e.g., LH C:\WINDOWS\MSCDEX.EXE /S /D:MSCD001 /M:10.

❏ Device drivers should be loaded in Config.sys using DEVICEHIGH (but make sure they're placed *after* the EMM386.EXE reference), for example DEVICEHIGH = C:\SB16\DRV\CTMMSYS.SYS.

Notice that the LOADHIGH (or LH) command is followed by a space rather than the = sign.

If you have a hard-disk compressed with DoubleSpace or DriveSpace, make sure you load the DriveSpace driver into upper memory with the Config.sys line DEVICEHIGH = C:\WINDOWS\COMMAND\DRVSPACE.SYS /MOVE.

Extended Memory & UMBs

Extended memory shouldn't be something you're short of, since it consists of your total installed RAM less (roughly) 1Mb. The point of this tip is to allow the use of UMBs (Upper Memory Blocks) to load real mode device-drivers and parts of DOS itself. When these are loaded into upper memory, they're releasing valuable space in conventional memory.

The reference to HIGH in the third line specifies that DOS is loaded into high-memory (HMA), saving another 40 + kilobytes of conventional memory.

As long as your program doesn't require Expanded Memory (EMS), place the following lines at the top of your custom Config.sys in this order:

```
DEVICE = C:\WINDOWS\HIMEM.SYS
DEVICE = C:\WINDOWS\EMM386.EXE NOEMS
DOS = HIGH,UMB
```

If this works as it is, fine. If not, replace NOEMS with FRAME = NONE at the end of the second line to add another 64K to your available UMBs. If you do this, start **System Editor**, find **System.ini** and also add the following line to the [386Enh] section:

```
NoEMMDriver = TRUE
```

Expanded Memory

The point of this tip is pretty much the same as the last: to make use of HMA and UMBs to free up as much conventional memory as possible. The difference is that the entries below sacrifice a little upper memory in order to provide Expanded memory (EMS). If your program needs EMS, place these lines at the beginning of Config.sys in this order:

```
DEVICE = C:\WINDOWS\HIMEM.SYS
DEVICE = C:\WINDOWS\EMM386.EXE RAM AUTO
DOS = HIGH,UMB
```

Another option is to specify a minimum setting for EMS by adding a space and MIN = ???, replacing the question-marks with the required figure. The default is 256k, so only use this addition if you need more. Extra experimentation may still be needed – you might have to raise the figure some way beyond the program's quoted requirements before it works.

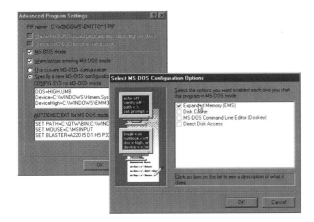

Screen 11.5 – **Let Windows insert your EMS configuration**

Auto Configuration

You can save yourself a bit of typing by clicking the **Configuration** button at the bottom of the **Advanced** page which launches the MS-DOS Mode Configuration Wizard. Checking the box labelled **Expanded Memory (EMS)** will insert the HIMEM.SYS, EMM386.EXE and DOS = lines automatically. (Sadly, you'll still have to specify your own device drivers though.)

To make the Wizard really earn his keep, grab a copy of the MS-DOS Mode Wizard Customizer (see page 332) and add all the drivers you need ready for one-click insertion.

One Last Option

If the previous tips for running the game from Windows in MS-DOS mode don't do the trick, try restarting the computer in MS-DOS mode from the **Shut Down** menu. To make sure the drivers you need are loaded, follow the previous tips for creating custom Autoexec.bat and Config.sys entries, but apply them instead to **Exit To Dos.pif** which you'll find in your Windows folder.

If this works, all well and good. Ideally, though, you may not want these same devices loaded every time you restart in MS-DOS mode – other games may not use them, so memory would be wasted – so **Exit To DOS.pif** isn't the best place to put them. Check out the next tip instead...

Custom Drivers?

If you have to restart in MS-DOS mode and need to use a mouse in the program you run, but you don't want to load the mouse driver every time you boot up, you could create a batch-file that loads the drivers you need and run it when you reach DOS. You could even create different batch-files that load different drivers and choose which **.bat** to run for individual games. The end result is practical, but the implementation is rather messy...

For the ultimate in choice, try the following. Create a batch-file in your Windows folder called **Dosgames.bat** containing all the devices you might ever want to load for any program, each on a separate line. Then create a second batch-file with the lines

```
echo on
command /y /k dosgames.bat
```

and save this to your Windows folder as **Dosmode.bat**. Go to the **Properties / Program** page for **Exit To DOS.pif** and type **Dosmode.bat** in the 'Batch file' box. (To do this, you'll have to first select 'Specify a new MS-DOS configuration' by clicking the **Advanced** button.)

Whenever you choose to restart in MS-DOS mode, you'll see a prompt asking if you want to run Dosgames.bat. Press *Enter*, and the program will step through each command in turn giving you the option to load or bypass each device by hitting *Enter* or *Esc* respectively.

DOS Drivers

If you install new hardware that you're going to need in MS-DOS sessions, don't forget to also install the DOS drivers that come with it or you might find the hardware isn't recognized when you run games and other DOS programs.

Memmaker

Another method of making more base memory available is to run **Memmaker**. Start the computer in MS-DOS mode and type **memmaker** at the command-prompt. (This is worth doing even if your games are running fine: you may still get a performance boost out of it.)

Memmaker reconfigures your Autoexec.bat and Config.sys to make maximum use of upper memory. This is the same as adding LH (LOADHIGH) to programs loaded in Autoexec.bat and changing all DEVICE= lines to DEVICEHIGH= in Config.sys. The dual benefits of using Memmaker are automation, and the chance to type **memmaker /undo** to revert to your previous settings at any time afterwards.

 If you don't have Memmaker on your system, you can find it on the *Windows95* CD-ROM in the **Other\Oldmsdos** folder. Copy the three Memmaker files to C:\Windows\Command.

Maximize Your DOS Memory

To make maximum memory available in DOS sessions, start **System Editor** and select **System.ini**. Find the section of the file headed [386Enh] and add LocalLoadHigh=1 on a new line.

Avoid Hotkey Conflicts

Some games use a variety of keyboard combinations for some of their functions which might conflict with combos used by Windows (such as *Ctrl + Esc*). Go to your game's **Properties** page, click the **Misc** tab, and take a look at the 'Windows shortcut keys' section: remove the checkmark from any of these that might be used in the game.

If in doubt, remove everything except *Alt + Tab* which can be useful to switch back to *Windows95* quickly if you need to.

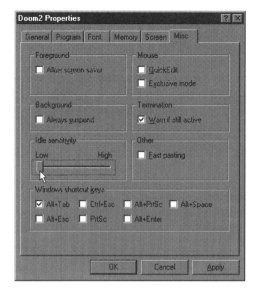

Screen 11.6 – **Cool it with the hotkeys**

Disable Windows ScreenSavers

If you're running a joystick-controlled DOS game under *Windows95*, make sure you disable your screensaver – most screensavers don't check for activity from the joystick-port, and might kick in while you're playing.

Go to the **Properties / Misc** tab, and clear the checkbox marked **Allow screen saver**.

Clear The Clips

If your DOS program won't run for lack of memory, take a look at the Clipboard/Clipbook: if the last thing you cut or copied was particularly large (perhaps a bitmap-image?) it could be filling enough memory to make the difference. Clear the Clipboard by hitting *Del* and clicking **Yes**, or by copying something small such as a single letter to replace it.

Idle Time

If your game doesn't seem to be performing as well as you'd hoped, open the **Properties / Misc** page and drag the **Idle sensitivity** slider to the left ('Low'). This ensures that maximum processor-time is allotted to the game rather than any other programs running in the background.

Tip

SCSI Compatibility

If you have an SCSI device installed on your system, you might need to enter the line DEVICE = SMARTDRV.EXE /DOUBLE—BUFFER in your Config.sys file before any DEVICEHIGH lines.

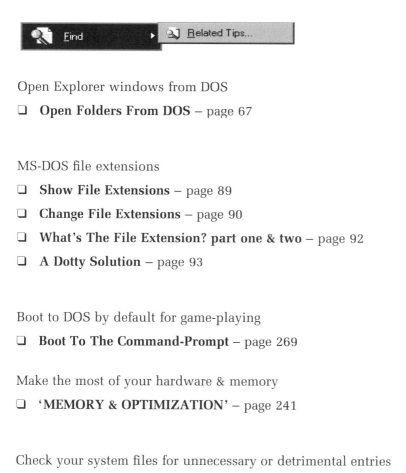

Open Explorer windows from DOS

❏ **Open Folders From DOS** – page 67

MS-DOS file extensions

❏ **Show File Extensions** – page 89

❏ **Change File Extensions** – page 90

❏ **What's The File Extension? part one & two** – page 92

❏ **A Dotty Solution** – page 93

Boot to DOS by default for game-playing

❏ **Boot To The Command-Prompt** – page 269

Make the most of your hardware & memory

❏ **'MEMORY & OPTIMIZATION'** – page 241

Check your system files for unnecessary or detrimental entries

❏ **'TWEAKING'** – page 278

12

Odds & Ends

A Good Start

Open the **Run** command-line applet and type **winver**. This unbelievably useful program will tell you which version of Windows you're running. Check the screen carefully: if it says **Windows95**, you're reading the right book.

Version Assertion

Once you've recovered your composure after typing 'winver' on the command-line, open a DOS-box and type **ver** (*Enter*). This little gem will give you the same information *plus* the build-number (final release being 950).

Desktop Mirror

Here's a cool trick using a few Windows features: mirror all your Desktop icons. Just arrange your icons to leave them well spread-out, and hit the *Print Screen* (or *Prt Sc*) key. Start **Paint** and press *Ctrl+V* to paste in the screen-grab. **Paint** will report that the image is too large, and offer to resize the bitmap – click **OK**.

Hit *Ctrl+R*, click the **Flip Vertical** radio-button and **OK**. Now save the file (anywhere you like, under any name) and select **Set As Wallpaper (Centred)** from the **File** menu. (Note that the image must be saved to disk before it can be set as wallpaper.) Exit **Paint**, and re-arrange your icons as shown in Screen 12.2 to form 'mirror-images'.

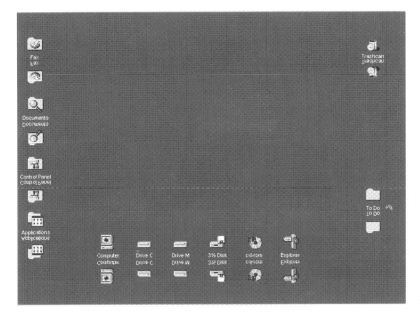

Screen 12.2 –
**Flipping fun
with Paint**

Registry
Tip

Logitech Logic

If you've got a Logitech 3-button mouse, you can opt to use a middle-button click to represent a double-click:

1   Open the Registry Editor.

2   Expand HKEY_CURRENT_USER, then **Software, Logitech, MouseWare**.

3   Expand the keys under **MouseWare** to reach the mouse-version you're using and you should see an item in the right pane named **DoubleClick**. Double-click on this item and change it's value-data from **000** to **001**.

4   Close Registry Editor and restart *Windows95* for this setting to take effect.

PIMs On The Rocks

To some, a Personal Information Manager is the only way to keep track of schedules, appointments, task and ideas. Others get a PIM, use it for a while, and gradually let it lapse: their lives aren't hectic enough to warrant loading the application and checking and updating its contents regularly. If this sounds like you, trash the PIM and try this tip, made possible by the combined wonders of long filenames, Desktop-folders and context-menus:

Right-click on the Desktop and select **New** and **Folder**. Name the folder something like **To Do**. Now open this folder, right click inside it and select **New** and **TXT File**. Name this file something meaningful like **Budget meeting Tuesday 10am** or **Feed the cat**. Create and delete these files as you need to.

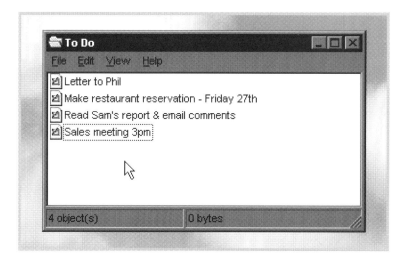

Screen 12.3 – **The DIY personal organizer**

If you want to add more details, just double-click on the icon and **Notepad** will open for you to do so. When you've saved the file again, add the word **READ** to the end of its name so you'll know there's more information available.

To create a priority list, either prefix each filename with a number (**01, 02** etc.) or use a code prefix: use *Shift+1, Shift+4 and Shift+7* (**!**, **$** and **&**) followed by a space to sort the list into a 3-level order of importance.

Make sure the folder-window is large enough to display long titles, and that you've selected **List** view (and **Sort by name** to create a prioritized list). If you find that the window is large enough, but the names are still being truncated, switch to **Details** view, move the mouse-pointer between the 'Name' and 'Size' buttons and drag to the right to enlarge the 'Name' field. When you switch back to **List** view the full message should now be visible.

Quick Messages

Use the 'New' context sub-menu to create quick reminder-notes on the Desktop (along similar lines to the 'sticky notes' accessories available): create the new file and type your message as the filename.

Custom Quick Messages

You could even create a new file-type with its own icon especially for the task. Go to **My Computer / View / Options / File Types** and create a new file-type called 'Desktop Message' with the extension **.mess** (since no other application is likely to use an extension like that!) and choose **Notepad** as the target application.

Now open the Registry Editor, expand **HKEY_CLASSES_ROOT** and find **.mess**. Right-click on **.mess** and choose **New** and **Key**. Name the new key **ShellNew**. Now right-click on **ShellNew** and select **New** and **String Value**. Name this new string **nullfile**. You can now create a new note on the Desktop by right-clicking and selecting 'Desktop Message' from the 'New' sub-menu.

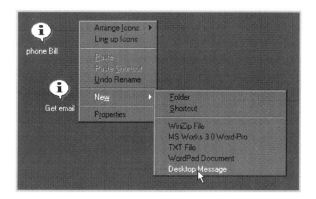

Screen 12.4 – **Reminder notes on the Desktop**

Snappy Tip Tactic

Remember **Welcome**, that cheery little applet that greeted you with a tip the first time you started *Windows95*? (Possibly the second time too, if you forgot to check the box to stop it happening again.) The applet itself lives in the Windows folder – you can start it up by typing **welcome** on the Run line – but its tips live in the Registry.

As tips go, they probably seem a bit tame by now, so why not replace them with new ones? Or make them educational: treat them as flashcards with each containing, for example, a word you tend to misspell? Or take a more sophisticated approach and enter a 'Joke Of The Day'...

I Start up Registry Editor.

2 Press *F3* ('Find'), type **you can solve** and press *Enter*. This will take you to the key containing the tips.

3   To edit or replace a tip, double-click on the tip's number and type your new text into the dialog-box. Type exactly as you want the finished text to look.

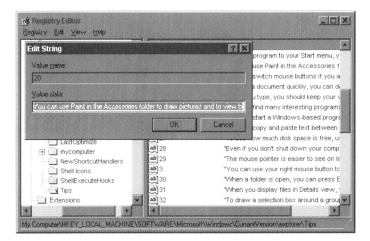

Screen 12.5 – **Double-click and type in a new 'tip'**

4   To add a new tip, right-click on the **Tips** key in the left pane, and select **New** and **String Value**. In the new value's label-area, type a new number for it (the original collection uses numbers 0–47.) Double-click on this new number to enter your 'tip'.

5   Close Registry Editor, and run **Welcome** to see the result.

Look Ma, No Icons!

Here's a trick to remove shortcut-icons from your Desktop entirely, and have your shortcuts represented only by their label. You might like to do this if you've selected a 'pictorial' wallpaper and don't like to see it covered in icons:

1   Open **Paint** and make sure you've got an empty white canvas (any size is okay).

2   Select **File / Save As...**, choose a convenient folder (such as C:\Windows\System) and save the file as **Blank.ico** (using the **.ico** extension will make Windows believe it's an icon file).

Screen 12.6 – **Icon practicality without the icons**

3   Now right-click on one of your Desktop shortcuts; choose **Properties /
Shortcut / Change Icon** and select your new **Blank.ico** file from its
folder.

 Remember that the result is a 'see-through' icon rather than *no* icon: it's
invisible, but you can still click/double-click on it.

**Registry
Tip**

Who Am I?

Forgotten your name? Can't find your way home? Let *Windows95* help. All the
information you entered when you installed *Windows95* is logged in the
Registry. To have a look at it, go to:

   HKEY_CURRENT_USER \ Software \ Microsoft \ User information.

The Big One

Want to find the largest (or oldest) file on your system? Open **Find** and hit
Return without entering any details other than your permanent drives: the

resulting list will contain every file and folder you have. Click twice on the **Size** (or **Modified**) button to bring the file to the top of the list.

 Find can't display more than 10,000 items at once. When it reaches this figure it'll stop searching.

Fake Program Manager

If you find the Start Menu slows you down after migrating from *Win 3.x*, but you don't want to sacrifice the long filenames and right-click options by returning to Program Manager, create a customized 'Progman'.

Right-click on **Start** and click **Open**, select all the folders in Start Menu and Start Menu \ Programs and drag them onto the Desktop to create shortcuts to them. (If you can't live without the **Documents** menu, create a shortcut to C:\Windows\Recent as well.)

You can now arrange or tile these folders as open windows or icons in true Progman style, with the added bonuses of being able to choose between different view options for the contents of individual windows and to create nested groups.

Screen 12.7 – **A fake ProgMan with Taskbar hidden**

To complete the 'fake', change the icon for each of the folder-shortcuts you created: right-click on a shortcut and choose **Properties / Shortcut / Change Icon**, then click the **Browse** button. In the **Files of type** box, select **Programs**, then navigate to your Windows folder and double-click **Progman.exe**. Program Manager's program-group icon is the 8th in the list.

Video ScreenSaver

Want to use an **.avi** video-file as a screensaver? Here's how...

1   Find your **.avi** file and double-click to start it playing. Then double-click its title-bar to open Media Player.

2   Press *Ctrl+O* to open the **Options** page and check the **Auto Repeat** box and **OK**. Press *Ctrl+D* to open the **Properties** page and click on **Full Screen** and **OK**. Now close Media Player.

3   Create a shortcut to the **.avi** file on your Desktop or Start Menu.

4   Right-click this shortcut and go to its **Properties / Shortcut** page. Enter a hotkey-combination in the 'Shortcut Key' box, and choose **Minimized** in the 'Run' box.

You can't set this 'screensaver' to start automatically like a normal screensaver would, but you can start it yourself using the hotkey or a double-click. When you want to resume work, press *Esc* and the video will minimize on the Taskbar. (Bear in mind it's still using resources so you'd want to close the file before going too much further – you might prefer to leave 'Run' set at **Normal** in step 4.)

Registry
Tip

Card Shark

The trick to winning at **FreeCell** is a successful start; that is, getting the aces to the home cells. You can tilt the odds in your favour by choosing a game in which the aces and low cards are easily reachable (games such as 27018, 10686, 7771, 11607, 1807 or 9558 for example). Just choose **Game / Select Game** (or press *F3*), type in the game number and start playing.

But if this whole 'playing' side of the deal seems too much like hard work, open the Registry and go to **HKEY_CURRENT_USER \ Software \ Microsoft \ Windows \ CurrentVersion \ Applets \ FreeCell**. In the right pane you'll see the strings **losses, lost, streak, stype, wins** and **won** (the last two will be missing if you haven't yet won a game!). Make any improvements to the score-sheet you think are necessary by editing these entries.

The entries are binary values (right-click on the **FreeCell** key and choose **New** and **Binary Value** if you need to enter one), but their data is entered in hexadecimal. Hex is a method of counting in base-sixteen using the numbers

0–9 and the letters a–f to enable counting from 0–15. Rather than a long explanation, a few examples are shown in Fig. 12.1.

Fig. 12.1

Hex	Decimal
05	5
0a	10
0f	15
13	19
1c	28

To change the figure in one of the FreeCell entries, double-click the value-name, press *Del* once and type in a two-digit hex number. You can check the result by pressing *F5* to refresh the Registry and selecting Game / Statistics (or pressing *F4*) in FreeCell. Figure 12.2 shows how the Registry values correspond with the Statistics chart.

Fig. 12.2

Registry Name	Statistics Entry
wins	Streaks / Wins
losses	Streaks / Losses
won	Total / Won
lost	Total / Lost
streak	Streaks / Current [figure]
stype	Streaks / Current [type]*

*Enter **01** for a winning streak, or **00** if you want to fake a losing streak!

If your losing streak just seems to be getting worse, make it better: simply go to the **stype** entry and change the **00** to **01**!

Registry Tip

Pinball Lizard

Have you got Microsoft *Plus!* with **Pinball** installed? Are you any good at it? Never mind – no one need ever know. Demonstrating commendable (if rather misguided) faith in our honesty, the scores are logged in the Registry in an easily read and altered form, making it easy to 'correct' a score that should have been better, delete one that couldn't have been worse, or change the name on one that should have been yours.

Go to **HKEY_CURRENT_USER \ Software \ Microsoft \ Plus! \ Pinball \ SpaceCadet** and you'll find the top five scores listed in the right pane from 0 – 4. Each score has two self-explanatory entries, **Name** and **Score**. Double-click any one of these and type something more appropriate.

Quick Catalogues

As you move files around your hard-disk, create partitions, install new software, you wind up with files of similar types scattered far and wide on the disk making a particular file that much harder to locate. You might try to solve the problem by creating a folder specially for all your **.bmp** files, for example, only to find it's more practical to leave some where they are, like leaving your wallpaper-files in your Windows folder. One way out is to create folders full of *shortcuts* (see 'Using Find Results' on page 18); a neater way is to use **Find** to create compact 'catalogues'.

Run a search to find files of the required type or extension and choose your preferred view from the 'View' menu. Put a checkmark next to **Save Results** on the 'Options' menu and choose **File / Save Search**. Run searches for other file-types in the same way.

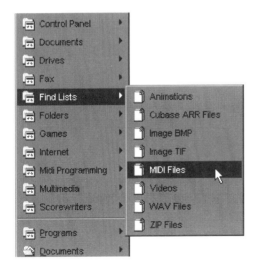

Screen 12.8 – **Automatic file lists, courtesy of 'Find'**

When you've run searches for all the file-types you need, create a folder on your Start Menu called something like 'Find Lists' and move all the result-files from your Desktop into this folder. You now have at-a-glance lists of all your most-used file-types one click away! If one of the lists seems to be a bit out of date, just re-run the search and replace the Start Menu file with the new one.

The benefits of using this method instead of creating folders full of shortcuts are twofold: firstly, of course, you'll save an immense amount of disk-space. Secondly, as the lists show the files themselves rather than shortcuts to them, you can carry out full file-management tasks from here such as delete, rename, open, print, and so on.

When you reopen a Saved Search in which the results were saved, files may be renamed, deleted and so on as mentioned above, but the changes won't be reflected in the list. The trick is to make all the changes you need to, then rerun and re-save the search to replace the original.

Registry
Tip

My Very Own Time Zone!

When you double-click the Tray's clock and the Time Zone tab, the heading you see is rather imprecise – perhaps **(GMT) Greenwich Mean Time; Dublin, Edinburgh, London**. If you'd prefer it to say something more specific like **My Office**, you can edit the entry in the Registry.

Go to **HKEY_LOCAL_MACHINE \ SOFTWARE \ Microsoft \ Windows \ CurrentVersion \ Time Zones** and find the key relating to your time-zone (**GMT** in the above example). In the right-pane, double-click on the **Display** entry and replace the string with your own.

Back To Write

If you installed *Windows95* over *Win3.x* you probably lost the **Write** application in the process: the *Windows95* installation replaced the original app (in C:\Windows) with a 5K stub diverting all calls to **WordPad** in C:\Program Files\Accessories. You may be quite satisfied with WordPad too, but it is unarguably slow to load and doesn't support page-breaks. Write is fast, supports full page and character formatting, and doesn't have **Notepad's** word-wrap problems when you load a text-file.

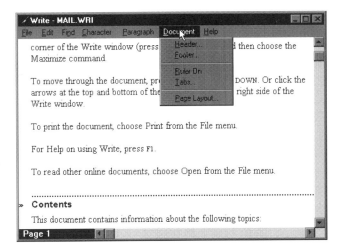

Screen 12.9 – **Write: unexciting, but fast & useful**

If you want to add Write to your collection again, hunt out your old *Win3.x* installation disks and find the one containing **Write.ex_** and **Write.hl_**. Then open a DOS-prompt window and type:

    expand a:\write.ex_ c:\windows\write.exe

    expand a:\write.hl_ c:\windows\help\write.hlp

(The first line will replace the 5K stub in your Windows folder with the Write application itself.)

Now go to **My Computer / View / Options / File Types** and decide what you want to do about file-associations. If you want to open any **.wri** files you come across in **Write** instead of WordPad, find the **Write Document** entry and edit its 'Open' and 'Print' actions to point to C:\Windows\Write.exe. You might want to add an 'Open In Write' option to the context menu for **.txt** files too (see 'Multiple Associations' on page 102).

Windows95 does the same thing to the old **Paintbrush** app. Compared with **Paint**, Paintbrush is extremely limited, but it can save files in **.pcx** format. If you fancy having Paintbrush back, find and expand the three **Pbrush** files in the same way, replacing the 5K Pbrush.exe stub in C:\Windows, placing Pbrush.hlp in C:\Windows\Help, and putting Pbrush.dll in C:\Windows\System.

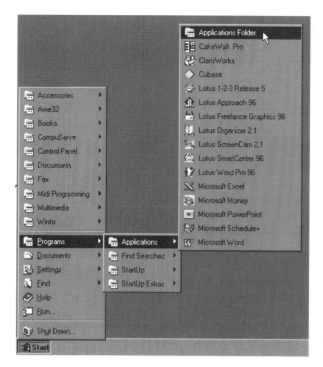

Screen 12.10 – **Straight to the folder you want to edit**

Start Editing

If you're in the habit of regularly add/removing/altering items in your Start Menu folders, the niftiest way to get at them is to add a shortcut to each folder *in* each folder! Taking Screen 12.10 as an example, this shortcut would have the command line:

> ″**C:\Windows\Start Menu\Programs\Applications**″

(not forgetting the quotes!). As you're cruising your Start Menu and you find something in this folder you want to change, just click the folder-shortcut.

Whodunit?

Windows95, like many other applications, has a hidden animated 'gang-screen'. What this one lacks in excitement it more than makes up for in sheer typing-exhaustion:

1   Right-click on the Desktop and select **New** then **Folder**.

2   Type the following name for the folder (precision is vital):

> **and now, the moment you've all been waiting for**

> and press Enter.

3 Right-click on the folder, select **Rename** and type:

we proudly present for your viewing pleasure

4 Press Enter and, again, right-click on the folder, choose **Rename** and type:

The Microsoft Windows 95 Product Team!

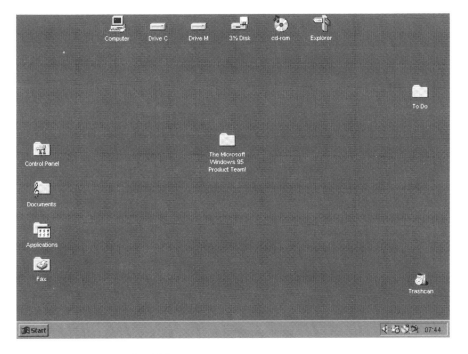

Screen 12.11 – **All that... for this?**

5 Press *Enter*, double-click the folder to open it, and settle back to enjoy this feast of music and animation.

6 When you've finished enjoying and started getting bored, close the window in the usual way.

You can move this folder anywhere you want to if you choose to keep it. You can also watch it in a two-pane view: open a two-pane Explorer window (using the /e, switch), navigate to your Windows\Desktop folder and double-click the 'gang folder' to see it play in the right pane.

Have an icon-free desktop

❏ **Clear Your Desk** – page 42

Put new file-types on the context-menu

❏ **Adding To The 'New' Sub-Menu** – page 108

Using Paint to customize the Windows boot & shutdown logos

❏ **Logo No-go?** – page 281

Use Program Manager as your shell

❏ **New Light Through Old Windows** – page 283

More 'Find' tips

❏ **'THE FIND COMMAND'** – page 14

More Paint offerings

❏ **'PAINT TIPS'** – page 151

13

PowerToys & Add-Ons

PowerToys

What Are They?

The **PowerToys** are a collection of accessories and utilities built by the *Windows95* team as late add-ons to the operating-system, and available for free download to anyone with Internet access from:

> http://www.microsoft.com/windows/software/powertoy.htm

You can also find them at a variety of other *Windows95*-related information and shareware sites on the web. Being free, these accessories don't officially form part of the *Windows95* operating system and therefore there's no warranty or support available for them: if something goes wrong, you're on your own!

The Toys can be downloaded as a single self-extracting compressed file or as separate items if you want only one or two. The following is a brief summary of each Toy's purpose and function to help you find out what you want, what you don't, and what you're missing.

Folder Contents

A utility that attaches itself to your context-menu: right-click on any folder or drive (or even a shortcut to one) and select **Contents** for a cascading sub-menu similar to that of the Start Menu.

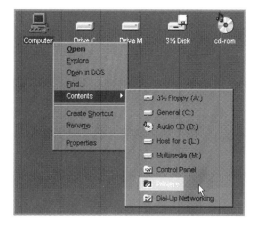

Screen 13.1 – **The context sub-menu displaying My Computer's contents**

Flexi CD

A 'replacement' for the **CD Player** applet. **Flexi CD** is a tray-icon accessory that comes alive when you put an audio CD in the drive: right-clicking the icon pops up a menu with controls for Play, Pause, Stop, Eject and Track-list. Hovering the mouse-pointer over the icon displays the current track's title.

The only shortcoming of the applet is in the track-listing: to display a track-title Flexi CD reads the details from CD Player's **.ini** file. And the details only get into the **.ini** file because you run CD Player and enter them. However, to run CD Player you have to first disable Flexi CD. So Flexi CD could be regarded as the tray-icon control that CD Player should have had (and could have better integrated).

Screen 13.2 – **Flexi CD's context-menu**

Target

Another context-menu add-on: when you right-click on a shortcut and select **Target** a sub-menu appears allowing you to open the folder containing the target file or application, select the properties for the target itself rather than the shortcut, and to Cut, Copy, Delete or create another shortcut to the target – and all without hunting through Explorer!

Desktop Menu

This is a solution to the common problem of needing access to the items on your desktop without the hassle of having to minimize, and later maximize, all the open windows you're using. **Desktop Menu** is an icon that lives in your Tray – click it with either mouse-button and a menu appears to display all your Desktop icons. For good measure, there's also a Minimize All Windows option, and an Undo Minimize All.

Round Clock

The name rather gives it away: it's a clock with a face of a certain shape (in analog mode at least). You can choose whether you want it 'Always on top' (using the Control Menu in the top left corner), and a right-click will make it vanish temporarily. The font for the digital option isn't resizeable in the ordinary way, but the 'window' itself is: with some hit-and-miss experimentation, it's possible to make the clock small but still legible.

Screen 13.3 – **The two faces of Round Clock**

Setting The Clock

If you're already the proud owner of 'Round Clock', you've probably had some trouble convincing it to remember its settings from one day to the next. Here's the solution...

Make sure the Clock isn't currently running, and find & delete **Clock.ini** (probably in your Windows folder). Now run the Clock and set up the position, font, size, and options such as seconds & date. Next, check **No Title** on the 'Settings' menu and make sure the finished result looks as you want it. (If it doesn't, double-click the clock-face to bring back the title-bar and menu.)

Finally, click once on the Clock's Taskbar-button and press *Alt + F4*. This will write the settings into a new **.ini** file. Find **clock.ini** again and check 'Read Only' on its **Properties** page to prevent these settings being changed. Now whenever you run the Clock it should always appear exactly the same.

CabView

An extension to the Windows shell (once again manifesting itself as an extra item on the context-menu) that allows you to view the **.cab** (cabinet) files on the *Windows95* CD-ROM and to extract individual items from them.

When you double-click a **.cab** file, its contents are displayed in an Explorer window. To extract a file (or group of files), right-click it and choose **Extract**; you'll then be prompted for a target-folder. Alternatively, you can use our best buddies, Drag & Drop.

The same thing can be done using **Extract.exe** from the Windows\Command folder in a DOS window (see 'Opening Cabinets' on page 131), but the familiar Windows environment makes the process more straightforward by miles.

Autoplay Extender

Audio CDs, as we well know, will start to play as soon as they're placed in the drive. A few CD-ROMs (the *Windows95* CD is an example) have an **Autorun** program that does the same. Nowadays most CD-ROMs have some form of graphic interface, but it may be run by a program called just about anything.

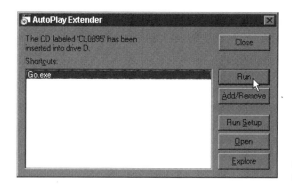

Screen 13.4 – **Extender recognizes another CD-ROM**

The **Autoplay Extender** is a method of allowing a CD-ROM to autoplay when it doesn't have a program called **Autorun**. When a data-CD is first loaded, the Extender's dialog appears prompting you to select the program on the CD that starts its UI. The Extender will then remember this program next time you insert the CD and give you the option to run it by clicking **Run**.

If you have a CD-ROM containing several executable programs, just add each to the Extender's list to save searching the CD for them.

You've also got the option to 'Explore' the CD instead, or to bypass the Extender and do nothing. A handy extra button is the 'Run Setup' button to install new software from a CD by starting its setup program.

The Extender also adds an **Autoplay Extender** option to the context-menu for your CD-ROM drive's icon with a submenu showing all the programs you listed for the disk plus the option to open the settings page.

Screen 13.5 – **The Quick-Res context-menu**

QuickRes

An unbelievably useful accessory for changing screen-resolution 'on the fly'. **QuickRes** places an icon in the tray: clicking the icon displays a menu containing the screen-resolutions and colour palettes available for your monitor setup: just choose the one you want and a few seconds later you've got it.

QuickRes is also included in the *Windows95* Resource Kit

XMouse

XMouse is a neat little utility that installs itself in the Control Panel the first time you run it. As you move your mouse over the sea of open windows on your Desktop, the focus follows.

XMouse gives an easy choice of options: highlight the window (the default setting), bring the window to the top of the stack, or function 'normally'.

Explore From Here

Adds the option **Explore From Here** to the context-menu. This is almost identical to the function of **Explore**, covered on page 65. The main difference occurs when you right-click on a folder in a dual-pane window: selecting **Explore** opens that folder in the same window, whereas **Explore From Here** will open a second.

The answer is nevertheless in this book: go to page 77 and follow the tip labelled 'Open New Windows Easily' (making sure you take the 'Option' at the end). This will give exactly the same results as **Explore From Here**.

If you really want to go for the 'fake', name the string-value **E&xplore From Here** instead of **New &Window** in step 3.

TweakUI

A compact accessory packed with useful switchable modifications to the *Windows95* user-interface, such as turning off window-animation, removing shortcut arrows, editing the Add/Remove list, and clearing Run/Find/Documents histories. However, almost all can be accessed via the Registry or Policy Editor if you know how (and you do: the instructions are in this book!). One of the real winning features of **TweakUI** is the facility to turn off the 'Shortcut to...' prefix permanently.

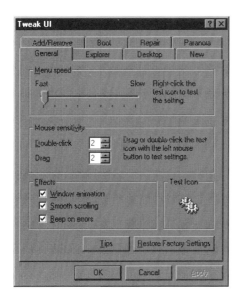

Screen 13.6 – **The multi-talented TweakUI**

DOS Prompt Here

This applet produces a result similar to 'Open In A DOS Window' on page 295, adding a 'DOS Prompt Here' option on the context menu of folders. Just select that option to open a DOS-box with the selected folder as the target. Because you often decide to open a folder in DOS after looking *inside* the folder (which would normally entail closing it again so that you can click on it), this little add-on also places the entire context-menu for a folder on its Control Menu (top-left corner) meaning that you can cut or copy the open folder, check its properties sheet, or create a shortcut to it without closing it, as well opening it in DOS. (When you create a shortcut to a folder from its control menu, the shortcut is placed on the Desktop.)

Send To AnyFolder

A definite king among accessories, this one: **AnyFolder** sits in your Send To folder. Any time you find a file or folder that you want to move or copy elsewhere, right-click it and choose **AnyFolder** from the Send To option. You can then browse an Explorer-like folder tree to choose the target folder or select one from a drop-down list of recent choices.

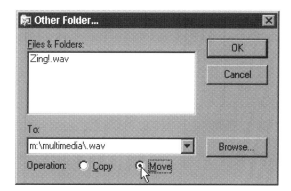

Screen 13.7 – **The simple and stunningly useful AnyFolder**

AnyFolder has recently reappeared in the PowerToys collection after a long absence, this time sporting a few extra additions (all of which are Send To options):

❑ **Clipboard as Contents** – Copies the contents of a file to the clipboard.

❑ **Clipboard as Name** – Places the path and name of the file on the clipboard.

❑ **Command Line** – Opens the Run window with this file as the command-line.

❑ **Mail Recipients** – Sends the file to an Internet, CMC or MAPI mail recipient.

Registry
Tip

AnyFolder Run List

If you've got a copy of **AnyFolder**, you'll know it features a drop-down list of the most recently accessed folders. In exactly the same fashion as editing the list for the **Run** command (see 'Shorten The Run List' on page 10), you can remove or re-order items in this list.

Open the Registry Editor, and navigate to

> HKEY_CURRENT_USER \ Software \ Microsoft \ Windows \
> CurrentVersion \ Explorer \ OtherFolder

In the right-pane, delete any entries you don't want, with the exception of the **(Default)** string. To change the order in which the entries are displayed in the drop-down list, double-click on **MRUList**, and type in a different letter-sequence.

HTML Driver

A printer-driver installed via the **Add Printer Wizard**. When you select this printer from an application and choose **Print**, the document is converted to HTML format and saved with an **.htm** extension ready to be published as a Web-page. Any embedded bitmap files in the document are converted to JPEG format and saved separately with a **.jpg** extension, and a pointer placed in the HTML file. The 'print' process will prompt you for a target folder and file name and, optionally, a separate folder for the **.jpg** files.

The current version (v1.0) lacks sophistication and tends to fall over badly on combined text/graphics files, but you can produce some great results using **WordPad**. The resulting **.htm** files are fully editable, so if nothing else, you can create the backbone of your Web-page this way, and then add missing codes, links and formatting manually afterwards by loading the saved **.htm** file back into **WordPad**, and save it as text when you're done.

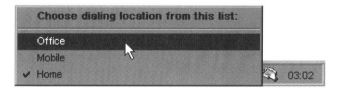

Screen 13.8 – **Quick relocation**

Telephony Location Selector

This impressively-titled accessory was built for portable-computers and runs as a Tray-icon (see Screen 13.8). A left-click on the icon lets you change your dialling-location; a right-click allows you to run **Phone Dialer** or open the Dialing Properties page of the **Modems** applet.

KernelToys

What Are They?

The **KernelToys** are add-on utilities created by the *Windows95* kernel-team, as an attempt to grab some of the adulation afforded to the shell-team for their PowerToys. These are unsupported extras, like the PowerToys, and can be downloaded separately or as a single archive from:

http://www.microsoft.com/windows/software/krnltoy.htm

Keyboard Remap

A small extension that adds a **Remap** tab to Control Panel's **Keyboard** applet. The main point of the extension is to allow users of standard keyboards to remap their *Ctrl, Alt, Shift* and *Caps Lock* keys to mimic the action of the Microsoft Natural Keyboard's *Windows* (Start Menu) and *Menu* (context-menu) keys, but if you've recently switched from an older keyboard and found your keys swapped about, this is the way to swap 'em back!

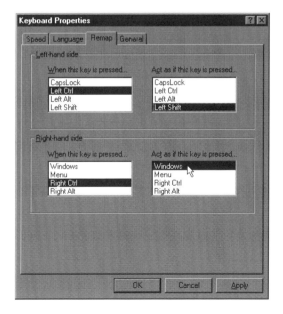

Screen 13.9 – **'Keyboard' sprouts a Remap page**

Conventional Memory Tracker

When you run the **mem /c /p** command in DOS, you'll see that a fair chunk of conventional memory is used by Vmm32.vxd. The Conventional Memory Tracker creates a text-file on startup listing the memory-addresses used by Vmm32, the virtual device-drivers by which these addresses are allocated and, most usefully, the memory-blocks grabbed by Vmm32 which are not used.

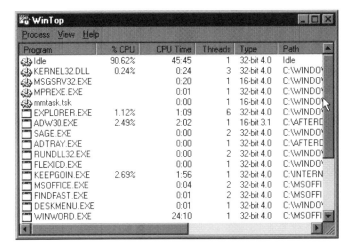

Screen 13.10 – **WinTop on watch**

WinTop

A clever little accessory that could be thought of as an advanced version of the End Task(*Ctrl + Alt + Del*) menu. **WinTop** displays which programs and processes are currently running, the number of threads created by a particular process, and, because it updates every two seconds, the percentage of CPU time used by a particular process or thread in the last two seconds. It's also possible to view the accumulated CPU usage-time of a process since it started. The processing-priority of each process is displayed (but can't be altered), and processes can be ended from here in a similar way to the End Task menu.

MS-DOS Mode Wizard Customizer

When you set a DOS-program to run in MS-DOS mode and click the 'Specify a new MS-DOS configuration, you can create a customized Config.sys and Autoexec.bat for the program. Clicking the **Configuration** button launches the MS-DOS Mode Configuration Wizard which will insert options into these files automatically when checked.

But the Wizard offers a very limited collection of settings – any mouse or CD-ROM drivers you want to add, or programs such as Doskey and Smartdrv, have to be entered by hand. The Customizer lets you add all the settings you want to the Wizard which can then be inserted into your custom system-files with just a single click.

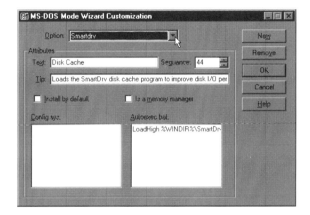

Screen 13.11 – **Adding new 'presets'**
to the **DOS-Mode Wizard**

Time Zone Editor

A small friendly utility that lets you edit or create time zones for the **Date/Time** applet in Control Panel. Options include the ability to change the name of a Time Zone, its difference from Greenwich Mean Time, and its Daylight Saving Time details such as start and end dates.

 You can change the name of a Time Zone with a simple Registry edit – read 'My Very Own Time Zone!' on page 318.

Resource Kit

What Is It?

The *Windows95 Resource Kit* is, in fact, a book accompanied by a **Help** file and a collection of utilities and scripts aimed at troubleshooting the deployment and management of *Windows95* in corporate networking situations.

Despite the technical nature of the Help file, it can be extremely handy to have around for the home or small-office user in troubleshooting situations.

In addition, if you haven't yet installed *Windows95* (or you've come over all nostalgic for the day you did install it), the Resource Kit explains the installation process in step-by-step fashion including screenshots of the main dialogs. If you have Internet access, you can download the Kit (minus the book of course!) from:

  http://www.microsoft.com/windows/software/reskit.htm

Click the 'Resource Kit Utilities' link to download the file named **rktools.exe** containing the help file and the utilities. This file weighs in at 3.7Mb and no, you can't just grab the utilities!

In addition to the Help file, the Resource Kit contains several utilities: **Cfgback** (also on the *Windows95* CD-ROM – see page 221 for details); **QuickRes** (one of the PowerToys covered earlier in this chapter); **Aniedit, Imagedit, Logview** and **Shortcut**. Here's a quick look at the last four.

 You can find the *Win95rk* Help file on the *Windows95* installation CD-ROM – see page 150.

Animated Cursor Editor

Aniedit does pretty much what you'd expect it to do: in true animation style, you select and assemble a group of cursor files and assign a display-time for each image to form an apparently 'moving' cursor which you can then save as an **.ani** file and select it from the **Pointers** tab of the **Mouse** applet.

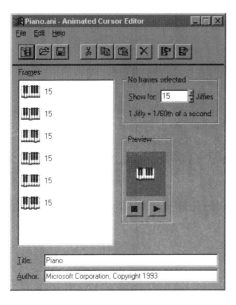

Screen 13.12 – **Aniedit doing what it does best**

Aniedit works hand in hand with **Imagedit** (unless you want to specify a different cursor editor) to let you create the original images and import them to be arranged, previewed and saved. Or, for the artistically challenged, you can import existing animated-cursor files and tweak them.

Image Editor

Imagedit is a basic bitmap editor for images of up to 256 × 256 pixels in size. Clearly, then, it can't compete with **Paint**, but its strength lies in its ability to create and save **.ico** and **.cur** files.

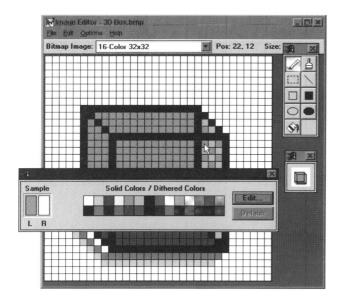

Screen 13.13 – **Image Editor with floating palette, toolbar & preview**

The **Image Editor** can be run as a stand-alone application, or started from **Aniedit's** Edit or Create buttons.

Log Viewer

This is a handy little utility for viewing the log files created by Windows as troubleshooting aids. **Log Viewer** is a sister-app to **System Editor** and is useful for exactly the same reasons: although any of these files could be viewed in **Quick View** or a text-editor such as **Notepad**, the Log Viewer opens them all simultaneously in a multiple-document interface to save you the trouble of hunting them down.

By default Log Viewer loads Bootlog.txt, Detlog.txt, Netlog.txt, Setuplog.txt, Scandisk.log and Ndislog.txt, but will open any text-based file without raising a sweat and allow you to print files or copy sections to the clipboard.

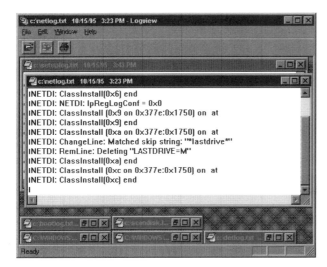

Screen 13.14 – **Log Viewer's multiple-document interface**

Installing Log Viewer

Log Viewer is included on the *Windows95* CD-ROM. If this is the utility your computer has been crying out for, navigate to **D:\Other\Misc\Logview** and just copy the file you find there to a convenient folder on your hard-disk.

At 17.5K it's hardly an extravagance, but you can, if you want to, run the program direct from the CD.

Shortcut.exe

An MS-DOS-based utility for keeping track of shortcuts. However, most of the options available can be accessed more quickly and easily within Windows by opening the shortcut file's **Properties** page.

The two primary differences are the inclusion of commands to fix a broken shortcut (ie. to force a search for a target file that has been renamed or moved), and to make a shortcut non-tracking (i.e., to prevent it from trying to keep up with renamed or moved targets).

Support Assistant

A second Help file, the *Windows95 Support Assistant* contains many of the troubleshooting and networking sections of the *Resource Kit*, together with solutions for installation and performance problems and a How Do I? section.

For the non-technical user it's probably a more useful acquisition than the Resource Kit, being a more compact reference with plenty of Question & Answer sections (and a much shorter download time!).

You can grab the *Support Assistant* from:

   http://www.microsoft.com/windows/support/assist.htm

Plus!

What Is It?

Plus! is a retail collection of add-on applications and accessories for *Windows95*. Since some of the tips & tricks in this book refer to elements of the *Plus!* pack, much of its contents have been covered already; the following gives just a brief overview of each item.

Add & Remove

When installed, *Plus!* automatically logs itself into the Windows **Add/Remove Programs** list enabling you to deinstall the whole package easily.

More usefully, though, you can re-run the *Plus!* setup program at any time to add or remove particular elements of the pack.

Desktop Themes

The **Desktop Themes** applet installs itself in the Control Panel, letting you switch between the various themes supplied with *Plus!* A theme consists of matched cursors, wallpaper, icons, colour-schemes and sound-events which all add to your computing atmosphere while subtracting from its resources.

Since each scheme requires a hefty portion of disk-space, you can select which schemes to install from the *Plus!* setup utility. Each theme can be customized to suit your taste or to save system resources, by opting not to use the Theme's sounds and icons for example. You can also create your own themes using the standard *Windows95* **Mouse, Sound** and **Display** applets and save them in the **Desktop Themes** applet.

System Agent

System Agent is an application intended ostensibly to schedule and run disk-utilities such as **Scandisk** and **Disk Defragmenter**, though it can in fact run any application you wish. It installs as an icon in the Tray which can be double-clicked to display and edit the scheduled programs.

A whole host of options allows you to specify exactly when each application should be run (e.g., at startup; whenever the computer has been idle for a time; hourly, daily, weekly or monthly at a particular time), how the program should run, whether it should stop or continue if interrupted, and how long it should continue trying to complete its mission.

If the program failed to run – perhaps because the computer was turned off – a dialog will tell you so next time you start up, and give you the opportunity to ignore it or reschedule it.

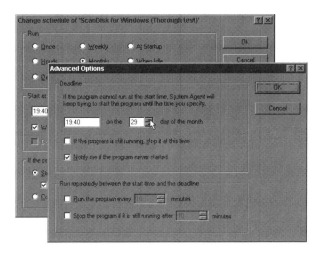

Screen 13.15 – **System Agent's advanced options page**

DriveSpace 3

An updated version of the DriveSpace utility included with *Windows95*, using more advanced compression-algorithms to maximize hard-disk space. The primary benefits of the new version are support for compressed drives of up to 2 gigabytes, and the ability to change the compression settings to gain maximum disk-space or fastest disk-access.

If your drive has already been compressed using an earlier version of DriveSpace under Windows or MS-DOS, **DriveSpace 3** can upgrade the same drive to its own compression-format.

Compression Agent

Compression Agent works hand-in-hand with **DriveSpace 3** to maintain compressed drives, and is automatically installed at the same time. When you compress a drive (or upgrade an existing compressed drive to **DriveSpace 3** format), **Compression Agent** logs itself into **System Agent** and runs regularly to recompress files according to the settings you choose.

The real bonus of **Compression Agent** (aside from automation) is the facility to choose different compression settings for different drives, or to select individual folders and files for maximum compression or zero compression.

Internet JumpStart Kit

The Internet JumpStart Kit contains two items: **Internet Explorer**, Microsoft's web-browser (see page 196), and the **Internet Setup Wizard**.

The Setup Wizard takes you through the process of creating an Internet connection via the Microsoft Network or an Internet Access Provider in true wizardly step-by-step fashion, and helps you configure your system to send and receive Internet Mail using Microsoft Exchange.

Microsoft are so keen to establish themselves in the Internet-software market that they're constantly updating **Internet Explorer**, and giving it away. So if the acquisition of IntEx is your driving motivation for wanting to buy *Plus!*, don't do it! You can download the latest version from the URL on page 206.

Screen 13.16 – **3D Pinball**

Extras

In addition to the Desktop Themes and applications, *Plus!* contains another little orphaned piece of the Dial-Up Networking jigsaw, a pinball game, and a collection of 'Visual Enhancements' accessed from an additional tab in the **Display** applet labelled **Plus!** This tabbed page also gives you the option to change the icons for My Computer, Network Neighborhood and Recycle Bin.

It's worth remembering that the use of any of these display-enhancements will consume more system resources than would sticking with the defaults.

❑   **Full Window Drag** – Allows you to see the contents of a window while moving or resizing it.

❑   **Font Smoothing** – Removes the jagged edges from screen-fonts to improve their look and readability. Requires high-colour mode.

❑   **Enhanced MS-DOS Font** – A more easily-readable font for the DOS-prompt window.

❑   **Animated Cursors** – Not unexpectedly, a cursor collection of the animated variety.

❑   **High-Colour Icons** – Replaces Windows' default icons with high-colour versions.

❑   **3D Pinball** – A realistic pinball game with sound-effects.

❑   **Dial-Up Networking Server** – Enables you to dial-in to your desktop computer.

Updates & Fixes

Service Pack #1

Although the word 'bug' is neatly avoided in all documentation, the **Service Pack** is a collection of 'problem' fixes for *Windows95*. These are updates that have appeared individually on Microsoft's web-site and have now been gathered together for easier installation. The 1.2Mb Pack can be downloaded from:

http://www.microsoft.com/windows/software/servpak1/enduser.htm

Installation of the **Service Pack** updates your Windows version to 4.00.950a and adds an 'Update Information Tool' to the Programs\Accessories\System Tools folder of your Start Menu to help you keep track of updated components. Here's a quick run-down of the Pack's contents as they pertain to the home and small-office user:

- ❑ **OLE32 Update** – Corrects a problem in which Microsoft Office applications allow portions of deleted files to creep into their own; these extra file-snippets are visible when the file is viewed in a text-editor such as Notepad.

- ❑ **Print Dialog Update** – Cures a situation in which 32-bit applications could crash when called upon to print using certain 16-bit printer drivers.

- ❑ **Password List Update** – A new encryption algorithm for storing network- access passwords that's considerably tougher to crack than the original encryption method.

- ❑ **System Agent Update** – A minor update to prevent the *Plus!* pack's System Agent interfering with floating-point calculations being carried out by another application while Sage is running.

- ❑ **Printer Port Update** – A virtual device driver update for certain ECP port laser-printers that support bi-directional communications. The file (Lpt.vxd) is also on the *Windows95* CD-ROM in the Drivers\Printer\Lpt folder.

Other Updates

Updates for *Windows95* have now been given a home of their own:

http://www.microsoft.com/windows/software/updates.htm

This is a page worth checking regularly – many of the updates that appear relate to a small percentage of users (addressing, for example, a compatibility problem with a specific network-client), but there is the occasional fix for a shell or accessory problem that most *Windows95* users should grab a copy of.

14

Clicks & Keystrokes

There are literally hundreds of possible keystrokes or key + mouse combinations available in *Windows95*. Consider all the underlined letters in all the menus of all the screens and applets – for example, in My Computer, to reach View / Options / File Types you can press *Alt + V, O, Ctrl + Tab-twice.*

This list concentrates on *shortcuts* – quick (or alternative) ways to reach the most common targets or carry out the basic tasks. For many of the shortcuts listed here there are sure to be other methods of getting the same result, some of which you may prefer.

General Keystrokes

Context-sensitive Help (in tabbed pages & dialogs)	*F1*
Open the Start Menu	*Ctrl + Esc*
Close the Start Menu	*Esc*
Navigate the Start Menu	*Arrow keys*
Open or run the selected item	*Enter or Return*
Move to (next) item beginning with **?** [initial letter/s]	**?** [initial letter/s]
'Run' command	*Ctrl + Esc* then *R*
'Find' command	*Ctrl + Esc* then *F*
Iconic list of currently open windows & applications	*Alt + Tab (+ Tab to select)*
Cycle through currently open windows, apps & dialogs	*Alt + Esc*
Close a window or quit an application	*Alt + F4*
Cut selected item	*Ctrl + X*
Copy selected item	*Ctrl + C*
Paste selected item	*Ctrl + V*
Close a menu or dialog without making a selection	*Esc*
Scroll through list of recent commands in Find & Run	*Up/Down arrow keys*
Drop-down the **Open** box in **Run**	*F4*

Drop-down the **Named** box in **Find**	*F4*
Drop-down the Computer/Drives box on a window's toolbar	*F4*
Open the **Look in** & **Save in** box in **Open/Save As dialogs**	*F4*
Defeat CD Autoplay or Autorun	*Shift + insert CD*
Move between options/buttons in a dialog box	*Tab*
Move backwards between options/buttons in a dialog box	*Shift + Tab*
Move through tabbed pages	*Ctrl + Tab*
Move backwards through tabbed pages	*Ctrl + Shift + Tab*
Shut Down Windows	*Alt + F4, Enter or Ctrl + Alt + Del, S*
Restart Windows	*Alt + F4, R, Shift + Return*
Restart in MS-DOS Mode	*Alt + F4, M, Return*
Close programs and log on as a different user	*Alt + F4, C, Return*

Boot Keystrokes

To prevent display of startup logo	Esc
To display Boot Menu on system startup	*F8*
To start *Windows95* in Safe Mode	*F5*
To boot to the command-prompt	*Alt + F5*
Boot with step-by-step confirmation of system-file entries	*Shift + F5*
To prevent Windows loading StartUp folder items	*Hold Ctrl as Windows starts*

Desktop & Explorer Keystrokes

Windows95 general Help	*F1*
Rename the selected item	*F2*
Send the selected item to Recycle Bin	*Del*
Delete the selected item, bypassing Recycle Bin	*Shift + Del*
Open the 'Find' command	*F3*
Show the context-menu for the selected item	*Shift + F10*
Show the properties page for the selected item	Alt + Enter

Move the selected item	*Ctrl+X* then *Ctrl+V*
Create a copy of the selected item	*Ctrl+C* then *Ctrl+V*
Create a shortcut to the selected item	*Shift+F10* then *S*
Refresh (update Desktop or Window contents)	*F5*
Undo last action (cut, copy, move, rename, delete, create)	*Ctrl+Z*
Select all items	*Ctrl+A*
Open parent folder	*Backspace*
Step from item to item	*Arrow keys*
Open the selected folder in a new window	*Ctrl+Enter*
Access the 'Open With' dialog for the selected item	*Ctrl+Shift+F10* then *E*
Close current window and all parent-windows	*Shift+Alt+F4*
Cancel a 'drag & drop' manoeuvre	*Esc*

Dual-Pane Window Keystrokes

Select and expand the drive-list	*F4*
Switch between left and right panes	*F6*
'Go To' a particular folder	*Ctrl+G*
(Left pane) Expand the selected folder (one level)	*+ sign (NumLock On)* or *right arrow (NumLock off)*
(Left pane) Expand the selected folder (all levels)	** sign (NumLock On)*
(Left pane) Collapse the selected folder	*− sign (NumLock On)* or *left arrow (NumLock off)*

Mouse Clicks & Combos

Move the selected item	*Shift+Drag*
Copy the selected item	*Ctrl+Drag*
Create shortcut to the selected item	*Ctrl+Shift+Drag*
Choose from Copy, Move or Create Shortcut	*Right-click+Drag*
Show the Properties page for the selected item	*Alt+Double-click*
Choose selected items from a window or list	*Ctrl+click each item*
Choose contiguous items from a window or list	*Click first item, hold shift+click last*

Open a folder in a new window   *Ctrl + double-click*
Close current window and all parent-windows   *Shift + click close button*
Open a folder in a dual-pane window   *Highlight, shift + double-click*
Add the 'Open With' option to the context-menu   *Highlight, shift + right-click*
Toggle a window between maximized / restored   *Double-click on title-bar*
Cancel a drag & drop manoeuvre   *Click opposite mouse-button*

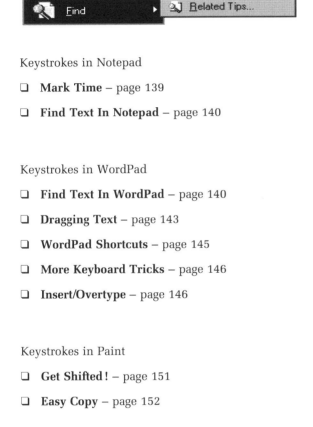

Keystrokes in Notepad

❑   **Mark Time** – page 139

❑   **Find Text In Notepad** – page 140

Keystrokes in WordPad

❑   **Find Text In WordPad** – page 140

❑   **Dragging Text** – page 143

❑   **WordPad Shortcuts** – page 145

❑   **More Keyboard Tricks** – page 146

❑   **Insert/Overtype** – page 146

Keystrokes in Paint

❑   **Get Shifted!** – page 151

❑   **Easy Copy** – page 152

Keystrokes in Calculator

❑   **Use The Keypad** – page 155

Keystrokes in Media Player

❑   **Media Player Quick Keys** – page 164

Mouse Considerations

How about a little animation...

Glossary

This collection of definitions and explanations is included as an aid to finding your way through the jargon- and acronym-laden world of computers – you could think of it as an extra tip thrown in for good measure. While many entries are not specifically related to *Windows95*, they are all relevant to Windows-based computing.

Since most of the items here will be interrelated, **bold** text in an entry indicates a Glossary definition for that word or phrase.

16-bit Older (pre-*Windows95*) applications access memory two **bytes** at a time – in other words, 16 bits at a time. 16-bit drivers and applications run in real mode.

32-bit A faster method of memory-access, upon which much of *Windows 95* is built. Memory is accessed 4 **bytes** at a time. 32-bit drivers and applications run in **protected mode**.

Archive (1) One of the **attributes** of a file set in its Properties page and stored as a single **bit** on disk (the 'archive bit'). When an archived file is altered the archive bit is created as an indication to file-backup programs. Next time the backup program runs it searches for archive-bits, replaces its backup copy of the changed file, and removes the archive-bit again.

(2) A name for a single file containing one or more compressed files. The archive formats you'll come across most often are **cabinet files** and **zip files**.

ASCII Acronym for American Standard Code for Information Interchange pronounced 'ass-key'. A universal convention that assigns a unique 7- or 8-**bit** code to letters, numbers and punctuation-marks, enabling ASCII-documents to be displayed accurately on all computers and text-based applications, at the expense of the text-formatting and font-selection options saved in a word-processor's own file-format. The basic ASCII character set contains 128 codes, of which 32 are assigned to non-printing characters such as carriage-return and tab.

ASCII file *see* **Text file**

Associations *Windows95* is intended to be document-driven rather than application-driven: double-clicking on a file's icon should launch both the file *and* the application that created it (or a different, but similarly compatible one) with that single command. This is done by *associating* each **file type** with an application. For example, a bitmapped graphics file can be given a **.bmp** extension. Files with this extension are of the type

347

'Bitmap Image', and Bitmap Image files are (by default at least) associated with Mspaint.exe.

AT command-set An almost universal set of modem command codes, so-called because every code begins with the letters AT (short for 'Attention'), such as ATM (mute modem-speaker) and ATZ (reset).

Attributes Characteristics of a file, such as **Archive, System, Read-only** or **Hidden**, set in the file's **Properties** page and stored in the **FAT**.

Autoexec.bat A **batch file** run automatically as you boot or restart the computer, to configure user-preferences, make system-settings, and launch memory-resident programs (**TSRs**).

Background task A task being carried out invisibly (such as printing or checking for the arrival of email) with a low processor-priority, while the user carries out another task in the foreground. Background-processing is a feature of a **multitasking operating system**.

Batch file A text-based MS-DOS program with a **.bat** extension containing one or more commands that are run in sequence when the program is started. Batch files are used primarily to automate simple, but mind-numbingly tedious, tasks.

Baud rate Usually used to express the data-transfer speed of a **modem**, measured in **bits** per second (bps).

BIOS Acronym for Basic Input/Output System. A small but vital set of instructions on a **ROM** chip in your computer that runs when you power-up, tests the computer and memory chips, and starts the **boot** process. The BIOS also handles data transfer between system hardware such as disk-drives and **RAM**.

Bit An abbreviation of BInary digiT. A bit is a single 1 or 0 in the computer's binary numbering system. These

digits are organized into groups of eight, called **bytes**.

Boot An abbreviation of *bootstrapping*, describing the process of starting the computer. A 'cold boot' takes place when you first switch on the computer; a 'warm boot' is effected by pressing the computer's Restart button or choosing 'Restart the computer' from the *Windows95* Shutdown dialog.

Boot disk see **Emergency startup disk; System disk**

Boot drive The drive containing the **operating system** files (usually C:). On bootup, the **BIOS** checks the floppy-disk drive (usually A:) first to see if a **system disk** has been inserted, followed by the boot drive.

Boot partition On a **partitioned** hard-disk, the partition containing the **operating system** files. This must be the disk's primary partition.

BPS *see* **Baud rate**

Browser *see* **FTP; World Wide Web**

Buffer A temporary holding-place in computer-memory for data being transferred from one disk, or device, to another.

Bus A network of wires on a circuit board in a computer carrying information between system elements such as **CPU**, disk-drive controller, and memory. The bus moves 16-bit chunks of data around at 8MHz which was fine in the days of MS-DOS but wildly inadequate for the graphics-intensive Windows environment, spawning the development of **Local bus**.

Byte A group of eight **bits**. A single byte contains the equivalent of a single character (number, letter or punctuation mark).

Cabinet files An archive file with a **.cab** extension containing compressed files, similar to a **.zip** file. This format is used by Microsoft on distribution disks for recent products including *Windows95*. Files can be extracted from the cabinets and de-compressed using Extract.exe from the Command folder or CabView from the PowerToys collection.

Cache memory A small amount of very fast-access memory (usually 256 or 512 **kilobytes** in current computers) that 'reads ahead', trying to guess what data the **CPU** will require next, acting as a **buffer** between the CPU and **RAM**.

CAD An acronym for Computer-Aided Design, a type of graphics-intensive application requiring fast processing and large amounts of **RAM** and **virtual memory**.

Cascading menu *see* **Sub-menu**

Checkbox A small selection-box which, when the corresponding option is chosen, shows a checkmark (tick). In contrast with **radio buttons**, any checkbox option may be freely selected regardless of the status of the others.

Client A term used in **OLE** to refer to the application that stores an **object** created by a **server** application. Also used to refer to software designed to handle a particular networking task, such as an **FTP** or email client.

Close An option usually found on the File **menu** in a **MDI**, used to close the active document-window rather than the application itself. Has the same effect as clicking the document-window's **close button**. (See also **Exit**.)

Close button The button in the top right corner of a window with a cross-icon, used to close the window or quit the application (with a prompt to save any unsaved work if necessary).

Cluster A small section of a file on a disk. The larger the disk, the larger the cluster-size, but every file on your disk must use at least one cluster and clusters are not shared. Floppy-disks use 512-byte clusters; many hard-disks use clusters of 32k, so if your hard-disk contains many small files,

of which shortcuts (.lnk files) are a good example, you could be wasting a lot of space (referred to as **slack space**).

A method of avoiding this is to **partition** the drive into several smaller drives thus reducing the cluster-size. Using DriveSpace to compress your hard-drive will similarly result in clusters roughly one sixty-fourth their original size.

CMOS Pronounced 'see-moss', an acronym for Complementary Metal-Oxide Semicondutor. The CMOS is a special **RAM** chip containing the computer's vital settings (such as size, type and configuration of its hard-disk), which are stored even when the computer is turned off. CMOS chips are fragile and known to fail, however, so the settings should be noted somewhere safe. You can usually view the CMOS settings when you first power-on your computer, often by pressing *Delete* or *Esc* before the boot-sequence starts.

Codec An amalgam of Compression/Decompression. Codecs such as Indeo, MPEG and **QuickTime** are used in graphics, sound, animation and (especially) video file-formats. Codec techniques reduce files to a more 'portable' size but are, as a result, **CPU**-intensive and may sacrifice picture quality.

Colour palette The number of colours your monitor and display adapter are capable of displaying at a given **screen resolution**. A 256-colour setting is usually sufficient; higher settings may cause a reduction in performance. (Also referred to as Colour Depth.)

Com Abbreviation for 'communications port'. Most computers have two communications ports (labelled COM1 and COM2). The mouse is usually connected to COM1, with COM2 used for a modem or serial printer. COM ports transmit data in a single bit stream (i.e., one bit at a time), in contrast with the **LPT** parallel port, and are therefore called serial ports.

Command-line interface   A user-interface, such as **MS-DOS**, in which the user interacts with the **operating system** by typing text-based command-codes, as distinct from a **GUI**.

Compound document   A document containing two or more types of data, created using **OLE**.

Config.sys   A text-file automatically run as you boot or restart the computer which configures the hardware elements of your system such as sound-card and CD-ROM drive, and sets the required levels of resources. Since *Windows95* includes its own drivers for most hardware devices, and is normally able to recognize these devices and install the necessary drivers automatically, this file is usually redundant in a *Windows95*-only environment.

Conflict   A term meaning that one piece of hardware on your system has been set to use non-sharable resources already allocated to another device: the most common conflict is that of assigning the same **IRQ** to two devices, which can usually be solved by simply changing a setting in Device Manager.

Two other possibles are conflicting base-addresses, and having the same hardware installed twice. The second of these is usually solved by uninstalling both devices and using Add New Hardware to *reinstall* one. The base-address problem may stem from two hardware-devices having the same base-address set in the hardware (in which case you might need to change the dip-switch or jumper settings), or may simply be that the base-address set in the software setup-routine for one device is incorrect – most non-Plug & Play hardware comes with its own installation software to identify and test available addresses and IRQs which can be re-run in the event of conflicts.

Context-menu   The menu that appears when you click the right mouse-button in *Windows95*, so called because the options it offers vary according to the object being clicked and the circumstances.

Control menu   A menu of options accessed by clicking the icon in the extreme top-left corner of an application- or document-window. The menu allows you to maximize, minimize or restore the window-size, switch to a different document window, or close the window (with a prompt to save any unsaved work).

Conventional memory   Of your installed **RAM**, conventional memory is the first 640K which is assigned to MS-DOS programs, TSRs and real-mode drivers. Lack of conventional memory is the usual stumbling block when trying to run game software. If you have to run your DOS program in MS-DOS mode or 'real' DOS, the most effective method of increasing the available conventional memory is to move DOS and real mode device drivers into **HMA** and **UMB**s using the Config.sys lines DOS=HIGH,UMB and DEVICEHIGH=.

CPU   An abbreviation for Central Processing Unit (or processor), the device in your computer that makes it compute. CPU chips vary in power (current popular chips are Intel's 80486 and Pentium) and clock speed (measured in MegaHertz) – the faster and more powerful the chip, the quicker it can perform operations on data.

CVF   Abbreviation for Compressed Volume File. See also **Host drive**.

DDE   An abbreviation for Dynamic Data Exchange. A DDE object is one that exists in a document as a *link* to a file. When the file is edited in some way, the linked data seen in the document automatically (*dynamically*) updates.

Desktop folder   Actually a **subfolder** of C:\Windows\Desktop, but the folder icon appears on the Desktop and is usually created by right-clicking the Desktop and choosing New/Folder from the **context-menu**. A Desktop folder is subtly different from other folders on your C: drive: for these to appear on the Desktop, they must either be moved there by **drag & drop** (thus becoming subfolders of C:\Windows\Desktop) or have shortcuts created to them.

Device driver   A small program that allows an **operating system** to communicate with, and control, an external device such as a CD-ROM drive, soundcard or printer by translating computer-data into a form recognized by the device.

Dialog   A window offering the user an option, or a choice of options, from which a selection must be made before the required task can be continued or completed.

Dial-up networking   The act of connecting your computer to a **network** (chiefly the Internet) by means of a telephone line and **modem**.

Disk cache   A small amount of a computer's *RAM* reserved as a temporary holding-place for chunks of data read from disk, such as portions of a document that an application needs to access frequently. The disk cache provides much faster access to the data than would be possible by reading it from disk each time.

Disk compression   A software utility (such as *DriveSpace*) that compresses the files on your disk to leave more disk-space. Compression involves searching for identical data repeated throughout a file and replacing it with the computer-equivalent of ditto-marks.

DMA   Short for Direct Memory Access. The computer has eight DMA channels by which data is passed (*directly*) between memory and hardware devices, bypassing the **CPU** and thus increasing the speed of transmission.

DMF   An abbreviation for Distribution Media Format, a read-only floppy-disk format for high-density disks that increases their capacity from 1.44Mb to 1.7Mb, used by Microsoft to distribute recent applications and operating system software.

DNS   Abbreviation for Domain Name Server, a system used by an **ISP** to translate **IP addresses** transmitted in the 'computer name@domain name' format to the decimal format.

Domain   The section of an **IP Address** following the '@' symbol, specifying your computer's location. The extensions included in the domain-name give you a few clues as to the country and the type of establishment of the computer, 'CO' being a UK company, 'COM' an American company, 'EDU' a college or university, 'AU' referring to Australia, 'FR' to France.

DOS extension *see* **File extension**

DOS   name *see* **MS-DOS name**

Download   To copy a file from a remote computer to your own over a network such as the **Internet**.

Drag & drop   The action of clicking on an item with a mouse-button, and moving the mouse with the button still depressed so that the item is carried with the mouse-pointer. When the pointer is in the required position (in an application window or over a folder's icon, for example), the button is released causing the item to be 'dropped' and interact with the target in some pre-determined way (e.g., to be opened in the target application, or moved to the target folder).

DTP   An abbreviation for Desktop Publishing, a type of software that allows text and graphics formats to be mixed and manipulated in a single document to create magazines, newsletters, stationery and so on.

DUN   An acronym for **Dial-up networking**.

EGA   Abbreviation for Enhanced Graphics Adapter, the forerunner of **VGA**, offering a **screen resolution** of 640 × 350 pixels with 16 colours.

Embedded object   In **OLE**, an embedded **object** is a file (such as a graphical image) stored in a document created by a different application (such as a spreadsheet). Double-clicking the embedded object will display controls allowing it to be edited. In contrast with a **linked object**, since the embedded object's data is stored in the same file as the host-document, editing this data will not alter any other copies of the file stored on your hard-disk. For the same reason, embedding an object can make for a larger file than would a linked object.

Emergency startup disk   A floppy-disk containing the system-files needed to get your computer started and reach the MS-DOS command-prompt in the event of hard-drive failure or corruption of the system-files on the hard-disk. Also known as a System Disk or Boot Disk.

Emm386.exe   This is a program provided by *Windows95* to manage **Expanded memory** and to move 16-bit drivers and TSRs out of conventional memory and into **UMBs**. It must be called from a DEVICE= line in Config.sys, with additional parameters added to specify the effect it should have, and must be called together with (and after) Himem.sys. The two most common parameters added to the Emm386 line are RAM and NOEMS: RAM specifies that both Expanded memory and UMBs are available; NOEMS specifies that no Expanded memory is required, thus freeing-up an extra 64K of UMBs.

EMS   *see* **Expanded memory**

Exit   An option found on an application's File **menu** (sometimes termed 'Quit'), that shuts down the application, prompting you to save any unsaved work first. Has the same effect as clicking the application's **Close button**. (See also **Close**).

Expanded memory   Often referred to by the abbreviation EMS, or as Enhanced memory. Expanded memory is provided by an Expanded Memory Manager (such as *Emm386.exe*) by converting **Extended memory**.

Expansion slot   One of (usually) several empty slots in a computer where additional circuit boards can be fitted, such as soundcards and graphics-accelerators. The expansion slot provides electrical connection to the **bus** to integrate these boards with the rest of the system.

Extended memory   Often referred to by the abbreviation XMS. This is the amount of memory in your computer above 1Mb (i.e., if you have 8Mb RAM, you have 7Mb of Extended memory). Of the first 1Mb, 640K is **conventional memory**, and the remaining 384K is reserved for **UMBs**. Because you have so much more extended memory than any other sort, and because *Windows95* loads 32-bit drivers into this extended memory and leaves more conventional memory free, DOS programs (and games in particular) are more likely to find the memory-resources they need when running Windows-DOS in a window or full-screen.

Extension   *see* **File extension**

FAT   An acronym for File Allocation Table, a vital file storing details of which disk-sectors a file occupies, which disk-sectors are used or unused, and which (if any) have errors.

File extension   The three characters following the dot (or the characters following the final dot in *Windows95* long filenames). These are used by Windows to determine the **file type**. File extensions are hidden by default.

File types   Files are sorted into types according to their **file extension**, with files of particular types **associated** with particular applications capable of displaying, playing and/or creating & editing them. File types are shown in Explorer's Details view.

Focus   Of the various applications and windows that might be open at any one time, only one of these is *active* (usually denoted by a differently coloured **title-bar** from all the others). This window is said to have the 'focus'. To switch the focus from one window to another, either click the required item, or the *Alt + Tab* or *Alt + Esc* hot-switches. When no windows are open (or all open apps and windows are **minimized**), either the Desktop or the **Taskbar** will have the focus: when the Desktop has the focus, a thin outline can (just about) be seen around an icon's label.

Folder   A notional storage place for the files and applications on your computer, to make for easy grouping and sorting. A folder can contain files of any type, and more folders (**subfolders**). Folders are known as *directories* within MS-DOS and earlier versions of Windows.

Fragmentation   When files are saved, they're placed on the disk in an ever-growing chain of **clusters**. So if you delete a file, its clusters may be used by the next file you save together with the next available clusters at the end of the chain when these are full. Similarly, if you increase the size of a file and resave it, it can no longer fit in the same number of clusters as before, so parts of it will be placed elsewhere. This scattering of file-portions on the disk is known as fragmentation and slows down disk-access as the read-head has to chase around to locate all

constituent clusters before it can open a file. Defragmenting programs search the disk and gather each file's clusters back into series.

FTP   An abbreviation for File Transfer Protocol, a communications language used to **download** a file from a computer connected to the **Internet**. Dedicated software (known as an 'FTP client') will handle the task, but many **World Wide Web** browsers have built-in FTP support.

GUI   An acronym for Graphical User Interface, pronounced 'gooey', of which the 'Windows' series of front-ends are examples, providing a friendly link between user and **operating system**. The user works with the software by means of *graphic* symbols, as distinct from a **command-line interface**.

Hidden   One of the **attributes** that may be assigned to a file or folder. Hidden files and folders are not visible in Explorer's windows, and cannot be selected, edited or deleted unless you specify their precise name and location. Certain files are hidden by Windows to protect the integrity of the system; you may choose to hide others for reasons of privacy or security. Hidden items may be displayed from Explorer's View / Options page.

HMA   An abbreviation for the High Memory Area, the first 64K of **extended memory** used chiefly by DOS. In most situations, DOS will be loaded into HMA with a line such as DOS = HIGH or DOS = HIGH,UMB in Config.sys, to relinquish over 40K of **conventional memory**.

Host computer   When you connect to the **Internet** through an **IAP**, you dial in to the access-provider's computer which acts as the go-between for data passing between your own computer and the Internet. This computer is termed the 'host'.

Host drive   An area on a compressed

hard-disk created by disk-compression software which contains the compressed volume file (CVF), a single file containing all the compressed files on the disk. This file is treated as an additional drive and given its own drive letter. For safety purposes, you can opt to 'hide' the host drive in *Windows95* by checking the appropriate box on its **Properties** page.

HTML Abbreviation for HyperText Markup Language, a continuously evolving text-based language consisting of formatting codes used to create **World Wide Web** pages.

HyperText The name for text containing an associated link: when the text is clicked with the mouse, the associated action is carried out (usually the retrieval or display of a file or document). HyperText is used in Windows Help-files and **HTML** documents.

IAP Abbreviation for Internet Access Provider, a company that allows individuals to connect to the **Internet** through its computer-system in return for money. (Also referred to as ISP, for Internet Service Provider.)

Icon A graphic symbol used in a **GUI** environment to represent items such as files, folders, devices and resources. (See also **WIMP**.)

Import The act of moving or copying data from one document into another (often from two different applications, via **OLE**).

Input/Output devices Devices that transmit data to the **CPU** for processing and/or receive data from it. Some devices, such as disk-drives, are input/output devices; others are input-only devices (such as a mouse) or output-only devices (a monitor). Each device has a unique **I/O address**, and many require a **device driver** file to act as translator between the device and the computer.

Insertion point A flashing vertical line in a text-based application such as a word-processor, showing where typed text or **imported objects** will be placed.

Installing software The dual actions of placing the files needed by an application on your hard-disk, and configuring the software to run correctly within Windows. In some cases, simply copying the files to your hard-disk is all that's required; in others, the files must be placed in particular folders and changes made to the Registry or system files. In the latter case, the software usually comes with a program called Setup or Install that handles this for you. (See also **Uninstalling software**.)

Internet Often abbreviated to 'Net', an INTERnational NETwork of computers connected by **modems** and telephone lines. Every computer on the network has a unique **IP address** allowing it to be accessed if the address is known.

Interrupt A signal sent to the **CPU** by a device (such as a soundcard) to interrupt the task currently being processed when an action takes place that requires processor-time (such as playing a **.wav file**).

IP An abbreviation for Internet Protocol, a communications language that determines how chunks of data (known as *packets*) are transmitted over the **Internet**, and ensures that each packet contains a source and a destination address. IP works in conjunction with a second protocol, **TCP**.

IP address Every computer connected to the **Internet** has a unique address, noted in either of two ways: either as a decimal series of four numbers separated by dots (such as 193.128.224.1), or as a computer-name plus a **domain** name (computer@domain).

IRQ Interrupt Request Line, a hardware connection from an installed device to the processor along which **interrupts** are sent. IRQs are assigned a priority status to enable the **CPU** to decide the urgency of the request.

ISA An abbreviation for Industry Standard Architecture, referring to the old 16-bit 8MHz **bus** and **expansion slots** in a computer, made obsolete by the use of increasingly fast **CPU**s.

ISP Abbreviation for Internet Service Provider, also known as an **IAP**.

Kilobyte (K) Along with **megabyte**, a measurement of disk storage-space or computer-memory equalling 1024 **bytes**.

LAN Acronym for Local Area Network. Computers on a LAN are physically connected by cable for high-speed data transfer, the LAN often forming part of a wider network **(WAN).**

Legacy A Microsoft-invented term used to describe software and hardware designed for *Windows 3.x* (or older) **operating systems**, and therefore not fully compatible with *Windows95* – in other words, parts of your system still surviving as a legacy of the older operating system after you upgraded.

Linked object In **OLE**, a linked **object** is a shortcut included in a document that 'points' to a file on your hard-disk. In contrast with an **embedded object**, since the link is only a *shortcut* to the file on your hard-disk, editing will change the file itself. Object linking allows you to place (for example) sound files in word-processor documents while keeping the word-pro document's size to a minimum (since the sound file's *data* isn't included).

Local bus An extra **bus** running at 33MHz built into a computer to speed up hard-disk access and graphics-processing to make more effective use of increasingly fast **CPU**s. The two variants are VESA local bus (or VL bus) and **PCI**.

Logical drive When you **partition** a hard-disk, the newly created partition is given a drive-letter and can be used as if it were an entirely separate drive. This new 'drive' is referred to as a logical drive.

Long filenames A naming convention new in *Windows95* whereby a filename may contain up to 255 characters, with the **extension** (i.e., the text following the final dot in the name) no longer limited to three characters.

LPT (Line PrinTer.) One of up to three parallel ports used for printing. Most computers have a single parallel port (labelled LPT1). The parallel port transmits data one **byte** (8 bits) at a time, in contrast to the **com** ports.

Maximize The button in the top right corner of a window with a square-icon, used to switch a window to full-screen size (or to fill the application window in a **MDI**). If the window is already maximized, this button becomes the **Restore** button.

MCI An abbreviation for Media Control Interface, a collection of device-independent commands for multimedia formats such as .wav, .mid, and .avi. Installed MCI drivers are indicated by corresponding entries on Media Player's 'Device' menu.

MDI Abbreviation for Multiple Document Interface. An application capable of having more than one document open at a time, each in a separate window within the main application window. The focus can be switched between documents by pressing *Ctrl + F6*. Each document window has its own **title bar**, **control menu** and **Maximize/Minimize/Restore/Close** buttons.

Megabyte (Mb) Along with **kilobyte**, a unit of measurement for disk storage-space and computer memory equalling 1,048,576 bytes (1024 Kilobytes).

Menu A list of available options.

Menu bar A row of drop-down **menus** situated below the **title bar** in an application's window.

MIDI An acronym for Musical Instrument Digital Interface, a method by which electronic musical instruments (and computers with MIDI-equipped **soundcards** or dedicated interface cards) can communicate with each other.

MIME An abbreviation for Multipurpose Internet MailExtension. A MIME message gives a convenient way to send various file-types (such as sound and video files) and non-**ASCII** text over the **Internet**, which the standard email message can't handle.

Minimize The button in the top right corner of a window with a line-icon, used to remove the window from the screen and display it only as a button on the **Taskbar** (or at the bottom of the application window in a **MIDI**).

Modem An acronym for Modulator/Demodulator, a hardware device that converts a stream of computer-data to sound for transmission down a telephone-line, where the receiving modem translates the sound back to data. A modem is required to send faxes or email from your computer and to connect to the Internet.

Motherboard The computer's main printed-circuit board, containing the processor, memory chips and **expansion slots**.

MS-DOS An acronym for Microsoft Disk Operating System, a single-tasking (as opposed to **multitasking**) **command-line interface** upon which the *Windows* series of **GUI**s are built.

MS-DOS name The MS-DOS naming convention consists of an eight-character name and a three character extension separated by a dot. When a file is named under *Windows95*, it's assigned an MS-DOS compatible name automatically. Names of greater than eight characters, or names con-taining spaces, are given an MS-DOS name consisting of the first six characters, a ~ (tilde) and a numeral to differentiate between other files in the same folder that might have the same six initial characters. **File extensions** consisting of more than three characters are also truncated.

MS-DOS extension *see* **File extension**.

Multimedia A collective name for various types of sound and graphics media, often (though not always) used in tandem. Media types include video, animation, digitally-sampled sound and **MIDI**. A computer's multimedia capabilities will depend on its power (in terms of processor-type, clock-speed, and **RAM**) and installed hardware (such as a **soundcard** and speakers to play digital or **MIDI** sound).

Multitasking An operating system's ability to handle the processing of several tasks, ostensibly at the same time, but in fact by switching rapidly between them or by allotting processor-time to the **background task** while the foreground task is idle (while waiting for keyboard or mouse input, for instance).

Name server *see* **DNS**

Network Two or more computers connected together allowing data to be passed between them. Computers in a network may be in the same office, or may be on different sides of the world. Networked computers may share resources such as drives, files and folders, and peripherals such as printers.

Network adapter A hardware interface in a computer that handles the transmission and reception of data over a **network**.

Network Interface Card or NIC; another name for the **Network adapter**.

Node Any computer with an **IP address** connected to the **Internet**.

Notification area   *see* **Tray**

Object   A file (or portion of a file) created by one application that can be linked or embedded into a document created by another via **OLE**. Object types include various text, graphics, sounds, video and animation formats. Double-clicking the object's icon in the document allows it to be read, displayed, played or edited according to its file-type.

OCR   Abbreviation for Optical Character Recognition, a software process of examining scanned images of text and converting them to 'live' text that can be edited in a word-processor.

OEM   Abbreviation for Original Equipment Manufacturer, used to describe hardware or software components included with one manufacturer's product that originated from another. For example, operating-system software and applications are often provided with a new computer on an OEM basis, the customer forgoing the right to automatic upgrades and support from the software-manufacturer in return for a (sometimes 100%) price-reduction.

OLE   An acronym for Object Linking & Embedding, pronounced 'oh-lay', a software technology that allows items created in one application (the **server**) to be included within items created in another (the **client**), such as including a sound or graphics file in a word-processor document. The **linked** or **embedded object** can be edited *in situ* by double-clicking it. A document containing such objects is referred to as a **compound document**.

Operating system   The software basis upon which applications are run (such as MS-DOS), supplying a means of interaction between the user and the system and peripheral elements of the computer. Access to the operating system is gained by the addition of either a **command-line interface** or the friendlier **GUI**.

OS/2 Originally a joint venture by IBM and Microsoft (now owned wholly by IBM), OS/2 and the latest version, OS/2 Warp, are packages combining a **32-bit operating system** with a graphical front-end (**GUI**).

Packet   *see* **IP**

Panes   A pun (of sorts) on Windows. In *Windows95*, files and folders are displayed in a window; the default-view (known as *Open view*) is a window showing the contents of a single folder only. The alternative view (*Explorer view*) also displays the tree-structure of the drive in an additional window-segment. The segments are referred to as 'panes'. (Throughout this book, the two view options are termed 'single-pane window' and 'dual-pane window' as an aid to clarity.)

Parent folder   The folder containing the currently selected folder.

Partition   Part of a hard-disk created to act as if it were a separate disk, and given its own drive-letter identification. A hard-disk can be partitioned using Fdisk under MS-DOS. (Creating new compressed drives using Drive Space does not create new DOS partitions – it simply creates a new large file on a **host drive** containing all your compressed files. MS-DOS sees this as just another file.)

Path   The full location of an item on a disk, specifying drive letter, folders and **subfolders**, and filename. For example the usual path to Mspaint is C:\Program   Files\Accessories\ Mspaint.exe.

PCI An abbreviation for Peripheral Component Interconnect, a type of **local bus** architecture introduced to transfer data between computer components faster as processor speeds increased and applications became more graphics-intensive. PCI runs at 33MHz but, unlike VESA local **bus**, handles data in more efficient 32-bit chunks. PCI also has the benefit of being compatible with **SCSI**.

PCMCIA cards Referred to more frequently now as 'PC cards', an expansion card that can be connected to a notebook-computer. These may be memory cards, soundcards, modems, network adapters, hard-disks and so on, depending on the type of card-slot(s) on the computer.

PIM Acronym for Personal Information Manager, an application acting as a computerized personal-organizer, containing a diary, address-book, planner, task-list and possibly many similar options depending upon its complexity.

Pixel An abbreviation of 'picture element', sometimes further abbreviated to 'pel', a single dot on the monitor-screen assigned a particular colour. As the screen is redrawn, pixels must be re-coloured according to the selected **colour-palette**. Combinations of pixels are used to create images on the screen, a file-icon, for example, being 32×32 pixels. (See also **Screen resolution**.)

Plug & Play A recent specification by which hardware components connected to your computer can be recognized and installed automatically, the system (usually) selecting correct, non-conflicting settings. The hardware itself must be Plug & Play-compatible, and both the **operating system** and **BIOS** must support the specification.

Pointer The on-screen symbol whose movements are controlled by the mouse or trackball. Pointer-shapes vary according to the tasks being carried out (such as Busy, or Working in background), and according to the object currently beneath the pointer.

POP3 *see* **SMTP**

Port A socket for connecting external devices such as printers and modems. Most PCs have two serial ports known as **com** ports) and one parallel

(**LPT**) port.

Processor *see* **CPU**

Properties The page accessed from an item's **context-menu**, displaying its **attributes**, general details such as creation/modification dates, location and **MS-DOS name**, plus specific information relating to the type of item selected.

Protected mode An operating mode supported by *Windows95*, allowing **multitasking** and the use of **virtual memory**. Protected mode has memory-protection features that prevent one program from accessing a memory address used by another (thus protecting the entire system from crashing when one program misbehaves). From the 80286, Intel processors have supported both protected mode and **real mode**.

Quick formatting A disk-formatting procedure which, rather than erasing the contents of the disk, deletes the **FAT** making the disk appear empty. Quick formatting can therefore be performed only on a previously formatted disk. (This method also doesn't scan the disk for errors.)

QuickTime An animation and video **codec** developed by Apple Computer Inc. QuickTime data is compatible with both Windows-based PC and Apple-Macintosh computers.

Radio buttons Small round buttons containing a dot when the corresponding option is selected. Radio buttons differ from **checkboxes** in that they allow the selection of only one of a group of mutually exclusive options.

RAM Acronym for Random Access Memory, a form of temporary storge space used by the computer to read/write data quickly. When RAM is short, *Windows95* uses **virtual memory** to supplement it, usually resulting in a noticeable performance hit. A minimum of 8 megabytes of

RAM is recommended to run *Win95*. In contrast with **ROM**, RAM is a readable/writeable form of volatile memory, requiring a power-supply to be able to store data.

Read-only   One of the **attributes** that may be assigned to a file or folder. A read-only item cannot be overwritten by an application. It can, however, be easily deleted in an Explorer-window.

Real Mode   An operating mode used by Intel's 80x86 series of processors providing single-tasking with no memory-protection features. Though superseded by **protected mode** (as used in *Windows95*), many real-mode applications are still used and continue to require operating system support. Real mode is the only operating mode supported by MS-DOS.

Restore   The button in the top right corner of a window, with an icon of two interlocking squares, that reduces a **maximized** window to its previous or default size.

ROM   An acronym for Read Only Memory, a microchip containing data that can be read, but not altered (hence 'CD-ROM'). Unlike **RAM**, ROM chips store the data permanently without the need for a power-supply.

Root folder   (Known as root directory in pre-*Windows95* operating systems.) The root folder is the primary folder on a drive, of which all the other folders on the drive are **subfolders**. Root folders are indicated by the drive's assigned letter followed by a backslash, such as C:\ or A:\.

RTF   An abbreviation for Rich Text Format, a universal format for text-files which allows the use of fonts and alignment, and character-formatting such as bold and italic.

Safe mode   A special 'troubleshooting' mode that enables you to start *Windows95* to put right whatever it was that prevented Windows booting normally. Safe Mode bypasses Registry files and network settings, and runs in 16 colours at 640 × 480 with only the basic generic drivers for mouse and display.

Screen resolution   The number of **pixels** that can be displayed on the screen, noted as *Horizontal Pixels × Vertical Pixels* (for example, 800 × 600). As the resolution is increased, items on the screen become smaller allowing more items to be displayed. Thus, more resources are required for higher-resolution displays. Available resolutions depend upon your monitor and display adapter.

Scroll bar   A narrow strip at the right or bottom edge of a window containing the **scroll box** and **scroll buttons**. Clicking the scroll bar itself, above or below the scroll box, has a similar effect to pressing the *PageUp* or *Page Down* keys on your keyboard.

Scroll box   A draggable rectangle on the **scroll bar** that slides a window's contents up and down or left and right to let you see parts of the document not currently visible.

Scroll buttons   Buttons at either end of the **scroll bar** that shuffle the contents of a window up and down or left and right to display information that extends outside the confines of the window.

SCSI   An acronym for Small Computer Systems Interface, pronounced 'skuzzy', a system used to control up to seven devices such as hard-disks and CD-ROM drives connected to a single SCSI controller card.

Selection-box   If you click on a white space in an Explorer-window and drag the **pointer** diagonally, an expanding dotted box-outline appears: this is used to select (highlight) a group of items in the window in preparation for carrying out an action such as deleting or copying them, or changing their **attributes**.

Server The central computer in a **network**, administrating access to the network and handling resources such as shared files that may be used by the **workstations** on the network. The server is typically a powerful high-specification machine with a large disk-drive.

Server application A term used in **OLE** to refer to the application that creates the **object** which is linked or embedded in a **client** application's document.

Shareware A method of distributing software, usually **downloaded** from a bulletin-board (BBS) or the **Internet**, which lets you try out the program to see if it's what you want before paying for (*registering*) it. To enforce this, the software may be restricted in some way (e.g., having the Save function disabled), or may display a 'Buy Me' screen at regular intervals – known as 'Crippleware' and 'Nagware' respectively. Another popular method is to time limit the software so that it ceases to run after a specified trial period has elapsed.

Shell A software program that allows the user to communicate with the **operating system**, such as Explorer in *Windows95*, Program Manager in *Windows 3.x*, and Command.com in MS-DOS.

Shortcut A small file with a **.lnk** extension that acts as a pointer to a file on your system, enabling you to access the file from various places (such as the Start Menu, Desktop or a variety of different folders) without sacrificing the disk-space required to make multiple copies of the file itself to each location. Shortcuts can be created to just about any item on the system and, in most cases, will act in exactly the same way as the item itself. If you rename or move the target file, *Windows95* uses information such as file-size and creation-date to find it

when you next use the shortcut, and updates the link with the new path.

SIMMs An acronym for Single In-Line Memory Module, a circuit board containing the computer's **RAM** chips. These are slotted into the computer's **motherboard** by means of pins, most recent computers using 72-pin SIMMs. A single module may contain anything from 4Mb to 32Mb, but modules usually have to be installed in specific combinations, resulting in a healthy market in second-hand SIMMs.

Slack space A term for the disk-space wasted by saving small files to a disk with larger **cluster**-sizes. For example, when you save a shortcut (**.lnk**) file, which is often about 300 **bytes** in size, to a disk with a cluster-size of 32k (32,768 bytes), you're creating 32,468 bytes of slack space which can't be used by any other file. Now imagine having several hundred shortcuts! To find out how much disk-space a group of shortcuts is using, open one of your Start Menu\Programs subfolders in a DOS-window and type dir /v /p. You should be able to work out the disk's cluster-size easily from here as well.

SMTP Abbreviation for Simple Mail Transfer Protocol; along with POP3, a method of transferring email on the **Internet**.

SoundBlaster A popular series of **soundcards** made by Creative Labs. So ubiquitous have these become that most game and **multimedia** software, and other brands of soundcard, take great pains to advertise their Sound-Blaster-compatibility.

Soundcard A slot-in expansion board adding sound recording and playback capability to your computer, often including **MIDI** compatibility, and sound-synthesis options via bundled software.

Start menu A user-configurable **menu** accessed by clicking on the Start button to the left of the **Taskbar**. The Start Menu contains the Run and Find commands, *Windows95* Help, and Shutdown. Two **submenus** show the list of recently used Documents, and the Programs folder. Further folders can be added to the Start Menu itself, and to the Programs folder, to create more submenus containing shortcuts to files and folders on your system.

Startup disk *see* **Emergency startup disk**

Startup folder A **subfolder** of **Start menu** \ Programs. Items placed in this folder (as shortcuts) will be run automatically every time *Windows95* starts.

Subfolder A **folder** contained within another folder. For example, C:\Windows contains folders such as System, Fonts, and SentTo; these are said to be *subfolders* of C:\Windows. Looking at it in reverse, C:\Windows is the **parent** folder of Fonts.

Sub-menu An extra 'flyout' **menu** to the left or right of the main menu offering additional choices, or the ability to refine the choice for a selected menu-item. Also referred to as a *cascading* menu.

SuperVGA Successor to **VGA**, offering **screen resolutions** of up to 1024 × 768 **pixels** with 16.7 million colours.

Swapfile A file created on your hard-disk and used by *Windows95* to move data not currently needed out of **RAM** to make room for data that is needed (in other words, 'swapping' it). This has the effect of giving you more memory than your hardware RAM supplies, but the swapfile can't compete with 'real' RAM on speed. Due to its wraith-like nature, the swapfile is referred to as **virtual memory**.

System One of the **attributes** assigned to a file by *Windows95* itself to indicate that the file is required by the **operating-system**. System files should not be deleted, and should always be backed-up before you edit them.

System disk A disk that contains at least enough of the operating system to start the computer and provide a user-interface. Also called a Boot Disk. (See **Emergency startup disk**.)

Taskbar A horizontal bar set at the bottom of the screen (though movable and resizeable by dragging or stretching). The Taskbar displays currently open windows and running applications as buttons which can be clicked to switch from one to another. At the right of the Taskbar is the recessed area called the **Tray**.

TCP An abbreviation for Transmission Control Protocol. The TCP passes data from an application to the **IP** to be transmitted over the **Internet** and ensures that it's received correctly. These two major protocols are often referred to as a single entity – TCP/IP.

Text file A file containing only the letters, numbers and punctuation marks, supported by the standard **ASCII** character set. All word-processor files can be converted to text-files, but the text formatting in the original (such as font-type and size, italics etc) will be removed. The text-file is therefore a 'universal' format used when text needs to be displayed on any computer using any word-processing or text-editing software.

Thumbnail A smaller representation of an image-file used to give a quick indication of what the full-size graphic looks like. Clicking or double-clicking the thumbnail usually opens (or **downloads**) the full image.

Tile A command that moves and resizes all open, non-minimized applications and windows to allow a portion of each to be visible on the screen at the same time.

Title bar The bar at the top of an application or document window that displays the name of the application and/or currently open file, together with its **Control/menu**, and **Maximize/ Minimize/Restore/Close** buttons.

Toolbar A collection of buttons often acting as shortcuts to options contained in menus on the **Menu bar** and usually sited below it, though a toolbar may be of the 'floating' variety (particularly in graphics applications) allowing you to move it around.

Tooltips Short information-messages or captions that pop up when you briefly hold the mouse-pointer over an item such as a **Taskbar** or **Toolbar** button, or **Tray** icon.

Tray The recessed area at the right of the **Taskbar** containing the clock, and icons for applets and accessories such as the volume control, or modem and printer status. Clicking, right-clicking or double-clicking one of these icons will usually present a menu of options or a properties/configuration page.

Tree A graphic representation of the folder-structure of a drive, showing how all its **folders** and **subfolders** are related.

TSR An abbreviation for Terminate and Stay resident, referring to a program that loads into memory but remains inactive until required to perform a task. It can then be called over the top of another application (of use in single-tasking **operating systems** such as MS-DOS).

UMBs Acronym for Upper Memory Blocks, the 384K of memory sandwiched between **conventional** and **extended memory**. UMBs are used to load 16-bit drivers and parts of DOS itself, to make more conventional memory available to the DOS program you're trying to run.

If your Config.sys contains the line DEVICE = EMM386.EXE NOEMS, the memory manager (**Emm386.exe**) will make this memory available for loading real mode drivers and sections of DOS. If the NOEMS parameter is re-

placed by the RAM parameter, extended memory is enabled as well as the UMBs, though a minimum 64K chunk of memory from the UMBs is sacrificed to make room for it.

Uninstalling software The act of removing an application from your system. In some cases, this can be as simple as just deleting the application's folder from your hard-disk; in others, constituent files might be scattered all over the disk, and changes might have been made to Registry and system-files during installation which need to be restored. In the latter case, the software usually comes with an Uninstall program to handle the task automatically.

Windows95-aware software will automatically log itself into the Add/ Remove Programs list in the Control Panel to make later removal easier still: make sure you always look here first before uninstalling anything – some of the least likely little third-party programs log themselves here without your knowledge! (See also **Installing software**.)

Upload To transmit a copy of a file on your own computer to a remote computer over a network such as the **Internet**; the term is usually used in the context of making the file available for other Internet-users to **download**.

V-series A series of modem specifications governing speed (**baud rate**) and data-compression. The current standards are V.34 (28,800bps) and V.32bis (14,400bps).

VESA An acronym for Video Electronic Standards Association. See **Local bus**; **PCI**.

Virtual memory A type of non-physical memory gained by using an area of hard-disk to emulate physical **RAM**. This hard-disk area contains a single file called a **swapfile** which (under the *Windows95* default settings) can expand and contract according to current memory-requirements.

VGA An abbreviation for Video Graphics Array, a video adapter with the same choice of modes as **EGA**, and the addition of 640 × 480, 16 colours and 320 × 200, 256 colours.

Virus A special program with the ability to clone itself undetected, and invisibly insert itself into other files, created with the express intent of altering data on your hard-disk to a greater or lesser degree. A virus may do no more than produce a beep from your system speaker once a year; on the other hand, it might trash every file on your system, depending on the warp-factor of the author's mind. The primary breeding-grounds for viruses are shared floppy-disks and files downloaded from bulletin boards and the Internet. Always check these with up-to-date virus-detection software before running or unzipping files.

WAN An acronym for Wide Area Network, a large **network** usually consisting of communications links with a number of **LAN**s. The **Internet** is an (extremely large) example of a WAN.

Wav file A digitally recorded sound file. The size and sound-quality varies according to the sample-rate and resolution setting, but files can be immense. A CD-quality stereo recording (44,100Hz, 16-bit) swallows hard-disk space to the tune of 10Mb/minute. (To hear a .wav file, you must have a **soundcard** and speakers.)

Wildcards Characters used to select a group of files by name, or to locate items whose exact name is unknown. The asterisk (*) is used to replace multiple characters; the question-mark (?) replaces a single character.

WIMP An acronym for Windows, Icons, Menus, Pointer – the four primary elements that make up a **GUI**, and probably not just a desperate attempt to prove that systems-design-

ers really do have a sense of humour.

Winsock An abbreviation for Windows Sockets, a software interface (Winsock.dll) needed in Windows **operating systems** to handle communication between applications and **Internet** protocols such as **TCP**.

Wizard The *Windows95* name for a type of program that takes you through an installation or configuration process in step-by-step question and answer fashion.

Workgroup Several computers that form one of (possibly) many similar groups on a network, each group being identified by its own name.

Workstations Computers connected to a network that make use of resources provided by the **server**. Also, somewhat confusingly, used to refer to a powerful stand-alone computer.

World Wide Web Often noted as the Web, WWW or W3. The name for the **Internet**'s collection of **HTML** documents containing a combination of graphics and text, all interconnected by **HyperText** links. The documents can be viewed in an application referred to as a 'browser'.

wysiwyg Pronounced 'wizziwig', an acronym for 'What You See Is What You Get'. The ability of an application to display the correct formatting of a document while you create or edit it, letting you see what the finished result will look like when run, printed, or published on the World Wide Web.

XMS *see* **Expanded memory**

Zip files A popular file-format (characterized by a .**zip** extension) used for compressing one or more files into a single archive file, usually to save disk space, and commonly used to transmit files over networks such as the **Internet**.

Index

Becoming a Prentice Hall Author

Getting published with Prentice Hall

1. Can I do it?

It is easy to think of the publishing process as a series of hurdles designed to weed out would-be authors. That may be true of some publishing houses, but not Prentice Hall.

- ❏ We do all we can to encourage new talent.

- ❏ We welcome unsolicited manuscripts.

- ❏ We carefully examine every proposal we receive, and we always write back to let the authors know what we think of it.

Although many of our authors have professional or educational experience, we look first for a passion for computing. Some of our most successful books are written by first time authors. If you have built up expertise in any computing-related topic, please get in touch. You'll be surprised how easy it is to get through.

2. Is Prentice Hall a successful company?

Prentice Hall is a highly respected brand in technical and scientific publishing, a status reflected in our relationships with the book trade and various professional bodies. Our reputation has been made with classic computing titles such as Kernighan and Ritchie's *The C Programming Language* (over two million copies sold) and Bertrand Meyer's ground-breaking *Object Oriented Software Construction*.

Becoming a Prentice Hall Author

We're part of Simon & Schuster, a $2 billion dollar global publishing company. Simon & Schuster is host to Macmillan Computer Publishing, home of renowned computer imprints such as Sams, Que, Waite Group Press, Ziff-Davis Publishing, Hayden and New Riders Press (NRP). Simon & Schuster is itself owned by Viacom Inc, one of the world's largest entertainment and publishing companies. Viacom owns film and tv studios (Paramount Pictures), world-wide cable networks (MTV, Nickelodeon) and retail outlets (Blockbuster Video).

3. What sort of books does Prentice Hall publish?

The computing revolution in the office and home has prompted a massive and diverse market for computer books. That diversity is reflected in our approach. We are happy to consider book proposals on absolutely any computing topic.

Essentially, Prentice Hall publishes books for anyone whose job or hobby connects them to a computer. We are already familiar with your intended readership, whether your book is written for professionals, students, enthusiasts or beginners. Our progressive editorial policy encourages new authors and gives us the flexibility required in a rapidly changing technological environment. However, we do have a 'books wanted' list – contact the editorial department for the latest copy.

4. What are the rewards of writing a book?

Prentice Hall royalty rates are among the most competitive in the industry, and many of our authors earn considerable sums through royalties. Payments are calculated along industry-standard guidelines, i.e. the author receives a percentage of the publisher's net sales revenue. We always offer preferential royalty rates for senior figures within the computing industry, or for books on hot topics written by experts. For the right book at the right time, the financial reward to the author can be extremely generous. This is especially true of books aimed at professional software developers.

If you are a computer professional or an academic, your livelihood depends upon your professional reputation. Successful Prentice Hall authors enjoy a constant stream of business and employment opportunities as a direct result of getting published. A book works like a business card, advertising the author's talent across a vast network of potential contacts.

5. How do I know my ideas are good enough to publish?

In assessing the market-readiness of book proposals or finished manuscripts, Prentice Hall editors draw upon a huge database of technical advisors. All of our reviewers are senior figures in modern computing, and their role is to offer free advice to potential authors, highlighting both the strengths and weaknesses of proposals and manuscripts. The aim of the review process is to add value to your ideas, rather than just approving or rejecting them.

We understand that errors are inevitable when writing books, but as a Prentice Hall author you need not worry about the quality of your finished work. Many of our authors have not written a book before, so we are there to help – we scrutinise all our manuscripts for grammatical accuracy and style.

6. How much control would I have over my book?

We understand that a book is a highly personal statement from the author, so we invite your participation at all stages of the publishing process, from the cover design through to the final marketing plans. A Prentice Hall book is a co-operative venture between author and publisher.

7. Will I get any help with the technical aspects of book production?

Our highly professional staff will ensure that the book you envisaged is the book that makes it to the shelves. Once you hand over your manuscript to us, we will take care of all the technical details of printing and binding. Beyond the advice and guidance from your own editor, our 64-page *Author Guide* is there to help you shape your manuscript into a first-class book. Our large and efficient production department is among the quickest in the industry. We are experts at turning raw manuscripts into polished books, irrespective of the technical complexity of your work. Technical queries can be answered by your production contact, assigned, where relevant, to you at contract stage. Our production staff fully understand the individual requirements of every project, and will work with you to produce a manuscript format that best complements your skills – hard copy manuscripts, electronic files or camera-ready copy.

8. How quickly can you turn my manuscript into a book?

The production department at Prentice Hall is widely acknowledged to be among the quickest in the industry. Our turnaround times vary according to the nature of the manuscript supplied to us, but the average is about four months for camera-ready copy, five for electronic file manuscript. For time-sensitive topics, we can occasionally turn out books in under twelve weeks!

9. Where would my book be sold?

Prentice Hall has one of the largest sales forces of any technical publisher. Our highly experienced sales staff have developed firm business partnerships with all the major retail bookstores in Europe, America, Asia, the Middle East and South Africa, ensuring that your book receives maximum retail exposure.

Prentice Hall's marketing department is responsible for ensuring the widest possible review coverage in magazines and journals – vital to the sales of computing books.

Our books are usually present at major trade shows and exhibitions, either on our own stands or those belonging to major retail bookshops. Our presence at trade shows ensures that your work can be inspected by the most senior figures within any given field of computing. We also have a very successful corporate and institutional sales team, dedicated to selling our books into large companies, user groups, book clubs, training seminars and professional bodies.

Local language translations can provide not only a significant boost to an author's royalty income, but also will allow your research/findings to reach a wider audience, thus furthering your professional prospects. To maintain both the author's and Prentice Hall's reputation, we license foreign language deals only with publishing houses of the highest repute.

10. I don't have time to write a book!

To enjoy all the advantages of being a published author, it is not always necessary for you to write an entire book. Prentice Hall welcomes books written by multiple authors. If you feel that your skills lie in a very specific area of computing, or that you do not have the time to write an entire book, please get in touch regardless. Prentice Hall may have a book in progress that would benefit from your ideas. You may know individuals or teams in your field who could act as co-author(s). If not, Prentice Hall can probably put you in touch with the right people. Royalties for shared-author books are distributed according to respective participation.

11. Could my company benefit?

Many Prentice Hall authors use their book to lever their commercial interests, and we like to do all we can to help. If a well-written book is an excellent marketing tool for an author, then it can also be an excellent marketing tool for the author's company. A book is its own highly focused marketing channel, a respected medium that takes your company name to all the right people. Previous examples of marketing opportunities with our books include:

1 free advertising in the back pages

2 Packaging in suitable corporate livery (book covers, flyers, etc.)

3 Mounting software demos in the back page on disk or CD-ROM

Although Prentice Hall has to keep its publications free of undue corporate or institutional bias, in general the options for cross-marketing are varied and completely open to discussion.

12. I have an idea for a book. What next?

We invite you to submit a book proposal. We need proposals to be formatted in a specific way, so if you have not received our guidelines, please contact the Acquisition Editor at this address:

Jason Dunne
Professional and Consumer Computing
Prentice Hall
Campus 400, Maylands Avenue
Hemel Hempstead, Herts.
HP2 7EZ
England

Tel: +44 (0)1442 882246
Fax: +44 (0)1442 252544

e-mail: jason_dunne@prenhall.co.uk